TAINTED WITNESS

GENDER AND CULTURE

GENDER AND CULTURE

A SERIES OF COLUMBIA UNIVERSITY PRESS

Nancy K. Miller and Victoria Rosner, Series Editors
Carolyn G. Heilbrun (1926–2003) and Nancy K. Miller, Founding Editors

For a full list of titles in this series, see pages 219–21

TAINTED WITNESS

WHY WE DOUBT
What Women Say
ABOUT THEIR LIVES

LEIGH GILMORE

Columbia University Press
New York

Columbia University Press

Publishers Since 1893

New York   Chichester, West Sussex

cup.columbia.edu

Library of Congress Cataloging-in-Publication Data

Names: Gilmore, Leigh, 1959– author.

Title: Tainted witness : why we doubt what women say about their lives /
Leigh Gilmore.

Description: New York : Columbia University Press, [2016] | Includes
bibliographical references and index.

Identifiers: LCCN 2016033453 | ISBN 9780231177146 (cloth : alk. paper) |
ISBN 9780231543446 (e-book)

Subjects: LCSH: Sex discrimination against women—Law and legislation. |
Sex discrimination—Law and legislation. | Sex discrimination in criminal
justice administration. | Witnesses—Public opinion. | Crime—Sex differences. |
Women—Crimes against—Public opinion. | False testimony. | Feminist theory.

Classification: LCC K3243 .G55 2016 | DDC 342.7308/78—dc23

LC record available at https://lccn.loc.gov/2016033453

Columbia University Press books are printed on permanent
and durable acid-free paper.

Printed in the United States of America

Cover design: Mary Ann Smith

FOR GILLIAN WHITLOCK

CONTENTS

ACKNOWLEDGMENTS

This project developed over more than a decade's interest in auto-biographical practices, cultural processes of judgment, and histories of testimony. It has traveled with me as I have moved from Ohio to California and back to Boston, and I owe a debt of gratitude to those who have stayed with me through these transitions, as well as those who have welcomed me to new places. At Ohio State University, where this work began, I thank Nick Howe, and remember him here, Jennifer Terry, Luke Wilson, and Dorothy Roberts for conversations that helped me to launch this project. Jim Phelan, Sandra Macpherson, Wendy Hesford, and Jared Gardner offered encouragement, often through their own fine work. I presented early drafts of some of the chapters during visiting appointments at UC Santa Cruz and UC Berkeley. I thank Judith Butler, Michael Lucey, Charis Thompson, Gayle Salamon, Carla Freccero, Jim Clifford, and Donna Haraway for their generosity. Other parts of the project took shape during visiting appointments and in conversation with Linda Blum, Laura Greene, Carla Kaplan, and Suzanna Walters at Northeastern University; with Amy Hollywood, Frank Clooney, and Ann Braude at Harvard Divinity School; and with Phillip Gould at Brown University. Many thanks to hosts and interlocutors who generously engaged with work in progress, including Teresa Brus at Wroclaw University in Poland, Clare Brant and Max Saunders at King's College in London, Sidonie Smith at University of Michigan, Kathleen Woodward at University of Washington, and meetings of the International Association of Autobiography and Biography in Sussex, Puerto Rico, and Michigan. I am especially grateful for Sidonie Smith's invitation to speak at the Presidential Forum at the MLA in Los Angeles in 2011 and to share that conversation with others whose work is important to mine, including Hillary Chute and Gillian Whitlock. I am grateful to Sid for a career-long intellectual conversation that has enriched and expanded every aspect of my understanding of life writing. I thank Julia Watson, with whom I too briefly overlapped at Ohio State, for the inspiration of her expansive archive. I thank Sid and Julia for their invitation to offer a keynote in Ann Arbor at a meeting of the IABA-Americas chapter. I have been inspired by the work of and conversations with Marcia Aldrich. My colleagues in life writing have pressed my thinking forward and dazzled me by the sheer range of their scholarly commitments; thanks especially to Craig Howes, Margaretta Jolly, Julie Rak, Anna Polletti, Kate Douglass, Laurie MacNeill, Eva Karpinksi, Laura Lyons, Cynthia Franklin, and John Zuern. Thanks to Lauren Berlant for the inspiration of her scholarship. Thanks also to a new generation of scholars whose thinking enlivens my own, including Joss Greene, Amulya Mandava, Jenell Navarro, Jose Navarro, and Surya Parekh. I thank my friends Shea Wilson, Matthew Sutton, Meredith Greiner, Pam Dickinson, Casey Near, Alejandra Kramer, and Robert and Anne Van Cleve. A special thanks to Brian and Patrice Taylor for respite under the oaks and design advice. Many thanks to those who welcomed us back to Boston, especially Bill and Helen Pounds, Morgan Mead, Bob and Alison Murchison, and Marlene Kenney and Josh Gray. I thank my editors, Nancy K. Miller and Victoria Rosner, for their skill and enthusiasm. I am especially grateful for the model of feminist collegiality and professionalism enacted by them and the director of Columbia University Press, Jennifer Crewe. I am honored that this book is included in a series I greatly admire. The anonymous readers of this manuscript took extraordinary care in their responses and greatly improved its final shape. They have my abiding gratitude. Closer to home, I thank my family, Tom, Finn, and William for support, patience, and lively engagement. I offer special thanks to

Beth Marshall who stood guard over this project from its inception and who has read every word with her keen editorial acumen.

The dedication honors a decades-long, continent-spanning intellectual and personal friendship with Gillian Whitlock, my brilliant interlocutor and steadfast editor. Writing is solitary work, but what feeds it draws on personal wells of encouragement, shared interest, and honesty. I thank Gillian for all of these.

Some of the thinking in this project builds on work that was published previously. I gratefully acknowledge permission to include revised versions of the following articles:

"'What Was I?' Literary Witness and the Testimonial Imperative." *Profession* (2011): 77–84.

"American Neoconfessional: Memoirs, Self-Help, and Redemption on Oprah's Couch." *Biography* 33, no. 4 (Fall 2010): 657–79.

"Jurisdictions: *I, Rigoberta Menchú, The Kiss*, and Scandalous Self-Representation in the Age of Memoir and Trauma." *Signs* 28, no. 2 (Winter 2002): 695–719.

TAINTED WITNESS

INTRODUCTION

Tainted Witness in Testimonial Networks

*The past is neither inert nor given. The stories we tell about
what happened then, the correspondences we discern
between today and times past, and the ethical and political
stakes of these stories redound in the present.*

—SAIDIYA HARTMAN, *LOSE YOUR MOTHER:
A JOURNEY ALONG THE ATLANTIC SLAVE ROUTE*

Ours is an age of testimony and witness. It is also an age of
judgment, which arises in response to the proliferating jurisdictions through which testimony circulates. Judgment falls
unequally on women who bear witness, as the well-known cases that
provoked controversy and litigation in the late twentieth and early
twenty-first centuries and that form the focus of this book reveal.
From Anita Hill's testimony at Clarence Thomas's confirmation hearing to Rigoberta Menchú's *testimonio* about genocide in Guatemala to
Nafissatou Diallo's claim that she was raped by Dominique Strauss-
Kahn, women's testimonial accounts demonstrate both the symbolic
potency of women's bodies and speech in the public sphere and the relative lack of institutional security and control to which they can lay claim.

Moreover, each testimonial act follows in the wake of a long and invidious historical association of race and gender with lying that circulates to this day within legal courts and everyday practices of judgment, defining these locations as willfully unknowing and hostile to complex accounts of harm. *Tainted Witness* brings a feminist perspective to bear on how women's witness is discredited by a host of means meant to *taint* it: to contaminate by doubt, stigmatize through association with gender and race, and dishonor through shame, such that not only the testimony but the person herself is smeared. By drawing together the fields of feminist studies, intersectional studies in race, law and literature, and life writing, we can reflect anew on the problem of how gender and race affect the mobilization of testimony and the public representation of women who offer it.[1] This book examines a series of contentious cases in which the conventional association of women with lying ignited the fire of scandal and provided an ample supply of incendiary material in the form of the suppressed histories of slavery and colonialism for it to burn brightly. In the conflagration of scandal, women who bore witness were besmirched even as those who distorted their testimony presented their bias as if it were illuminating and rational. However, even as these cases migrate from scandal to yesterday's news, women's testimony continues to move in pursuit of new venues, jurisdictions, and publics where it may bear witness anew. *Tainted Witness* charts what happens as and after women's testimony is discredited. It follows the search for an adequate witness after the terms of public reception have shifted in order to show that the adequate witness testimony seeks is a moving target.

Antifeminist views on sexual violence and sexual agency exist alongside women's acts of testimony within the jurisdictions where they bear witness. When police, attorneys, family members, or readers, reviewers, and courts of public opinion greet women's testimony and life narratives about sexual harassment or political violence with a response that seems to moot fair judgment, on what grounds can testimony emerge? When testimony is cast outside credulity by a formulation like "nobody knows what really happened" that is simultaneously commonsensical and capable of derailing thought, where can women turn? This book attends to recurrent stories of sexual violence in relation to the large story of women's and girls' inequalities before the law without making every story seem like a reiteration of the same story and without compromising the force of specific stories and their idiosyncrasies, or the epistemological demand of reading their dense textuality. It follows specific testimonies across the varying jurisdictions and publics in which they were heard. In so doing, it connects affective response and judgment to truth telling as a racial and gendered formation intertwined with histories of permissible violence. It questions the adequacy of empathy as a response to testimony and concludes by arguing for the importance of a literary witness capable of generating an ethical response that is not primarily grounded in identification or compassion. A literary witness asks readers to engage at a level that is not limited to identifying with pleasing or displeasing characters and their stories.

The movement of testimony—those verbal acts in which a person bears witness to harm in a public forum—reveals what propels and impedes the search for an adequate witness. Through a focus on testimony as event and practice, we begin to see what is often obscured: testimonial networks of autobiographical narrative, documentary film, national and international courts, and extralegal settings within which testimony is mobilized, in relation to the practices and spaces of legal and illegal detention, rendition, and incarceration that shadow the testimonial network.[2] I propose that we conceptualize testimonial networks as circulatory systems that connect the discourses and sites through and across which persons and testimony flow. Instead of thinking of the rules of evidence that structure how witnesses may testify in courts, the norms of reviewing and commenting in print and online reviews of memoirs and first-person literary accounts, and the fog of scandal and acrimony that often greets new accounts of sexual and racial violence as belonging to separate orders of judgment, *Tainted Witness* focuses on the pathways through which witness accounts reach diverse audiences. Official and formal structures, like national and international courts, coexist with news media and a host of online sources. Judgments are reproduced as testimony is cross-referenced by a click on a link here, that takes one to a site there, that reveals the presence of an ongoing case, or that seems to indicate the end of testimony in the form of cold, dropped, or discredited cases, even as testimony and witnesses continue to circulate online in a virtual and extrajudicial exercise in habeas corpus. By linking testimonial networks to carceral spaces and histories, we expose more clearly the risks undertaken by those who bear witness: who becomes vulnerable, where, and how. Here, we confront histories and practices that remind us of the testimony offered by bodies. When verbal records are impossible to make, or are destroyed, or remain untranslated or uninscribed, a testimonial record nonetheless exists within the body and in the history of bodies of those excluded from the public square as full citizens. Testimony emerges from diverse experiences of violence and multiform exposure to risk and in various forms we must struggle to read; its fate, like the fate of those compelled by circumstance to offer it, is both dynamic and insecure.

By working across specific cases, the histories of how each one bears witness, and in what jurisdictions, emerge; we observe where testimony is obstructed, as well as the institutional, epistemological, legal, and geographical boundaries and frames it crosses as it relocates in search of a hearing. By following testimony—verbal, embodied, and silenced—as it moves across publics, we can anatomize a testimonial network through which life story travels. Composed of literary and legal accounts moving through official and improvised jurisdictions, measured according to genre and rules of evidence but sped or halted by politics, and heard in courts and media, testimony moves in relation to a network of legal punishments. Testimony can be prosecuted as fraud and is subject to laws of libel and slander. Via unequal and racist policing in the United States, and legal practices of punishment, the persons who seek to offer first-person accounts of harm often share the same fate as their testimony: silenced by legitimate, which is to say both permissible and required, violence. The penalties one risks differ in official settings and the court of public opinion, and the shape of testimony reflects a dialectical relation between what one says and where one says it.

In written and oral forms, in eloquent speech and broken utterances, in protest and in pain, in courts and police stations, as well as the lecture halls, TED Talks, editorial pages, blogs, and online comments sections representing courts of public opinion, those who put forward personal accounts of suffering and those who encounter them form a transactional dynamic of testimony.[3] This dynamic emerges in the interaction of judges, attorneys, plaintiffs, defendants, and witnesses in criminal and civil courts; as refugees and migrants face immigration services and learn the approved narratives that enable them to negotiate the barriers in their path; in the interaction of memoirists, publishers, reviews, and readers; and with political activists, human rights advocates, humanitarian workers, and those on whose behalf they work. The locations and their formality vary, as do the actors and the rules of evidence and engagement, but one caveat persists: in summary and popular judgment, the person who has suffered harm and writes, speaks, displays bodily, or otherwise performs a first-person representation about it will be tasked with doing more than bearing witness to this injury. When the witness is a woman, and especially when the harm includes sexual violence, she will be subjected to practices of shaming and discrediting that preexist any specific case.[4] As the case studies in this book testify, attacks on her credibility will draw from a deep reservoir of bias that connects gender and race to status across popular culture and informal spaces as well as institutions. Judgment as a cultural practice is participatory, rule-governed, and binding. Testimony moves, but judgment sticks.[5]

Testimony does not begin and end with a single speech act, nor is its lifespan limited to its duration within a particular forum of judgment. Rather, testimony moves—sometimes haltingly, sometimes urgently—in search of an adequate witness. An adequate witness is one who will receive testimony without deforming it by doubt, and without substituting different terms of value for the ones offered by the witness herself. An adequate witness meets a basic threshold. Like the "good enough mother" in D. W. Winnicott, the adequate witness creates a holding environment for testimony.[6] An adequate witness is no echo chamber, empty of knowledge and passive in the face of the other's demand, nor is she credulous. She would not simply credit all testimony about sexual violence, for example, believing it to be the one thing about which no one could ever lie. Instead, when confronted with the charged demands of testimony, an adequate witness resists the rush to judgment and learns how to attend to accounts of gendered harm and agency made by impure victims in conditions of complexity. An adequate witness can preempt the processes of judgment that taint a witness but can also undo that stigma by altering the practice of judgment itself.

Testimony possesses vitality and agency and may find new life even in bleak circumstances, but judgment moves, too. It sticks to testimony and weighs it down. Judgment has a bodily connotation of viscosity and is couched in a rhetoric of animate gunk: reputations are tarnished or smeared, critics sling mud and throw dirt, shit hits the fan. Scholars working to theorize the norms through which identities are produced in relation to bias and stigma include Sara Ahmed's notion of sticky judgment in "affective economies"[7] through which stereotypes about race stick to black bodies via repetition over time. Chandan Reddy accounts for how such stickiness emerges in law and policy through the process of attaching amendments, often with powerfully divergent political meanings, to laws.[8] Thinking of how judgment, following Reddy, amends testimonial identities with negative judgment helpfully conceptualizes the sticky logics of legitimate violence and compassion that can be given and withheld to persons, bodies, and speech. How judgment is added to testimony takes a specific form within modernity; namely, that stigmatized aspects of identity will be added to witnesses as weight their words cannot bear.[9] Race, gender, and sexuality align with citizenship to produce sinking doubt and to permit legitimate violence against persons whose identities can be freighted in these ways.

Two of the stickiest judgments that circulate in response to claims by women of sexual violence are "he said/she said" and "nobody really knows what happened." These arise in response to narratives of sexual violence, claim harm, identify perpetrators, and demand either a response within the terms permitted by the jurisdiction or simply the right to tell one's story in the public square. They render as unknowable and undecidable both physical evidence and verbal testimony. They deflect a more rigorous engagement with narratives, persons, evidence, and scenes of abuse that are complicated. Physical evidence is discounted when, for example, "she said" the sexual contact that the evidence confirms was rape, but "he says" it was consensual. The evidence, often undisputed and ample in rape cases, is removed in this formulation into a realm of doubt that favors the rapist. Often courts possess adequate evidence to bring criminal charges of rape and sexual assault but decline to prosecute them, or lose these cases, when the evidence is argued to confirm sexual contact merely. Consent, this view argues, is a matter of interpretation. "Maybe he misinterpreted her response as consent" operates as a purposeful and strategic intervention in rape prosecution. It represents the introduction of reasonable doubt, the legal standard by which rape is judged in criminal court. But we should remember also that "he said/she said" simply identifies how witnesses in an adversarial legal structure are positioned. How "he said/she said" has come to be seen as something other than the prompt from which due process begins suggests that women lie outside the frame of justice from the beginning.

Similarly, the vernacular formulation "nobody really knows what happened" makes a legal claim that has been successfully adopted in everyday life as a reasonable response to news about rape. Yet, again, legal proceedings have rules of evidence to address precisely whether or not the evidence can meet a burden of proof (reasonable doubt in a criminal proceeding or by a preponderance of the evidence in a civil case), and "nobody knows what really happened" is the starting point of a trial. Like the presumption of innocence, it names a suspension of judgment rather than the imposition of doubt. Only in cases of sexual violence do people feel virtuous, objective, and fair when they claim that the conditions that typically initiate and guide a legal proceeding moot it from the outset.

The intensity with which women witnesses are vilified and the repetition of this spectacle is difficult to understand without reference to the celebratory and shaming responses to testimony engendered within "intimate publics."[10] Shaming, victim blaming, discrediting, and denunciation attach to women's testimony so predictably, and are so regularly associated with it, that these negative affects function as prolepsis: they are a threat that prevents women from testifying. When joined with doubt and directed at women who testify about sexual degradation, victim blaming has the epistemological status of an objective and ethical response. That such judgment can be sticky and seem neutral is a crucial feature of how women's witness can become tainted without also tainting doubters or the institutions through which doubt is legitimated.

In networks through which "human rights and narrated lives" circulate, the individual comes increasingly to represent the rights-bearing construct synonymous with the human.[11] There is a paradox here: the figure of the girl or woman of color as deserving and representative victim seems to be enjoying an unprecedented level of credibility and visibility. As I write these words, Malala Yousafzai is one of the most admired human rights campaigners worldwide, Nicholas Kristof regularly reaches an international audience when he addresses the horrors of an international sex trade in his op-ed column in the *New York Times*, and when many humanitarian organizations and NGOs seek to put a human face on suffering, they choose girls and women from the global South in appeals directed at Western audiences. Yet, even as these new optics suggest an openness to women's testimony, the mechanisms through which their testimony is tainted are increasingly widespread and efficient, as the case studies in this book demonstrate. This paradox is consistent with enactments of legal violence in the United States and, in differing ways, globally. Indeed, the presence of racialized women and girls as representatives of harm functions as a concession to the actual harm they experience from state-sanctioned violence: their unequal exposure to violence and unequal access to justice coincide in the compromised project of eliciting their testimony. Here, as I will show through a discussion of Greg Mortenson's now-controversial campaign for girls' education in Afghanistan and Pakistan, undertaken through his Central Asia Institute and chronicled in the best-selling *Three Cups of Tea*, it is often the voices of Western humanitarians that substitute for the voices of women and girls on whose behalf they elicit support.

We come here to the importance of neoliberalism as an analytical lens through which to view the rhetoric of individual agency and responsibility. In neoliberalism, the state benefits from abandoning "the individual" to his or her own care and promotes that exposure as the freedom to choose in the absence of a safety net of appropriate support. The individual who does not need the state's support because he can adequately accumulate capital remains the empowered white male subject of classical liberalism. Only he is enabled to claim that the position he inhabits is freely open to all through hard work. The narrative

engine that propels neoliberalism is the autobiographical account par
excellence of the rise.

Autobiography as a genre—along with its allied forms of memoir,
slave narratives, captivity narratives, *testimonio*, and other permuta-
tions of "the story of my life, told by me"—notably twins the "I" who
narrates with the "I"'s narrative. When that narrative conforms to dominant cultural notions of legitimacy, the "I" who narrates it will accrue
authority. Despite the claim the "I" makes to the legitimacy of personhood, it is more the story than the self that generates social opprobrium
or affirmation in the reception of autobiography and not the other way
around. A variety of subjects can claim the power of the form by telling the "right" story, but telling a dissonant story, one that challenges
tolerances around who may appear in public, will place marginalized
subjects at greater risk of being doubted. Racial logics construct identities—"Black," "Indian," "Muslim"—that are further amended by colonial
hierarchies—"peasant," "slave"—in modern liberalism. Lisa Lowe notes
that the construction and stigmatization of such "identities" does not
simply sort populations into those who need to be brought from a "state
of nature" into civil society. Instead, the construction of those identities hardens into the impermeable outside of civil society, with identity naming the intractability of one's diminished status and the basis
of exclusion from the law.[12] Autobiography is more flexible than legal
testimony. Because it permits innovation, writers have historically made
use of its literary elasticity to assert legitimacy, to challenge power, and
to enable counterpublics to coalesce around life stories. Life stories have
been vehicles through which to expose the racial and colonial exclusions
of liberalism, as Olaudah Equiano showed in the eighteenth century,
Frederick Douglass and Harriet Jacobs in the nineteenth, and Rigoberta
Menchú, Patricia Williams, and Saidiya Hartman in the twentieth and
twenty-first. Thus the force of liberalism, and its potent afterlife in neoliberalism, is interwoven with the genre of autobiography, which, in turn,
is bound up with legal and extralegal testimony. This is the testimonial
condition: the decontextualized individual who stands apart from histories of oppression to assert the right to speak and to claim political and
personal freedom is a fiction. One can attempt to wield this fiction for

one's own purposes, of course, but the dynamic exclusions that derive from and continue to propound racial, gendered, and colonial histories are inseparable from the enactments of testimony this book examines.

How do liberalism and neoliberalism, filtered through and expressed in autobiography, contribute to shaping a new era in doubting women in public inaugurated, in many ways, by Anita Hill's testimony in 1991? Her testimony at Clarence Thomas's confirmation hearings before the Senate Judiciary Committee exemplified the promotion and policing of new norms around individual freedom, violence, testimony, and justice in the post-Reagan years and previewed the expanded role of media in victim blaming.[13] Victim blaming obscures the context surrounding any specific person; it is consistent with a neoliberal distortion of responsibility. Generally, victim blaming seeks to degrade individual women's capacity to receive sympathy, understanding, and justice by shifting focus and responsibility away from perpetrators and onto victims. Women who are victims can be blamed as individuals (when they are seen as "asking for it") or as members of an untrustworthy category (women are compromised as women). That is, women can be blamed by association with other compromised women witnesses but also denied the benefit that comes from helpful generalizations about women's unequal vulnerability that might explain their actions. Women victims are routinely asked if they knew the men who harmed them, if they tempted those men, and why they didn't leave if they felt endangered. Seeing victimization as cooperation or participation asks of women, what did you do to deserve this? And, in so doing, falsely represents women's vulnerability to harm as their culpability and recasts the compromised situations in which they live (relationships, workplaces, homes of various kinds) as willful choices or even risk-taking behavior. The transformation of the harm women suffer into the harm they tempt others to do is characteristic of the cultural processes through which women are discredited, and their testimony called into question. Women victims recast as wrongdoers, instigators even, of the harm in which they are caught up find themselves unable to access the benefit of the doubt. Victim blaming represents an inverted image of the individual to whom choice is attributed. In the same way that it renames victims as catalysts of their own harm who are "asking for it," or temptresses who render men incapable of restraint or judgment, neoliberalism presents an aspirational but false agency to an individual cleansed of history.

The notion of intimate publics marks a critical intervention in reading women's culture in the post-Reagan years because it identifies how the relation between a new notion of the individual and the state was experienced as communal activity among fellow citizens. In *The Queen of America Goes to Washington City, The Female Complaint*, and *Cruel Optimism*,[14] Lauren Berlant elaborates a framework for understanding the pairing of private and public life. Berlant identifies both a time and a particular mode of being-in-public within the history of sentimentality in the United States and its racialized and gendered investments and expression. Public life is saturated with feelings associated with private life. The feeling of inclusion, for example, central to feeling at home in the world could be experienced as communal and even civic engagement. One could feel good about joining with others and weighing in on the crucial issues of the day by castigating Monica Lewinsky, for example, or assessing whether Hillary Clinton should stay with or divorce her husband.[15] The melodrama of this particular situation "felt like" national political discourse in no small part because structurally it was: the discourse around sex in the White House was reported as news, debated widely, and as simple to follow as a popular song about cheating. Through public spectacles like the Clinton impeachment hearing and the confirmation of Supreme Court justices, audiences could experience their recycling of racist and sexist views as political participation.

A series of substitutions moved public awareness away from racial and gendered policies restricting access to voting, education, employment, and health care and charged venues of change like the law with therapeutic energies. Berlant identifies how the juxtaposition of law with the rise of popular confessional media makes the shifting line between public and private an issue of national political import.[16] Sexual harassment crystallizes the feelings that define this shifting line: the feelings of romantic hope and disappointment that arise within the workplace meet not simply with asymmetries of interest but with power over subordinates. The narrative of sexual harassment as an artifact of love and longing gone wrong circulates the false notion that harassment arises from innocent, unknowing, and therefore nonresponsible stirrings, awkward, perhaps, but hardly actionable. In such an interpretation, we are deflected from engaging with the economic and hierarchical conditions of working life.

Such deflections emerge around women's testimony in literary texts and legal settings. Truly, the word "responsibilize" is an awkward artifact in the lexicon of critique, but it captures how individuals are tasked with responsibilities they can never fully assume or discharge because they are positioned too far from the levers of actual responsibility to effect change. And yet, when young women are told to watch their own drinks at parties, to designate someone to watch out if another woman disappears from a party, and to wear or not to wear particular clothing in order to avoid rape, "responsibilize" describes the anonymous voice that deceptively labels ready-made blame as helpful advice for women who are seen as potential victims of violence, and who will be blamed and discredited thereafter because they should have known better. After all, they were warned. Even in the most generous interpretation, those warnings are only about evading harm rather than stopping those who perpetrate it.

In the current context of brutal and widespread attacks on people of color in the United States by police, no advice about how not to inflame police can be foolproof. The inadequacy of advice to prevent violent and deadly encounters with police derives from how culture and law disproportionately create impunity. Some young and older men can assault some women with impunity. Some police officers can assault some people of color with impunity, whether these people are college students like *New York Times* columnist Charles Blow's son, who was detained by campus police at Yale; or Martese Johnson, an undergraduate at the University of Virginia who was bloodied during an arrest by state liquor agents; or Eric Garner, a nonviolent citizen known to the police with past citations for the petty crime of selling unpackaged cigarettes; or children playing in a park in a way children play in parks across the United States, like Tamir Rice; or a young man buying Skittles and an Arizona tea at the local convenience store, like Trayvon Martin; or Michael Brown, a young man in Ferguson on a summer night who did not get out of the street—a public street in his own neighborhood—fast enough. These outcomes do not result in any coherent way from a failure to follow good advice. In these cases, the African American men and boys involved were never even permitted a hearing. Presumptions about who they were and the potential illegality or danger of their presence accelerated the actions of police and vigilantes.

I connect these disparate cases in order to materialize how judgment disproportionately affects the vulnerable. Sometimes advice dematerializes harm and makes it hard to conceive of who is responsible, who is vulnerable, and how. Declarations for the necessity of state and legal responses to testimony often emerge in concert with the restriction of the movements of the bodies and speech of women and people of color. It is no surprise that gender, race, and sexuality coincide with the construction of reliability and credibility before the law and in the intimate publics of press and media. Feminist studies and critical race studies insist on analyses that focus on lived, embodied experience, less through a focus on identity than on the structural inequalities of race, gender, and sexuality. Therefore, when intersectional analysis, for example, takes black women's experience as paradigmatic, as Brittney Cooper argues, it does so as politics and methodology.[17] It asserts that race as black women experience it reveals the intersection of race and gender as an inseparable and interwoven dimension of culture and power, imbricated with the lived and representational politics of public and private life, in domestic and international spaces, and, tellingly, in the construction of identity as a commonsense entity.

Critical language continues to evolve to provide more precise terms through which to analyze the associative capacities of power and the shifting force of histories that inform institutions like the law with what Raymond Williams called "structures of feeling."[18] The cases I read across are embedded in diverse critical methodologies and disciplines, including literary and legal analysis, that sometimes meaningfully assist understanding as cases migrate to new audiences, but often cause confusion. We need a critical language as elastic as the spatial, temporal, and embodied demand of bearing witness. First-person accounts carry histories of violence within them that they cannot fully articulate within a forum of judgment. It is also the case that these rights-bearing subjects, when they are able to appear as such within a jurisdiction, are shaped by the histories that have excluded them from freedom and agency. For this reason, as witnesses circulate within a testimonial network, the truth they can tell and the testimonial power to which they can lay claim will require audiences to be able to read race-gender together. They will need to say race-sexuality, for example, when the magnetized association of divergent affect is more the issue than convergence. The figure of the "I" can stand as such a magnetic figure: less the point of convergence visualized by intersectionality than the magnetic bar with poles of attraction and repulsion at either end. Here, too, we need a more supple term than either subject or object. We need to say simultaneously that the subject-object exists in order to name identity as a politics generated by histories of exclusion and resistance, in which personhood (subject) is entwined with the historical status of property (object) for the enslaved. Such a subject-object is always seen to generate a field of opposing and powerful forces to which both sympathy and antipathy stick. Thus the sense that there is a legal subject who differs from a literary subject who differs from other locationally or formally defined person-positions is less applicable as we track testimonial ambits than the notion that the "I" itself has certain properties that will be permitted or denied depending on who judges. For example, as I will show with Rigoberta Menchú, the function of the "I" in *testimonio* enables one person to stand in for the collective. Yet even as the "I" connotes a plural eyewitness, a hostile audience can substitute the test that some*one* is or is not telling the truth as the criterion of judgment for that *testimonio*.

First-person accounts as different as memoir and sworn testimony, for example, circulate within the testimonial network. Although they share a family resemblance and benefit from comparative readings that contextualize the range of genres in which witnesses testify, they elicit different standards of judgment.[19] Expectations about the elasticity of factual recall, the adequacy of evidence, or even the place of invention in testimony differ across accounts and audiences. Testimonial accounts are anchored in experience, but they do not simply draw their authority from how well or fully they comport with verifiable facts.[20] Instead, because testimonial truth often exceeds empirical evidence, we look to testimony for both more and less than the facts can document.[21] Testimony acquires meaning and authority from the historical force of genre. We learn how to listen, understand what is being asked of us, and respond in the context of genre. Within liberal politics, the human has rights. Within neoliberalism, the human has a story. How the story comports with genre—familiar or dissonant, conforming to expectations or unable to meet them—can determine how much access to credibility and care a witness can achieve. Testimonial truth is indexed not to facts but to power.

Tainted Witness argues that the everyday association of testimony with the test that someone either is or is not telling the truth operationalizes a political claim about who gets to decide the question. Thus this seemingly admirable truth-telling test is allied with what Donna Haraway described as the "god-trick" through which a specific epistemology is rendered seemingly free of bias by aligning it with objectivity and thereby obscuring how it is situated.[22] The thesis that a witness is either telling the truth or lying functions as a proxy for veiling the conservation of the power to judge.[23] The history of testimony, in particular, demonstrates objectivity's alignment against the dispossessed. It is not only the asymmetrical attribution of lying to women and people of color, among others, that accounts for how witnesses are mobilized within testimonial networks. The network itself is structured to speed legitimate forms of harm. To say this is to call into account the racial and gendered histories of unpunished harm that haunt the courts and weave sovereign violence into popular and institutional forums of judgment.[24] As Saidiya Hartman observes in her autobiographical narrative of searching for traces of her family's history along the Atlantic slave route: "The past is neither inert nor given. The stories we tell about *what happened then*, the correspondences we discern between today and times past, and the ethical and political stakes of these stories redound in the present. . . . If the ghost of slavery still haunts our present, it is because we are still looking for an exit from the prison."[25]

The history of slavery, Jim Crow, and civil rights in the United States, for example, significantly shaped the nomination of Clarence Thomas to succeed Justice Thurgood Marshall, the first African American to serve as a Supreme Court justice. How Thomas was able to represent his life story as an exemplary tale of postracial success and, in effect, to both reference race and also evacuate it of historical meaning illustrates the power of avowed neutrality to suppress actual histories of violence. Witnesses who require audiences to learn or to remember the history of state-sanctioned racial violence as the necessary context for bearing adequate witness to their testimony can be made to seem, in the absence of this context, incomprehensible. In contrast, those who, like Thomas, testify that they personally overcame racism offer majority audiences the opportunity to trumpet the end of slavery's lingering effects.

Given the ease with which a personal truth that promotes a postracial, postfeminist vision of history can be substituted for the evidence of sexism and racism's lively presence, *Tainted Witness* questions whether we can any longer resort to *truth* as an adequate term to describe what women's witness seeks to represent, or the grounds of ethical witness testimony requires. Although truth possesses a potent and commonsensical authority, testimonial truth and empirical evidence frequently diverge. In cases where the witness narrates traumatic experience, it is often not only trauma but the demands of testimony that drive a wedge between the event and its retelling. If we want to insist on the capacity of women witnesses to offer accurate descriptions of fact, as I believe we must, then we ought also to recognize the work they have to do to make those facts legible within a testimonial framework. There is pressure to produce an account that fits the facts and to do so in such a way that conforms to the format necessary to move forward in the search for justice. "The facts" seem to speak for themselves, but when women testify, they are rarely sufficient. Courts of public opinion weigh in on whether victims suffer the right kind of harm, the kind for which sympathy can be elicited or relief provided; or whether they suffer in the right way; or survive in a way that corresponds with the burden of proof victims are required to meet. Although truth appears to name the deep essence that witness accounts must offer and which audiences seek to plumb, the practices by which these accounts are produced and judged lie on the surface, and they demand scrutiny. When we trace how women's testimony travels within the circulatory systems of institutional and vernacular judgment, as well as literary and everyday accounts, we can recognize how women in the most constrained conditions find inventive ways to bear witness within and across the jurisdictions that define and delimit their humanity. A focus on the individual alone, therefore, misses the complexities of the network in which her testimony seeks a witness and mutes volumes of contextual, resistant knowledge.

This book begins with Anita Hill, who testified before the Senate Judiciary Committee in October 1991. Despite the case being widely described as one of he said/she said,[26] Clarence Thomas said he did not watch Hill's televised testimony. What "he said" was a robust refusal to engage wtih Hill's testimony that he sexually harassed her during the time he served as her supervisor and head of the Equal Employment Opportunity Commission. Although what "she said" may have been stringently managed by the Senate Judiciary Committee to minimize its force, Hill was questioned at length throughout a long afternoon. Similarly, Rigoberta Menchú's *testimonio* circulated widely for over a decade before it became controversial in 1991. The events about which Anita Hill and Rigoberta Menchú provided testimony unfolded over years, as is typical in histories of ongoing abuse and episodes of political repression and revolt. In such cases, a threshold of believability is briefly held open before the powerful flow of judgment finds its target and sticks. In the protracted experience of bearing witness, women's invisibility and silence serve as metaphors for thwarted agency. Scandal shifts blame onto them. Testimony provides witnesses the occasion to target those who may hold abusers to account. As the act unfolds, however, witnesses themselves may become the target of doubt and censure. A radical decontextualization of testimony occurs when an audience is prevented from grasping an individual in context. Histories unequally known and shared, politics, and institutional norms all produce complexities of positioning that provide material from which understanding develops. Neoliberalism actively dismantles such positioning as a ground of meaning.

As the figure that animates this book, a tainted witness is not who someone is but what someone can become. "Tainted witness" names the identity produced in an encounter between testimony and judgment.[27] This encounter is staged in conditions where women bring forward accounts rooted in experience, and where the general meaning of that experience is already ambivalent or polarizing; where women witnesses would benefit from ethical norms of compassion but cannot rely on them; when the experience to which she bears witness emerges from crisis, or where she is disempowered and/or "foreign," then women may become tainted witnesses. Witnesses are tainted in the act of testifying, for it is the public forum in which the testimony initially circulates that establishes the rules by which it will be judged. When Anita Hill testified, she insisted she had come to "inform about conduct" and not to "press a legal claim."[28] When Rigoberta Menchú traveled to Paris to give the interview that would become the international best seller, *I, Rigoberta Menchú*, she was trying to bring comparable international awareness to the genocide in Guatemala that was already circulating about El Salvador and Nicaragua. Yet by appearing in a volatile forum over which they would be able to exert little control, Anita Hill and Rigoberta Menchú were vulnerable to concerted political attacks to undermine the suasive force of their testimony. Certainly their truthfulness was attacked, but primarily as a means to advance an alternative political program or analysis (the interpretation of the U.S. role in Latin American politics and an anti-Marxist agenda by Menchú's attackers and the conservative, Republican ideology of Hill's enemies).

Women are often seen as unpersuasive witnesses for three related reasons: because they are women, because through testimony they seek to bear witness to inconvenient truths, and because they possess less symbolic and material capital than men as witnesses in courts of law. An intersectional analysis incorporating race and class with gender is crucial in the cases I examine because issues of power can be made to seem to be issues of individual identity only. However, cross-racial solidarity among men can also be a feature of sexual violence, and class privilege can rapidly dissolve in interactions with police (including in multiracial police forces where "thin blue line" solidarity is fostered). Take, for example, a cluster of cases about students that, despite often being lumped together, offer up instances of dense and specific textuality with complex race/gender dynamics. From the rape of a white high school student in Steubenville, Ohio, by popular football players who took video of the assault on their cell phones and shared them, to the recent case of an undergraduate claiming gang rape in a fraternity house on the University of Virginia in an inadequately verified and then discredited article in *Rolling Stone*, to the protest by a Columbia undergraduate who carried a mattress, to represent the one on which she claims she was raped, through her classes and onto the stage when she graduated as a performance of public witness, publics have confronted cases that cause affective whiplash. Before we can consider what we are to do when confronted with terrible incident after terrible story about women's vulnerability to violence and inadequate justice, we are often confronted by doubt about a woman's motives or innocence. Before further facts are brought to light, judgments are recycled as if they were truth. How are we to read each case so that we pause the rush to judgment? The very ubiquity of these acts and accounts reinforces already held positions: feminists are likely to recognize the dynamics of sexual violence enabled by a range of community and cultural investments that ride within the caveat that boys will be boys, while other audiences, like the district attorney and many school officials at the University of Montana, families, and young people in Missoula, Montana, are as likely to sanction such violence against women as part of the routine shielding of criminal male behavior from prosecution.[29] The epistemological work of reading these cases differently must be enjoined as part of the pragmatic task of what we must do differently if we are to preempt the mechanisms in the testimonial network predisposed to speed judgment along with sexist and racist bias.

Although the focus of this book is on contemporary cases, the dynamic I describe is long-standing. Tainting women's testimony is a familiar element in ancient and modern cultures. In the law, both unreliable witnesses and degraded evidence are said to be tainted. The term carries both the physical properties of stain and impurity as well as the metaphorical suggestion of ruination. Women's testimony is frequently associated with unreliability because it is women's testimony. Doubting women is enshrined in the law, represented in literature, repeated in culture, embedded in institutions, and associated with benefits like rationality and objectivity. Quite simply, women encounter doubt as a condition of bearing witness.[30] On the whole, women's testimony is greeted individually and in aggregate as messy, conflictual, and compromised.

The victim who is presumed to be complicit can never be pure enough. One thinks of Eve, of her sin of disobedience to God and her temptation of Adam; of Helen of Troy, and the compromised sexual barter of a hostage; of Jocasta, Antigone, and Ismene outside the main action of power and war but compelled to act in ways that accelerate their demise; of the impossible binds and actions of Clytemnestra and Medea and their jealousy; of La Malinche's dual reputation as traitor and survivor, and the ways in which myth and literature offer example after example of women for whom one can feel little compassion, but whose compromises emblematize the gender and race of unreliability and the limitations of agency. Think, too, of how the figures Jezebel, Mammy, and Sapphire form a repertoire of stereotypes repeated in popular culture and imposed as identities on black women.[31] These figures represent amalgams of the impossible incoherence of feelings associated with women. They make no sense. Not only are these figures of women ruled by others, their outsize emotions, actions, and forms of reasoning are presented as irrational or prerational. Their emotional excesses populate legal storytelling with cautionary tales about how people will act and how objective and dispassionate judgment must correct and rationalize their doing and their being.[32] Yet surely these figures absorb and personalize the impossibility of the situations in which they find themselves. From the concatenation of wars of conquest, hostage taking, slavery, and genocide, a pantheon of figures with seething desires and bloody hands emblematizes histories of violence projected onto women. Yet the notion that "others" and their emotions represent a threat to the law and state would have surprised an audience of ancient Athenians for whom these figures' emotions would not have been outside the law but rather a central fact of the social relations law sought to address and through which it determined how the body might be punished, imprisoned, executed, or exiled. Indeed, women's anger was frequently associated with the exercise of justice in cases where the stateless and noncitizens were on trial.[33]

While a legacy of contradictions shapes testimony historically, the global crisis affecting immigrants, refugees, and asylum seekers brings urgency to a focus on testimony and the long histories of justice in the context of noncitizens. This political catastrophe, borne as collective and personal suffering, means that witnesses will be bringing stories of harm with them as they flee. They will also be sending stories ahead of them, and these stories will mingle with precirculated stories about who they are, what they seek, and what they might do. We must pay attention both to how bodies are and are not permitted to cross boundaries, including which bodies are forbidden entry and by whom, as well as to whose stories circulate and through what intermediary voices and technologies. As Menchú insists, testimony is a crucial vehicle for propelling knowledge of atrocities to distant audiences, but to share that knowledge she became a body in motion with a story to tell as she traveled from home in Guatemala to exile in Mexico and then to France. The instant Anita Hill saw a barrage of flashbulbs erupt the first time she altered position in her seat, she knew that in photographs of her testimony, her body could be made to tell a story that would compromise her. Nafissatou Diallo appeared in prim business suits, her hair flat ironed, and worry etched into her expression as her testimony against Dominique Strauss-Kahn initially flowed into the press. Months later, when she exited civil court as the beneficiary of an unspecified financial settlement, she wore a headscarf, a flowing dress, and a confident smile. Bodies and stories move in a choreography of testimony whose temporalities are not coordinated in advance. The conflicting notions of who can be harmed, who can harm, and how such harm is best addressed raise fundamental questions about the conduct of daily life: what it means to be a person and a citizen, to have a body, to act and be acted on by others, to know oneself as vulnerable and to experience oneself as beyond the reach of judgment, and to have such knowledge extend over time until it becomes both personality and social positioning, defining the horizon of potential becoming.

A focus on tainted witness is not simply a reiteration that we should listen to women's voices. It is an analysis of how women's voices emerge as subject to doubt. Indeed, the prima facie case for twinning doubt and rationality arises in the skepticism directed at women's testimony, specifically and persistently. Not all stories are the same story, and *Tainted Witness* takes up the challenge of tracing how specific bodies and stories move within testimonial and carceral networks. Testimony can end in one location only to be revived in another; people can disappear, but their stories survive; people can survive, but bereft of stories that enable them to make sense of their survival, they falter. Focusing on specific stories accentuates the mass of accumulated meaning that sticks to testimony as it moves. Not only are attacks on women and on women's credibility concerted and ubiquitous, they follow scripts that induce fatigue by producing the effect of endless repetition and the affect of hopelessness. The swiftness with which women who bear witness attract an effective besmirching contributes to that enervating sense of sameness and repetition.

The cases I examine concern the use of the woman witness as a figure of potential credibility or doubt and take up how women's testimony grapples with issues of representational authority. Chapter 1 begins with Anita Hill, situating the study at the beginning of the 1990s (with roots in the 1980s). I argue that Anita Hill's testimony initiates a new phase in the history of discrediting women's public accounts of agentic response to sexual harassment. Sexual harassment offers a test case of how the social contract, based as it is in a public/private split, is confounded by the presence of women in the workplace as citizens, workers, professionals, colleagues, and sexual agents rather than objects.

Chapter 2 traces Rigoberta Menchú's search for an adequate witness from the interview she gave that became an international best seller to her recent vindication in Guatemalan court. I trace two histories—the history of scandal and the history of testimony—as Menchú's life story and life work move from book to documentary film to court. Through her example, we can better understand how testimony travels within a network, how it halts or continues, and how multiple audiences receive it.

Chapter 3 analyzes how the memoir scandals of the late 1990s were invoked to discredit Rigoberta Menchú's *testimonio* but also focused additional vitriol at women who wrote about incest and sexual violence within families. The response to Kathryn Harrison's *The Kiss* demonstrates how judgments about women's credibility operate across legal and cultural courts of public opinion. It did not take long for the memoir boom to generate a backlash rather than a bust. From Kathryn Harrison, who blew up the memoir boom, to Elizabeth Gilbert and Cheryl Strayed, who revived and redefined it, respectively, women's memoir now permits a traumatized heroine, but she must be resilient and sexually well-adjusted if her life story is to skirt critique. This chapter follows women's life narrative as it migrates into the twenty-first century, via Oprah Winfrey's Book Club and television show, to the genres of self-help and the redemption narrative.

Chapter 4 takes up the interest in secondhand life narratives of girls exemplified by Greg Mortenson and David Oliver Relin's *Three Cups of Tea* and Nicholas Kristof and Sheryl WuDunn's *Half the Sky*[34] and argues that humanitarian campaigns now promote ever purer (and younger) victims as deserving of empathy and Western intervention. Blameless witnesses, sufficiently innocent to arouse nearly universal sympathy and often the victims of profoundly unsympathetic criminals, populate accounts by Mortenson, Relin, Kristof, and WuDunn. For Mortenson, girls in Afghanistan ground his appeal. Kristof and WuDunn draw more broadly from a global archive of traumatized girlhood, but one thinks also of Malala Yousafzai, shot on her way to school; of schoolgirls kidnapped by Boko Haram in Nigeria; of a young woman gang raped on a bus in India. Often young, seeking education or employment, these girls and women spark international awareness campaigns, as they should, but not necessarily in concert with local efforts at feminist reform. Thus Mortenson, Relin, Kristof, and WuDunn expose the appeal of the proxy witness: the man who speaks on behalf of girls and women and who, in a turn of the humanitarian screw, is not so much their proxy as they are his.

Chapter 5 examines two examples of unsympathetic women witnesses and the transits of their testimony across an assemblage of legal and literary modes of judgment. I follow the rape case brought by Nafissatou Diallo against former head of the International Monetary Fund and former French presidential hopeful Dominique Strauss-Kahn as Diallo and her testimony traveled from criminal court, through the court of public opinion, to civil court. I read Diallo's search for an adequate witness in relation to the autobiographical fiction of Jamaica Kincaid. Kincaid offers a literary witness who generates an ethical response that is not primarily grounded in identification or compassion. A literary witness emerges from a close engagement with the textuality and the trajectory of testimony and offers an ethical stance toward unsympathetic witnesses. *Tainted Witness* asks not only who is she and what her story is, but what we owe her.

Tainted Witness concludes with a discussion of embodied witness and its representation in protest, online, and in literary texts and argues for the copresence in testimonial networks of contemporary forms and figures of witness and judgment and the weight of submerged histories in search of an adequate witness. I read the prospects for bearing embodied witness through a constellation of powerful contemporary examples that center black women's voices, embodiment, and protest in a range of forms and across different platforms, including #BlackLivesMatter, Sandra Bland's protest captured on a police car dashboard camera, Bree Newsome's act of civil disobedience when she took down the Confederate flag from the state capitol grounds in Charleston, South Carolina, and Claudia Rankine's *Citizen: An American Lyric*.[35] The example of #BlackLivesMatter underscores the labor of turning histories of racial violence and the grief and lamentation to which they give rise into protest.

Testimony represents a fulcrum where the value of life weighs in the balance: on one side, harm; on the other, rights. Testimony names a form through which those who have been harmed claim a right to speak, to be heard, and to seek justice. Judith Butler, in a sustained examination of "grievable life,"[36] argues that the human as a rights-bearing construct is compelled to appear through a series of frames that delimit its access to that category. Butler makes a case for the co-construction of harm and rights: rights matter not only when we are injured but because we can be harmed. *Tainted Witness* takes up women's witness, specifically, not to essentialize the harms to which women can and cannot bear witness, or to link them falsely across time and space, but to analyze what has remained a blank in the historicization of trauma and testimony: that norms of justice and personhood do not fully include women, and their agency, value, and even existence are often denied through this exclusion. Testimonial accounts arise in relation to judgment and not simply as an expression of truth. This matters for how we think about neutral standards of judgment, including whether someone is telling the truth. We do not always tell the same story even when we narrate the same event.

Empathy is typically taken to be necessary to sociality. Putting oneself in the place of another and, in a sense, overcoming alterity through voluntary understanding enable some of the complex interactions required to ease the friction of social differences. Yet in the refusal to bear witness to stories in which race, gender, harm, and credulity interact, empathy often extends to perpetrators of violence rather than to their victims. Thus empathy is both an inadequate ground for an ethical engagement with unsympathetic witnesses, as women are likely to be, and also a form of sociality that reproduces historical asymmetries in race, gender, and credibility. It may seem counterintuitive to oppose truth and empathy in a book about why we don't believe what women say about their lives, but truth and empathy move through testimonial networks along well-mapped routes and can be transformed into additional material with which to strengthen social hierarchies, institutional norms of law, and the disinhibition of bias rather than its amelioration into justice.

1

ANITA HILL, CLARENCE THOMAS, AND THE SEARCH FOR AN ADEQUATE WITNESS

*For insight into the complicated and complicating events
that the confirmation of Clarence Thomas became,
one needs perspective, not attitudes; contexts, not anecdotes;
analyses, not postures. For any kind of lasting illumination,
the focus must be on the history routinely ignored or
played down or unknown.*

—TONI MORRISON

The trick is then just to keep the light shining.

—ANITA HILL

What justifies a return now to the notorious hearings in which Anita Hill testified in Clarence Thomas's confirmation process, twenty five years on? For some, what played out in the 1991 hearings in Washington remains a paradigmatic example of "he said/she said." Broadcast in televised hearings, reported in newspapers, and talked about by seemingly everyone, the event riveted a national audience.[1] For others, feminist critics in particular, the case endures as an indelible reminder of what Toni Morrison refers to as a "history routinely ignored or played down or unknown," and a display of legally permissible and intertwining forms of racism and sexism. By "keeping a light shining" on Anita Hill's testimony, we trace how sexual harassment was carved out as an issue for white feminists, while racism was represented as a threat to black men in legal proceedings. Anita Hill was associated with feminist legal reformers targeting workplace discrimination rather than with working women of color, while Clarence Thomas presented himself as a postracial, anti–affirmative action black candidate for the Supreme Court. Hill was managed into a knowable enemy—a feminist—as Thomas's team tried to prevent him from turning into one—a black man. That is, until Thomas characterized the proceedings as a "high tech lynching for uppity blacks."[2] After that comment, Hill shed race but became saturated in gender, while Thomas claimed blackness but struggled to retain the privilege of masculinity granted by law. As Anita Hill put it: "I had a gender, he had a race," an analysis to which I will return. Following Hill's advice "to keep a light shining" on race and gender in the hearings, I read how the dueling life narratives Hill and Thomas offered, first as testimony and later as memoir, expose how race, gender, sex, and doubt travel together.

In testament to the continuing relevance of the hearings in public memory, a 2014 documentary, *Anita*, brings the event to members of a new generation who have no memory of the hearings and lack knowledge of how sexual harassment law improved workplaces over the past twenty-five years. With reference to the documentary, Hill argues for the benefit of historical context in understanding the processes through which sexual harassment can be exposed and the need for vigilance in ensuring legal means through which to seek relief from it. Yet, as Morrison argues, the history of slavery also informs the "unknown" recent history of feminist efforts to create protections for sexual harassment. The context for understanding the raced and gendered witness of the hearings, then, extends back to slavery and its sanctioned forgetting in public life, includes the contemporary context of sexual harassment law and its recent forgetting, and extends into the future in the form of Justice Clarence Thomas's jurisprudence, which is characterized by an intolerance for prisoners' rights, civil rights, and reproductive freedom.

Here we find a potent case for understanding how the testimonial network teems with histories of violence and legitimacy that exceed any specific case, and how judgments about race, gender, bodies, and the power of life story stick to witnesses who move through it.

Testimonial networks are never neutral. Testimonial accounts achieve a hearing within jurisdictions they never control, although they may expose their limits. When Anita Hill participated as a witness in Clarence Thomas's nomination process, her testimony exposed the limits of the confirmation hearings to provide an adequate witness to racism and sexism in law, work, history, and intimate life. Hill's testimony disrupted the carefully managed construction of Thomas as a post–civil rights nominee to succeed Justice Thurgood Marshall, the first African American on the Supreme Court and legendary civil rights advocate who argued *Brown v. Board of Education* before the court in 1954, the case that ended the legal basis for racial segregation. Thomas and his handlers gravely underestimated the volatility of Hill's testimony that he had sexually harassed her when she worked for him as an attorney at the Equal Employment Opportunity Commission, an agency of the federal government created by the civil rights act. The legacies of slavery, racial segregation, and civil rights legislation were brought into view by testimony about sexual harassment rather than by a claim about racial bias. As Avery Gordon's approach to haunting suggests, the racist past overloaded a proceeding about sexual harassment with an intensity of affect it could not address or discharge.[3] Yet reminders persisted. The exclusion of people of color from the corridors of power was visually represented by the exclusive presence of white men on the Senate Judiciary Committee. Only Clarence Thomas's assertion that Hill's testimony had transformed his confirmation into a "high tech lynching for uppity blacks" materialized the confluence of legality and racial violence. When Anita Hill testified about sexual harassment, she also forced the careful management of race in Thomas's nomination into view.

During the course of the hearings Anita Hill became a tainted witness. To understand this, we must examine the testimonial network in which she bore witness, its investments in presenting racism in the United States as what Thomas had overcome in his personal journey, and its argument that sexual harassment was an artifact of the feminist movement rather than a part of a racial history the nomination process rescripted in order to suppress the threat to civil rights Thomas's ideology posed. A fuller examination of the context that Anita Hill was prevented from providing during the hearings reveals how affect, race, gender, law, and history impact witnesses within testimonial networks, which incubate histories of racism that can erupt in formal spaces like the Senate, in testimonial forms like memoir, and in the jurisprudence and ongoing work on rights that have become the opposing postconfirmation legacies of Clarence Thomas and Anita Hill.

Senator Alan Simpson, a member of the Senate Judiciary Committee, was right when he predicted that Anita Hill would "be injured and destroyed and belittled and hounded and harassed, real harassment, different from the sexual kind, just plain old Washington variety harassment" when she testified.[4] On October 11, 1991, Anita Hill testified during the final days of Clarence Thomas's confirmation hearings. She stated that while she was Thomas's employee at the EEOC, he had sexually harassed her by importuning her for dates and, after she refused, discussing in graphic detail the kinds of pornography he enjoyed, his own sexual prowess, whether he found her sexually appealing in particular clothes, and his continuing insistence that "you should date me." During the afternoon in which she testified, the committee reframed Hill's description of how Thomas had sexualized the workplace, and the claim of sexual harassment generally, by reinterpreting *his* conduct as *her* fantasy, *her* mistaken impression, or *her* fabrication. In an effort to manage Hill's damaging testimony into a he said/she said frame where it could be dismissed with a shrug of undecidability, the committee unleashed a secondary "real harassment, different from the sexual kind," in Senator Simpson's terms, to destroy her as a credible witness. In his formulation of "real harassment," Simpson revealed the game plan for tainting Hill as a credible witness ("to injure, to destroy, to hound, to belittle"), as well as his view of the lesser harm of the "sexual kind" of harassment, the kind of harassment that is less than real. The Republican senators on the committee and a host of other participants belittled both Hill and her claims of sexual harassment. By remaking both into vague rather than substantive entities, they cast Hill as someone whose motives made no sense and sexual harassment as a workplace invention of feminists who shouldn't be there in the first place. A man's sexual conduct, according to this logic, as we shall see, should remain private no matter where it occurs, sealed within a bubble of impunity in which he floats from home to office, to government, and court. Under the chairmanship of Senator Joseph Biden, witnesses who would have corroborated Hill's testimony and burst that bubble were not called, while hearsay about her alleged behavior in other workplaces and in social settings was actively sought and found its way into the record. In other words, her ability to create a context in which her testimony would be credible, notably by allowing another woman whom Thomas had treated similarly to testify, was refused. There would be no meaningful movement of information across the frames of friendship, office, government, and court. Confusion about what would be allowed for Thomas and disallowed for Hill, as well as the commingling of hearsay and testimony, was so rampant that at one point committee member Howard Metzenbaum, an Ohio Democrat, asked the fundamental procedural question of the hearing, "What are the rules?"[5]

Returning to this case now enables us to take Metzenbaum's exasperated rhetorical query seriously and to pose critical feminist questions from the vantage point of twenty-five years after the hearings burst in klieg-lit intensity onto the public stage. Here we see how women's witness is tainted through the permissible protocols of legal processes, as well as a range of tactics that amount to smears. These smears rely on stereotype and bias, often have little relation to truth, and can be fed into legal processes where they discredit women as if they were factual.

The time frame of scandal is crucial to tainting women witnesses. Scandal's temporal signature is acceleration. The rush to judgment encourages framing testimonial conflicts in terms of who is telling the truth and who is lying, with the presumption that this is an adequate and meaningful testimonial test. Such a framing, however, prevents witnesses from providing adequate context for their testimony. The coproduction of tainted and adequate witnesses underscores that testimonial networks embed multiple audiences who use different and conflicting criteria for determining legitimacy. Witnesses cross into jurisdictions in which their accounts lack adequate context. Formal processes restrict what they can say, to whom, and in what language, but they cannot purge the past of its deep damage. However, when the haunting histories that obscurely animate proceedings burst into view, the disruption they engender can continue to mobilize witnesses outside the frame of the jurisdiction in which testimony is initially circumscribed. Haunting can imply hope for new encounters with the painful past.[6]

We can now, in retrospect, review the hearing itself in slow motion and break the tempo of scandal. A number of documents fill the archive: from the transcript of testimony given during the confirmation hearings, to comprehensive investigative reporting by principals who continue to speak to the legacy of the hearings, to edited collections of essays in support of Hill, to memoirs by Hill and Thomas, and the memoirs of those involved in the hearings in many different capacities. From this perspective, we see better what was managed to the sidelines: how Clarence Thomas prepared a path to the nomination over several years and how Anita Hill became collateral damage in a conservative Republican strategy to place an anti–affirmative action African American justice in Thurgood Marshall's seat; how slavery, Jim Crow, and post–civil rights racism would haunt the hearings; how Anita Hill's testimony was blocked until a group of women senators demanded that she be heard; how witnesses who would have corroborated her account were not permitted to speak; how Thomas's and Hill's postconfirmation paths continue to shape the race-gender-citizenship nexus through Thomas's jurisprudence and Hill's public speaking, teaching, legal and popular writing, and film. Anita Hill's testimony provides a historical opening for this book in order to mark how the hearing shaped the terms for how women would be doubted in public in the post-Reagan years even as they were increasingly present and credible on a public stage. All these processes, though, can still fail to provide adequate context unless the afterlife of slavery and Jim Crow is engaged in thinking on race and gender.[7] Anita Hill's testimony demonstrates how a professional African American woman, a graduate of Yale Law and a law professor, a person who understood the forum in which she gave testimony as well as it could have been understood, could be tainted as "a little bit nutty and a little bit slutty" in order for a conservative African American justice with a meager record and no major accomplishments to secure a Republican vote on the court.[8]

In subsequent critical reflection on the hearings, opinion has pursued two lines of analysis: a feminist analysis that places race at the center of inquiry, and a political analysis of the hearings as a struggle to secure a conservative vote on the Supreme Court.[9] Feminist analysis has attended to the figure and person of Anita Hill, while analyses of Washington politics, often offered by journalists and legal scholars, focus on Clarence Thomas.[10] Taken separately, these analyses focus on the movement of persons and testimony through professional, legal, familial, and media networks and reveal how power smoothed and blocked the paths of witnesses. Each specifies how belief attached to Hill and Thomas variously, how it stuck initially to him, and how it shifted to her.[11] A critical question looms large here: what is the relationship between gender and racial violence? How did Hill's gendered testimony about sexual harassment interrupt Thomas's scripted narrative of race and expose the narrative of law, gender, and race that Thomas's narrative sought to tell?

Clarence Thomas's campaign for nomination to the Supreme Court began early in his career, and its central feature appears to have been the strategic use of his life story. The "Pin Point strategy," named after the small, rural town in Georgia where Thomas was born into poverty, enabled Thomas to offer a story rooted in the history of slavery and Jim Crow that presented his climb from humble beginnings as something more than the individual narrative of the rise.[12] The Pin Point strategy also offered a way for white conservative politicians to brush aside the history of race entirely. Thomas was a self-made man, and if he could make it on his own, all African Americans could and should. The story, honed over years, moved to tears President George H. W. Bush, who nominated Thomas, and inspired him to bungle his prepared nomination statement, replacing the scripted "best man" for the job to "most qualified," a glaring falsehood, but one that represents the power of this narrative to travel beyond the frame of life story and substitute the affective glow it was designed to offer in place of professional expertise and experience. The American Bar Association offered Thomas the lowest rating for a nominee: a barebones "qualified." He had risen within the conservative political network to his appointment to the EEOC and then a judgeship independent of much of a legal record.

The personal narrative of humble beginnings represents politics by other means. It sends coded signals of reassurance to like-minded audiences. It focuses attention on the preprofessional life of the candidate to deflect scrutiny from an inspection of what the past actually was prologue to. Following Robert Bork's failed confirmation, nominees to the court adopted a "say nothing" strategy about their views. In the absence of discussion of legal principle and precedent, life story represented a pool into which the committee was invited to peer and see only the burnished image of the nominee they sought reflected back to them.[13] In Thomas's case, as in others following the unabashedly conservative Justice Bork's contentious nomination, life narrative provided a Teflon coating over the ideology of nominees and placed what was often the reason for their selection off-limits for actual discussion.[14] More pitch than life story, the nominees' narratives were honed to elicit the right affect.

The up-from-poverty story begins with Thomas's birth in rural Georgia. His parents were not married, and Thomas had a sister and brother. His father left when Thomas was young, and his mother worked as a maid for low wages, long hours, and no better prospects despite her toil. With no other options to feed and clothe her three young children, she asked her estranged parents for help. They took in the two brothers, exacted stern discipline and regular corporal punishment, provided private Catholic school education, and gave Thomas and his brother a foundation of care based on the unacknowledged sacrifice his sister and mother made to obtain support for the boys. Thomas did not place his mother's sacrifice into his public narrative despite the fact that her decision to send him to her parents set his success story in motion. Thomas's grandparents provided a stable life. His grandfather owned two businesses and supported civil rights and labor, both movements

Thomas would disavow to his grandfather's disappointment.[15] While the Pin Point strategy suppressed his mother's and sister's ongoing poverty, it implied a narrative of persistent poverty when he lived with his grandparents. Thomas's characterization of ongoing economic deprivation surprised people who knew his financially stable grandparents in Savannah or attended school with him. Despite his assertions that he "fended for himself" and received "active opposition" rather than government assistance, Thomas's actual circumstances were transformed by the advent of civil rights and the affirmative action program that enabled him to attend Holy Cross and Yale Law School. Thomas spoke against *Brown v. Board of Education* and in support of segregated schooling, despite having escaped the worst version of that system by attending a segregated parochial school founded in 1878 and staffed by white, civil rights–minded nuns.[16] Thomas and his narrative circulated together through conservative Washington circles and assured conservative white contacts that he was reliably anti–affirmative action, indifferent to civil rights, and uncommitted to labor. The packaging of conservative political ideology as a narrative of humble origins magnetized patrician white patrons like President George H. W. Bush and Senator John Danforth to Thomas. Used as a set-piece in his public appearance, Thomas's narrative also circulated in popular media during the confirmation hearings, remained the standard version in the press and his paid lectures thereafter, and was later revived in Thomas's memoir.

Clarence Thomas represented a convenient paradox for white Washington politics: the self-made man who benefited from the opportunities of affirmative action but disavowed them as corrosive to self-worth. The paradox between the claim of being self-made and the benefit of civil rights legislation would need to dissolve in order for the self-made man narrative to succeed as his political autobiography. In an effort to resolve the juxtaposition of a self-made man who had pulled himself up on his own *and* benefited from affirmative action, Thomas denounced affirmative action programs publicly and frequently in emotionally charged statements. He identified affirmative action as an injury: neither racism, poverty, paternal abandonment, nor the loss of living with his mother and sister would figure as strongly.

The Pin Point strategy celebrated virtue and moral rectitude as the fruits of Thomas's disciplined rise from poverty. It did not include three key issues: his evolving views on civil rights, his enthusiasm for watching and discussing pornography, and his history of using the work places he supervised as dating pools. First, his early commitment to civil rights and his friendship with Lani Guinier, the civil rights and social justice theorist, with whom he had planned to pursue civil rights law after law school, fell outside the official narrative, and his evolving views of civil rights were not discussed during his confirmation.[17] Second, the well-known fact that Thomas enjoyed pornography and talked about it with friends and at work, as Anita Hill testified, similarly fell outside the authorized narrative. Third, Thomas's behavior as a supervisor included sexualizing the workplace, as Angela Wright was prepared to confirm, though she was blocked from testifying. Thomas's friends recognized the man and behavior Hill described, and not the pure nominee on view up until she testified. Yet the Pin Point strategy, which restricted attention to a pinpoint-sized frame of its own creation, was so successful that Thomas's patron Senator John Danforth was shocked to think Thomas could even utter a profanity and could not reconcile the prayerful, somber Thomas he knew with the pornography enthusiast.[18] The life story had done its intended work, but it rendered the person it purported to represent unrecognizable to those who knew him.

Thomas's life story was not the only one shared with a national audience. Indeed, the hearings offered twin autobiographical narratives of the rise from poverty by African Americans in the South through elite education to professional success. Both Thomas's and Hill's experiences were rooted in Jim Crow; both had living relatives who remembered a family member who had been enslaved. Both spoke of family love and support, and the sustaining presence of church and faith (Catholicism for Thomas and the Baptist church for Hill). Yet there were differences. Anita Hill had an equally compelling story of rising from humble origins, but no "Lone Tree strategy" had been prepared for her. Instead, her life story spoke in the key of history rather than myth. She was the thirteenth of thirteen children born to African American parents in Lone Tree, Oklahoma. Her great grandparents and maternal grandmother were born into slavery in Arkansas. The family had a strong Baptist faith. Hill was the valedictorian of her high school graduating class, earned honors at Oklahoma State, and attended Yale Law, like Thomas. Yet, as Hill would later say, her life story could not find traction during the hearing: "I had a gender, he had a race." It was as if the story of a woman's rise, unburnished by strategists, carried too much historical reality. His story shed history, as well as other people, and rose to myth; hers was rooted in family and care, confirmed her discipline and talent, and remained stubbornly particular. Rather than engage with her actual life story, Thomas's supporters presented Anita Hill as incoherent and baffling: either she was a liar outright, as Thomas insisted, or she was a careerist, a professional woman willing to maintain ties with Thomas for the sake of her professional network. That she could also have been sexually harassed was denied.

The he said/she said framework of judgment that was organized through ignorant and hostile questioning, and reported in news accounts, replaced the testimonial significance of how race and gender informed these his-and-hers life stories. As Anita Hill commented, the prominence of Thomas's life story coupled with the perfunctory treatment of her own repressed the connections between race and gender. But their stories provided far more context for understanding the routes by which they arrived at the Senate confirmation hearings than could gain adequate witness. Although their humble beginnings inspired comparison, Thomas's upbringing was defined by paternal abandonment, and Hill's, by a large and supportive family. Whereas Thomas is recalled as a boisterous consumer of porn and something of the "class clown" in his needling of straitlaced colleagues in his first job working for Senator Danforth, Hill was "bookish" and "sheltered," as her relatives described her, protected by her mother and immersed in moral lessons drawn from life and the Bible.[19] There are no stories of her breaking out of this mold when she arrived in Washington, of telling a lie, or behaving unethically. Thomas's life story framed race as apolitical: Thomas was not angry, militant, or activist; or, if he did have an activist period, it was enfolded into a developmental narrative as a youthful enthusiasm. In contrast, Hill's politics stuck to her in this public forum: she was a pro–civil rights feminist.

"LET ME TRY TO EXPLAIN AGAIN"

Let us turn now to the substance of Hill's testimony. During the final days of the Senate confirmation hearings, she testified that when she worked for Thomas at the EEOC, he had used his position to pressure her for dates. She described how he sexualized the workplace through consistent reference to his sexual desires and preferences, including the kind of pornography he enjoyed (featuring bestiality, rape, and group sex). During these encounters, Thomas commented on her body and comportment, including whether certain outfits or hairstyles made her more or less sexually attractive to him. Thomas's behavior took place in the office, during work hours, and during meetings addressing EEOC business. Thomas interrupted meetings when Hill was present to pursue the topic of his sexual interests, talked over her protestations, and disregarded her presentations on legal matters as she consistently attempted to conduct a one-sided professional relationship.

While she worked at the EEOC, Hill confided to a few close friends that Thomas's behavior was unwelcome, rebuffed, and unstoppable. It undercut her effectiveness on the job and made her sick. Like many working women who experience sexual harassment, she was trapped; however, as the subordinate of a political appointee in Washington, D.C., where patronage and connections rule, her entrapment was not simply restricted to a single place of employment. If Hill wanted to work in Washington, she would need to survive working with Thomas in order to move on. Although some commentators expressed disbelief that anyone who had been sexually harassed would retain any contact with such an employer, would ask for a letter of recommendation, would not widely bad-mouth such an employer, or would not otherwise burn her bridges, Hill chose to behave at the EEOC exactly as she behaved when she testified before the Senate Judiciary Committee and in the twenty-five years since she worked for Thomas: she said as little about it as she could in public in order to make her point.

When Hill did bring forward her public account of sexual harassment, it was because she was subpoenaed. Arizona Democrat Senator

Dennis DeConcini explicitly misrepresented how Hill's account of sexual harassment reached the committee. On October 7, as her statement was provided to committee members in response to requests from the committee itself for information, DeConcini said, "If you're sexually harassed, you ought to get mad about it, and you ought to do something about it, and you ought to complain, instead of hanging around a long time and then all of a sudden calling up anonymously and say, 'Oh, I want to complain.' I mean, where is the gumption?"[20] Her description of why she informed about Thomas's conduct baffled members of the Senate Judiciary Committee. Their response became a tactic, intentional or merely reflexive, to shift the focus away from Thomas's conduct and place it on Hill: How did she feel when she was subjected to unwanted conversation about porn? Why did she continue to work for Thomas? What kind of dating relationships did she have? Was she, in Alabama Democrat Howell Heflin's memorably florid characterization, "a scorned woman . . . a zealoting civil rights believer . . . [someone with] a militant attitude relative to the area of civil rights . . . [someone with] a martyr complex . . . [seeking to become] a hero in the civil rights movement"?[21] Heflin and others concocted extreme scenarios to explain away a simpler version of events and motivation. Witnesses in support of Thomas were encouraged to speculate without basis about motive, too, as if to render the details of workplace harassment increasingly specular and unstable. Interpretation replaced testimony. In this new construction, Thomas had not sexually harassed her, or, if he had, she was a participant. She was lying about it happening at all, or she was lying about her previous participation, or she had fantasized such interest from Thomas and invented an account of it with which to punish him. Her motives were either political, intended to block the nomination of a conservative justice to the Supreme Court, or merely personal. Thomas went the furthest in his characterization of Hill and his denunciation of her testimony: a friend turned betrayer, she was in league with a conspiracy to undo him: "Senator, I believed that someone, some interest group—I don't care who it is—in combination, came up with this story and used this process to destroy me. . . . I believe that in combination this was developed, or concocted, to destroy me. . . . [M]y view is that others put it together and developed this. . . . All I know is that the story is here and I think it was concocted. . . . The story is false, the story is here, and the story was developed to harm me."[22] Yet in the nearly twenty-five years after Thomas alleged that Hill perjured herself, no one has brought forward any evidence that Hill lied, that she had been a part of any conspiracy, or that anything other than exactly what she reported happened. How, then, could such an elaborate smokescreen successfully occlude her testimony?

Hill's testimony revealed huge gaps in public knowledge about sexual harassment, a workplace dynamic that was coming into view as women were challenging discriminatory practices and everyday sexism in the workplace. Hill's experience at the EEOC was saturated with unwanted sexualization. There was no sexual harassment law to which she could appeal for relief, no sexual harassment prevention workshop or human resources officer to whom she could report. If she wanted to stay in the job, and also if she wanted to move to another one, Anita Hill had to wade daily through the sticky, ugly atmosphere, knowing that her boss was likely to say something vulgar that would knock her off her game, distract her from work, and diminish her professionally and personally. When Hill appeared before the committee, the senators lacked an understanding of sexual harassment and used public unknowing about sexual harassment strategically to facilitate victim blaming. The lack of an available public and feminist discourse through which to make the significance of this widespread harm knowable showed in the questioning. Hill called attention consistently both to what had happened and to how to understand it. In an unmistakably lawyerly method, Hill returned to the facts, established principles, and pressed her points. Her signature phrase, "Let me try to explain again," threaded throughout her testimony in response to the false leads and blind alleys down which the Republican senators were intent on journeying.

Because Thomas's vulgarity was central to her testimony, Hill was compelled to find his words in her mouth. His notorious comment, "Who has put pubic hair on my Coke?," had the kind of real-world specificity that persuaded some commentators that Hill was credible.[23] The stereotypical sexual harassment scenario at that time featured the handsy male boss chasing a female secretary around the desk. Thomas's preferred mode was verbal harassment, and his preferred subject was dating and pornography. In her recollection, Thomas enjoyed using his power over her, punishing her with this talk, and subjecting her to discomfort. With comments about rape scenes in pornography and whether he found her outfit sexy ringing in her ears, Hill would leave Thomas's office rattled, but she disciplined herself to remain professional.

Hill lacked an advocate in the hearings who could have filled in the context crucial for a new understanding of sexual harassment to emerge in public. At least an advocate could have educated the other committee members, deflected their most egregious statements, and called for greater fairness to Hill in the process she joined under subpoena. Massachusetts Democrat Edward Kennedy would have been an obvious candidate for the role, but his role in a recent rape scandal involving his nephew muted him. Even without providing advocacy, Senator Joseph Biden as chair failed to balance the hearings: " 'He was basically playing judge,' Susan Deller Ross, a Georgetown University law professor and expert in workplace sex discrimination, said of Mr. Biden, adding 'the other side was playing advocate' for Mr. Thomas. 'I'm sure you remember nobody played advocate for her. I don't think he did well and he bears responsibility for Mr. Thomas being on the court.' "[24] Instead, Biden introduced the standard of a criminal proceeding to face Hill's testimony. Thomas would enjoy the presumption of innocence.

Biden has been described as tilting the process to favor Thomas in multiple ways. In a crucial decision, for example, Biden did not permit Angela Wright to speak. Wright was the key suppressed witness who had worked for Thomas, dated him, recalled his pornography enthusiasm, broken up with him, been fired by him, and then been actively managed by Thomas's team into a quid pro quo for her ongoing silence with a positive letter of recommendation from Clarence Thomas.[25] Wright's testimony could have diluted the taint of Hill alone having to speak Thomas's words that she found so degrading. In a further concentration of responsibility for bearing witness to sexual harassment to Hill alone, Biden did not permit affidavits from an expert on whether a pattern of behavior needed to be established to prove sexual harassment. Susan Deller Ross, also a member of Hill's hastily composed legal team, concluded: "He did everything to make it be good for Thomas and to slant it against her."[26]

Despite her admirable life story, unblemished record as a government employee and law professor, and uncontroversial life as a private citizen, Anita Hill was subjected to two forms of witness tainting: one on view within the hearing and the other a hastily undertaken smear campaign that fed misrepresentations, wild allegations, and theatrics into the hearings through committee members' questions.[27] The boundary of the hearing would prove porous when the project was tainting Hill. The first unfolded under Senator Biden's control as committee chair and the second as he presided over the hearing. Thomas's team had prepared for the hearings well. One task had been to manage Angela Wright offstage and to buy her silence with a positive job recommendation. Further damage to Hill was permitted through the failure to uncover what journalists Jane Mayer and Jill Abramson documented and what could have informed the proceedings once Hill began to testify. The second took the form of all-out character assassination as Thomas's supporters, shaken by Hill's testimony, stirred outright lies, hearsay, and calumny into a "witch's brew"[28] and flooded the media with misrepresentation. Among these participants was Senator John Danforth, Clarence Thomas's patron and supporter throughout his confirmation hearing. As Danforth described in his posthearing memoir, he sought to dig up as much dirt as he could throw at Hill. He actively sought affidavits from former and current students at Oral Roberts University and University of Oklahoma College of Law and from former peers at Yale Law School meant to incriminate Hill.[29] Danforth even provided Wyoming Democrat Alan Simpson with a couple of dubious faxes and letters, which Simpson multiplied to "sound like an outpouring of seriously disturbing truths about Hill. But almost all of them were from students who had never studied with her and had no firsthand knowledge."[30] Danforth took it as his mission to generate what he knew to be unsubstantiated and scurrilous smears of Hill: "getting those affidavits was my obsession that afternoon. I knew that Anita Hill was going to be demolished. . . . In my quest for affidavits I was showing no concern at all for fairness to Anita Hill."[31] Because the time from

Hill's testimony to the confirmation vote was brief, no one could run so many assertions to ground in a few days' time.

The jurisdiction in which Hill testified was an amalgam of parliamentary procedure and stagecraft. The event had all the trappings of an official hearing, including the swearing in of witnesses, but kept mutating with an improvised quality that gave rise to genuine befuddlement and exasperation, as Metzenbaum's query, "what are the rules?" reveals. The improvisation that informed the hearing drew on the practices of both private and public prosecution.[32] The majority of the members of the Senate Judiciary Committee, Anita Hill, Clarence Thomas, and many of those whose testimony was elicited were trained as attorneys, and the reserves on which they drew to shape their questions and statements reflected this expertise. Through the public prosecutor's role, the state expands its power to punish individuals. Through private prosecution, an individual can press a claim. Hill was treated by many of the committee members as if she were pressing a claim, despite the facts of how her testimony reached the committee. It was offered in response to a question about Thomas, Hill insisted it be sealed and that she retain confidentiality, and she became publicly known only when NPR correspondent Nina Totenberg acquired Hill's statement as it was about to be leaked to the press and asked Hill to comment on it. Her testimony was all the more shocking for the tight control Thomas's supporters and handlers had exerted over all aspects of the nomination and confirmation processes. Yet from the moment Anita Hill placed her hand on the Bible and submitted to questioning, punishment hung in the air because that is what legal proceedings, backed by the power and legitimacy of the state, deliver.

The hearings were described as traumatic and mesmerizing, which alerts us that while harm was unfolding in real time, another history was looming there, too, in search of an adequate witness and contemporary forms through which to make itself felt.[33] Within the testimonial space of the hearing, the racial past sought a witness. The relationship between racial violence, segregation, sexual violence, and workplace harassment represented the necessary context for understanding Anita Hill's and Clarence Thomas's intertwined lives. Although this context was never permitted to appear, it haunted the proceedings. The jurisdiction that took shape around and fostered judgment against Hill was animated by the histories of racial and sexual violence and the legal cover offered by slavery, Jim Crow, and lack of adequate law to protect against their reorganization after civil rights. From the all-male, white committee members intoning about processes they were improvising for their own benefit, to the presence of Hill's family seated in silence behind her as she was compelled to repeat the words of Thomas, to the dueling life stories of southern African American families who had emerged from slavery to forge lives in Oklahoma and Georgia in which women were still unable to protect and provide for their children, the past broke through the managed forum of the hearings and was opaquely reenacted. In the Hill-Thomas hearings, a black woman's sworn speech informing about the conduct of a nominee to the Supreme Court in his position at the EEOC became both vivid testimony about sexual harassment and a proximate and public reenactment of it.

The array of gendered and raced power became a forum of judgment organized around Hill's speech, despite the fact that she was neither on trial nor pressing a legal claim. A tainted witness is not who someone *is* but who someone can *become* in the process of bringing an account into the public sphere. Inadequately in control of the forum of judgment, unable to offer appropriate context, and reliant on ethical norms that are unequally applied to witnesses, Anita Hill as witness found herself in a precarious position. As a tactic to taint her, Senators Orrin Hatch and Arlen Specter most vigorously pursued shaming and suggested Hill herself had a penchant for pornography, on which she drew to create her account of Thomas's behavior. Both Specter and Hatch suggested Hill sought contact with Thomas; or, if she did not seek it, she tolerated it; or, if she did not do either, her inability to make it stop represented a kind of assent.

The volatility of this testimony was evident as it pitched and circulated around the testimonial cast of characters. To whom could it be made to stick? Who could be tarnished by this particular muck? Toni Morrison observes that by virtue of the association of racialization and sexualization, Clarence Thomas himself was in danger of becoming a tainted witness. Once the "dirt," as he called it, of Hill's testimony was conjured, it threatened to stick to him through the racial stain associating black masculinity with sexual depravity. He and his supporters ensured that the stickiness of this judgment would attach to Hill. They questioned her motives and her actions; they told lies about her past and his. Morrison observes that Hill's testimony was not witnessed so that it would reveal truths; instead, "it produced an exchange of racial tropes."[34] Kendall Thomas observes that the "metaphorics of dirt" that saturated the hearings in the "associated figures of pollution, contamination, and defilement" were figures of judgment drawn from the sexualization of racism.[35] The persistent association of filthiness with black skin threatened the "purity" of the hearings with excremental fantasies of pollution represented by the presence of Hill and Thomas in the chamber.

Specter and Hatch took the main roles in shifting responsibility and blame onto Hill. Thomas's persistence was presented as something Hill failed to stop, and, more than that, her failure to halt Thomas's behavior redefined his ongoing harassment as if it were something she incited. Her failure to stop him was placed on one side of a scale, with his harassment on the other to create a false appearance of balance. The creation of a false appearance of equality conforms to the popular notion that culpability in cases of sexual violence is notoriously difficult to determine because only the parties present know what really happened. When their stories conflict, the shorthand judgment "he said/she said" misrepresents a cultural bias against women's testimony as the false equality of rational skepticism and objectivity. He said/she said represents the creation of a false pairing of culpability in the face of unequal harm, action, and exposure to risk. If she was sexually harassed, the proof would be in her actions: she would cut off contact with Thomas, bad-mouth him, or otherwise burn her professional bridges. Here is where the twenty-five-year gap is relevant to reassessing Hill's testimony and Thomas's: currently, by law, places of employment require training to inform about and prevent sexual harassment. Additionally, whistle-blower protections prevent retaliation against the kind of information Hill brought forward. None of these protections were in place in 1991 when Hill risked both professional harm and retaliation. Yet many senators argued that Hill shared responsibility with Thomas precisely because she failed on her own to make him stop harassing her. Obviously, it would have been more favorable to Clarence Thomas in his confirmation hearing if it could be demonstrated that the sexual harassment simply did not happen. To create this impression, Anita Hill had to be shown to have invented the story out of her thwarted desire to gain Thomas's attention. To this end, Senators Hatch, Specter, and Heflin painted Hill as a "scorned woman," a fantasist, and a retaliator. In the end, the committee recommended Thomas and he was confirmed by the full Senate by 52–48, the slimmest margin ever.

Although the hearings followed Thomas's historic nomination, Hill's testimony dominates cultural memory. The image of an African American woman testifying at length on television was unprecedented. Her image became iconic: the blue linen dress, professional demeanor, and calm delivery of details that were unfamiliar in American public discourse.[36] Hill's family traveled from their home in Oklahoma to act as a gallery of silent witnesses to her testimony. With her large family arrayed behind her, Anita Hill offered her life story. With that formality dispatched, she was asked to repeat again and again the raunchy remarks Thomas had so frequently made and heard herself characterized as part of a political conspiracy against Thomas, a liar, an opportunist, and vengeful fantasist. Commentators often mention the racially charged tableau created by the fourteen white male senators grilling an African American woman, but there is a more potent image created by looking beyond Hill at the witnesses seated behind her who also faced the all-white figures of law and power. The image of a black woman being made to describe her own sexual degradation by a panel of white men while her family sat in silent witness provides the indelible testimonial image of the hearings. It offers a *tableau vivant* of the racist association of black bodies and sexuality. Kendall Thomas has described how the "racial pornography" of the hearings was purposefully exploited by Senator Orrin Hatch, who persistently asked both Hill and Thomas to delve into the pornography's association of racism and sexuality in the guise of a fact-finding innocent, as an enactment of white supremacy.[37] By using sexuality as an instrument of racial power, Hatch demonstrated legal power over both Thomas and Hill.

This past burst through when Thomas called the hearing a "high tech lynching for uppity blacks." Hill's betrayal of him, he asserted, orchestrated by a political conspiracy and enacted in a televised and public hearing, represented lynching by means other than the noose. Thomas had so successfully rewritten racism in the United States into his own story of rising above it that its appearance in the hearings in the form of Thomas's anger and his use of the word "lynching" was all the more startling. Once uttered and elaborated through his language of embodied affect, race became his sword and shield, not Hill's. She would not refer to race or display emotion. Instead, she was a textbook witness: unshakeable and consistent, her answers were precise and closely restricted to the questions posed. She was unable to claim an explicitly raced position as a form of protection, as Thomas had done, artfully and explosively characterizing Hill's testimony as a "lynching" in a way that rendered his anger apotropaic and proleptic. "I had a gender," she said, "he had a race." In this formulation, prying race and gender apart meant she was further exposed.

Hill recognized how the disaggregation of race and gender worked to promote and protect Thomas and to vilify her. Thomas's supporters cast Hill with the feminist movement as a social movement composed of white women whose interests lay in workplace equality and reproductive rights, and they also encouraged the narrative of her racial disloyalty. Hill was not extended the deference Senator Biden offered Thomas.[38] In contrast, Hill remarked that she was turned from credible to tainted witness by lack of a patron or a proxy to power: "The ease with which I was transformed from respected academician to malicious psychotic in the eyes of the public illustrates the tenuousness of my association with power." Notice how Hill indexes Thomas's credibility to power rather than truth. "In sum, my license to speak before the committee as a credible witness was revoked by the tribunal and the process. I was cast as just another African American woman who was not to be trusted to describe her own experiences truthfully and who had no place in the decidedly political arena of the moment."[39] The lack of protection for

Hill permitted the senators to humiliate and degrade her by drawing out her testimony at length concerning what Thomas had said to her, how she felt when he said it, how she felt about the pornography, and so on. By managing Hill's and Thomas's testimonies into another performance of the age-old and undecidable struggles of "he said/she said," the hearings rendered the victim unpersuasive and her harm unknowable. By prying apart race and gender, the hearings effectively obscured the connections of sexism and racism within larger formations.

The "high tech lynching" comment represents a key to understanding how racial violence haunted the hearings, a history Thomas sought to suppress through his autobiographical narrative. Although the history of slavery, Jim Crow, and racial violence in the South was suppressed during Hill's testimony, it was nonetheless vividly on display in the form of an all-white male panel that compelled Hill's family to sit in stoic silence as their brilliant, successful daughter had to say things like "who has put pubic hair on my Coke?" When Thomas said "lynching," that history burst into the courtroom. When he characterized an official proceeding of the U.S. Senate to confirm a justice to the nation's highest court, he branded the proceeding with a rhetorical weapon forged through slavery. Yet in his refusal to answer to Hill's account, Thomas suggested an additional historical context that would be important in understanding the hearings.

The laws of ancient Greece help to contextualize how this peculiar jurisdiction was charged with emotions it contained but did not resolve, specifically, in the animated affect that magnetized to Hill. Law in ancient Greece was proximate to theater and to tragedy, and feelings are central in both. Anger was very much on the minds of the Athenians as they crafted law to deal with feelings like wrath and desire, and they extended to male heads of household considerable sway to manage and punish strong feelings. The invented notion that private and public realms are separate is exposed by the ability of male citizens to exercise and enjoy freedoms in both, including the freedom to restrict women to the home. The public realm in which equals enter into contract exists in contrast to the private realm in which individuals are imagined to be bound by affection. Yet everything about the social contract is predicated on the notion that women have unequal access to enter into it while men are granted a lifetime of relief from it in their relations with women and children. Rationality is thought to be the affective register in which relations in the public realm take place. Here, *homo economicus* and the rational man dispense and receive justice, engage in contractual relations, and vote. Those denizens of the private realm and their interactions—wherever they occur—are imagined as supporting rationality as what enables civic life to proceed in the midst of conflict.[40] The emotions have a specified role to play in civic life: they are constrained by rationality and morals, sanctioned by family ties, and expressed in art. However, the extent to which emotions exceed and supercharge the public sphere was formally acknowledged as a feature of law in Athens. Anger, passion, and desire were treated as substantive, personal, and permitted to male heads of households.[41] The air of in-house privilege that characterizes the formulaic civility among the men on the committee continued to extend to Thomas in the form of deference for his dealings with Hill and his intensely emotive response to her testimony. It did not extend to Anita Hill in the same ways. For her, punishment seemed always to be organizing itself in the form of judgment about her motive and credibility.

In 1993 Hill sat for a two-and-a-half-hour interview with journalists Jane Mayer and Jill Abramson. In 1994 they published *Strange Justice: The Selling of Clarence Thomas*. Over four hundred pages trace Thomas's rise in Washington and run every accusation hurled at Hill to ground. *Strange Justice* effectively dismisses Thomas's allegation of a conspiracy and documents that he and his supporters lied. The first gauntlet the authors pick up is the one with which Thomas led off. Thomas claimed if he had sexually harassed Hill by using such "grotesque" language, surely someone would have overheard it or he would have directed it at other women as well. Since no pattern was admitted into evidence, her story must be a lie, Thomas declared. Mayer and Abramson were able to document precisely the pattern Thomas singled out as exculpatory in absentia: he sought to date women who worked for him, he consistently saw his workplace as a site for relationships, he enjoyed porn, including hardcore, and talked about it, and these, as with Hill, amounted to a persuasive contextualization of her sexual harassment account.

Yet of the alleged conspiracy to humiliate him and the concoction of Hill's testimony to bring down a conservative African American man, Mayer and Abramson found no evidence, nor has anyone else. Mayer and Abramson conclude that the balance of believability on the facts brought to light in the aftermath of the hearing goes to Anita Hill. The natural extension of their analysis is that Thomas perjured himself during his nomination hearings.

For Mayer and Abramson, the truth was an especially relevant issue. Picking up the story three years after the hearings, they were spurred to investigate: "Since two people with such completely contradictory accounts cannot possibly both be telling the truth, it is clear that not only one of them lied under oath but is continuing to lie." After researching the history of the Thomas nomination for two years, they recognize that the "narrow question of who lied, Hill or Thomas"[42] failed to provide adequate perspective and analysis. Once the scope of inquiry widened to provide context and corroboration of what he said/she said in the hearings and a fuller study of materials and witnesses available but excluded from the hearings, as well as follow-up on some of the surprise witnesses who were heard, Mayer and Abramson reached several conclusions, none of which have been challenged. First among these was that Thomas had rather consistently used the "grotesque language" Hill alleged.[43] Angela Wright, who had a similar experience working for Thomas, let it be known after she saw Hill testify that she would be willing to corroborate the conduct from her own experience, offered a sworn statement, and waited on site during the hearings. Biden never called her. For Mayer and Abramson, Thomas's lying, Senator Danforth's complicity in smearing Hill, the orchestration of a baseless attack on her character, and Biden's mismanagement of the hearings tells an old story of politics as war, with winning at all costs as the goal. The hearing was always a political battleground, Mayer and Abramson conclude, and never a legal process designed to weigh evidence and sift for the truth. Their conclusion, shared by other journalists, is that Clarence Thomas perjured himself in his confirmation hearing. From this we see that questions of who lied and who told the truth deserved to be weighed on a scale not already rigged to balance he said versus she said.

In a further revelation, Mayer and Abramson contextualize Thomas's consistent habit of diminishing his appointment to the high court as "a job" he had neither sought nor particularly wanted: "Mere confirmation, even to the Supreme Court, seemed pitifully small compensation for what had been done to me," Thomas remarks in his memoir.[44] As friends and colleagues reported, Thomas not only frequently expressed his ambition to sit on the court, he also put together a resume, cultivated political contacts, and assiduously presented his conservative anti–affirmative action bona fides throughout the Washington network of conservative politics in order to achieve it. Whereas the Pin Point "I" loathes affirmative action, Clarence Thomas made very good use of it, as was his right, on his rise in Washington. Yet something of the anger associated with the struggle for civil rights percolates as spectral harm within the up-from-poverty account of his singular and self-propelled rise, unattached to racial violence and displaced onto the damage done to African Americans by affirmative action. Thomas's memoir, published sixteen years after his confirmation, preserves the "seething, aggrieved, wounded"[45] persona associated with any direct reference to race. He has rendered his own history, as well as his place within history, unspeakable. It is as if the ghost of history can only shake in anger when it is given no voice or place. Thomas's memoir tells one story, but his anger has a life of its own.

Thomas and Hill both published memoirs after the hearings.[46] In his, Thomas repeats the Pin Point strategy and amplifies it to memoir length in the voice of the wounded postconfirmation "I." In introducing Hill in his memoir, he minimizes his awareness of her presence and refers to her as his "subordinate."[47] He portrays her as mediocre at her job at the EEOC, possibly due to her "immaturity" but also due to her temperament, which he finds prickly and pestering. She is a minor character. During the time he supervises her, he presents himself as distracted and disorganized. He travels regularly to Savannah to see his ill and aging grandparents and then to organize his grandfather's funeral. Thomas complains that Hill followed up on a letter of recommendation for a new job while he was caring for his grandparents: "In the midst of my grief, Anita Hill had been nagging me to write her a letter of recommendation, and the sooner I did it, the sooner she'd be out of my hair."[48] He takes offense at a routine professional request from an employee but notes that he was not especially attentive at work: "It was excruciatingly difficult for me to concentrate on the day-to-day problems at EEOC that had come to seem to unimportant, especially since I had to fly back to Savannah several times that spring [1983] to settle my grandparents' affairs."[49] Thomas procrastinates long enough in responding to Hill's request that she has to follow up with his secretary. He opines: "I also had to do something about Anita Hill, who'd been pestering Anna Jenkins" for the letter.[50] Thomas promotes Hill's request for professional courtesy on her way out the door into a narrative of her "nagging" him when she wanted something from him.[51] Indeed, all the bothersome examples Thomas offers are of routine professional requests. Yet by relying on the language of "nagging," a term of stereotype straight out of a *Lockhorns* cartoon in which the beleaguered husband endures his shrewish wife's endless importuning, Thomas diminishes Hill as a professional and recasts her as a player in a domestic drama.

SEXUAL HARASSMENT AND THE JURISPRUDENCE OF RACIAL PAIN

The hearings in 1991 remain vividly alive to so many because they represent the unfinished business of engaging with the racial past, specifically, by the law and within the law. By placing Thomas's nomination within the context of Washington politics, we see how easily public opinion was distorted and manipulated by a rush to answer the question, "Who is lying and who is telling the truth?" In the absence of the kind of reporting that followed Thomas's seating on the court, sympathetic and skeptical audiences alike were ill-served by a lack of information about the behind-the-scenes actions of Thomas's supporters and the broader nomination process. By reconnecting histories of sexual and racial violence, we can pose different questions, as we must: What is the relationship between gender and racial violence? How can the links between them that the hearings forced apart and then obscured be restored? More specifically, sexual harassment became raced and gendered as "white and female" by its association with professional work spaces into which women had recently gained entry. Yet such harassment persistently and dangerously defines the low-wage, unwaged, and forced work all women historically perform. When we restore these connections, we read the hearings as a part of a testimonial network in which whitewashed histories and life stories circulate. Following this analysis and with reference to the politics of life story that Thomas continues to elaborate, we find a new context in which to understand the civil rights politics and anti–prisoners' rights jurisprudence that define Thomas's career on the Supreme Court.

Thomas's wounded feelings formed a consistent core of his public remarks: they informed the Pin Point strategy, swelled operatically during his response to Hill's testimony, are showcased in his memoir, and, as we shall see, entwine with a jurisprudence of racial pain whose central feature is permissible injury to incarcerated prisoners, notably African American men's shackled and abused bodies. Embodiment is key here. Of his efforts to recollect any behavior about which Hill testified, Thomas expresses bafflement through embodied metaphor: "[I had to] tear away at myself trying to think of what I could possibly have done." The betrayal by a friend is a "blow" that "sapped" all his strength and was a source of "enormous pain." The resultant misery is "so debilitating."[52] Thomas attests to the staying power of negative emotion in his memoir in embodied terms. Because he is embittered by racism and by affirmative action, he refuses to visit Yale Law, his alma mater. When he is rejected by law firms, he recalls in a speech that he saved all the rejection letters and remarks, "I felt beaten."[53] Thomas consistently pled injured feelings and described emotional displays in grandiose and embodied terms: he lay prostrate on the floor of his hotel room following Hill's testimony. He wept and struggled. He appeared biblical.

Hill presented a sharp contrast to Thomas's heightened display of anger and outrage. During the hearing she realized that even her slightest bodily movement set off a hail of clicking shutters and popping flashbulbs. She knew any movement would betray her: sweat would indicate

deceit, mopping her brow would suggest she was withering under scrutiny, and so on. So she willed herself to become still: "'Don't move,' I told
myself, freezing almost in midmotion. I resolved to become as motion-
less as possible. I had to be impervious to the lights and to the heat as
well as the natural reactions of my body. Though I felt each one of the
senators' attempts to humiliate me, I vowed not to so much as twitch." As
she recounts in her memoir, Hill suffered from fibroid tumors, a painful
and recurrent condition that she experienced during her testimony:

> I ignored the numbness in my legs and even the pain from the tumors
> in my abdomen. From that moment on, I did not even take a drink in
> front of the camera. I ignored my dry throat. I sat through the "conver-
> sations" with the Republicans and Democrats with my hands in front
> of me and only occasionally would I even lean forward. Oddly enough,
> this exercise in self-control enabled me to focus on the questioning.
> Or perhaps it took some sort of divine intervention, some source from
> outside myself that took over when I needed it. And, of course, years of
> being impervious to and immobile in the face of hurt.[54]

Her physical and emotional control mirrored each other and contrasted
to Thomas's intensive lability. She was still and focused; he overflowed
with emotions.

Given his eloquent rage before the committee, it is surprising that
Thomas is typically silent during oral arguments before the court. He so
frequently concurred in dissents penned by the late Justice Scalia and
by Justice Alito that some have concluded that he has no clear jurispru-
dential views or voice. This would be a mistake. Thomas has authored a
coherent, if compact, body of legal writing as a Supreme Court justice
denying relief to prisoners who protest their brutal treatment in prison,
including being badly beaten by prison guards while they are restrained
and, most recently, receiving inadequate painkiller as the first drug in
the three-drug sequence used in executions. Without the painkiller,
the second two drugs cause great pain. Yet neither claim amounts, in
Thomas's reading, to "cruel and unusual punishment." If prisoners
recover from beatings at the hands of guards, he does not regard such

beatings as "unusual." Thomas's willingness to permit the punishment of black prisoners is central to how he understands law. Prisoners bringing suit for relief from pain inflicted as part of incarceration and execution find no hearing from Thomas. When inmates are shackled and beaten, Thomas is unmoved by their testimony. Thomas's ability to feel monstrously wounded translates to a capacity to be infinitely punishing. The centrality of negative affect in his life gives rise to a jurisprudence of racial pain.

Thomas minimizes claims to pain and suffering by black male prisoners subjected to sadistic and brutal treatment by white prison guards in southern U.S. jails. He is unmoved by the experiences of prisoners chained in the sun for seven hours without food, water, or bathroom breaks, or beaten while shackled, including a prisoner pummeled so savagely after the request for a grievance form that other guards intervened. Yet when Thomas testified at his confirmation hearing, he reflected: "You know, on my current court, I have occasion to look out the window that faces C Street, and there are converted buses that bring in the criminal defendants to our criminal justice system, busload after busload. And you look out, and you say to yourself, and I say to myself almost every day, But for the grace of God there go I. So you feel that you have the same fate, or could have, as those individuals. So I can walk in their shoes, and I can bring something different to the Court."[55] By the time he is on the bench, he is not similarly moved. When the issue is the restriction of the Eighth Amendment's protection against cruel and unusual punishment and whether and how it applies to prisoners, Thomas adds a particular twist to the definition of cruel and unusual. Linda Greenhouse documents his consistent objection to the application of the Eighth Amendment to protect the rights of those incarcerated, but his callous view toward pain is key. Thomas argues that the men who were punched, kicked, beaten, and otherwise abused in jail had not been treated either cruelly or unusually because their punishment did not cause permanent damage. And, one must conclude, the routine abuse of prisoners does not concern Thomas as an Eighth Amendment issue.[56] In contrast to his assertion during his confirmation hearing that he was the adequate witness who could temper justice with mercy and fellow feeling, Thomas refused to countenance prisoners' civil rights claims when they came before him on the court.

As legal scholars from Noah Feldman (Harvard Law) to Peter Edelman (Georgetown Law) to Eugene Volokh (UCLA Law) agree, "Thomas is . . . the *most conservative* justice, willing to regularly strike down long-accepted case law that has been in place for decades, in some cases for as much as a century." Thomas is

> the only justice willing to allow states to establish an official religion; the only justice who believes teenagers have no free speech rights at all; the only justice who believes that it is unconstitutional to require campaign funders to disclose their identity; the only justice who believes that truthful tobacco advertising and other commercial speech may not be regulated, even when it is aimed at minors; the only justice who voted to strike down a key provision of the Voting Rights Act; the only justice to say that the court should invalidate a wide range of laws regulating business; and he is the only justice who voted to allow the president to hold American citizens in prison indefinitely without charge and without review by the courts.[57]

Overwhelmingly, Thomas's jurisprudence favors originalism, conservatism, and anachronism and is rooted in the slaveholding history of the nation. His views about prisoners' rights and civil rights mark an especially sharp contrast to Justice Marshall, whom he followed. Marshall wrote key decisions in cases involving prisoners beaten or denied essential medical care, declaring such treatment a violation of the Constitution's ban on cruel and unusual punishment. Although Thomas's comment in his confirmation implied fellow feeling toward criminal defendants being brought to court, just two months following his confirmation, Thomas "dissented from a decision upholding an $800 damage award to a prisoner who was beaten so severely by prison guards that his teeth and dental plate were broken. Thomas, joined only by Scalia, said 'a use of force which causes only insignificant harm to a prisoner . . . is not cruel and unusual punishment.'"[58]

Thomas consistently writes separate concurrences or dissents when the subject is race. He often votes against civil rights claims, where his feelings of being harmed by racial preferences emerge in affirmative action cases. When the Supreme Court, for example, "reaffirmed the use of race as one factor that can be used in university admissions, Thomas railed that these programs were 'nothing more than a facade, a cruel farce of continued racial discrimination that stamp minorities with a badge of inferiority.'"[59] Thomas's protections of those who would harm people of color through legal means has drawn repeated dissent from Justices Sandra Day O'Connor before her retirement and Justice Ruth Bader Ginsberg.

Thomas's rare and consistent selection of prison abuse makes his jurisprudence absolutely about race. As Michelle Alexander argues in *The New Jim Crow*, because more African Americans are currently incarcerated than were enslaved in 1850, the modern prison is a microcosm of racism.[60] For Thomas to weigh in against the right of prisoners to be treated without abuse, especially when he comments on no other issue with this consistency, flags this issue as singularly compelling to him.

Tainted witnesses serve as larger-than-life, public examples of what can and will happen to women who bear witness. Commonsense notions like "Nobody knows what really happened" and "It's a case of he said/she said" deflect inquiry into what we might come to know and even what we already do know. Moreover, they participate in narrowing attention to the immediate time frame of crisis or scandal, restricting the frame temporally, and ensuring that no adequate context for understanding will emerge. For these reasons, Toni Morrison's comment on the hearings provides pivotal guidance: "For insight into the complicated and complicating events that the confirmation of Clarence Thomas became, one needs perspective, not attitudes; contexts, not anecdotes; analyses, not postures. For any kind of lasting illumination, the focus must be on the history routinely ignored or played down or unknown."[61] Shame was one of the negative affects set loose in the hearings, and it was produced asymmetrically. Hill and Thomas were positioned differently with respect to the risk and benefit of explicit reference to his sexually harassing comments to Hill. She had to report them and be questioned about them. By refusing to answer her testimony, Thomas never said those words in the hearing. Instead, he refused to acknowledge that the process had any authority over him. In so doing, he ensured that the only sexually explicit remarks would be made by white men and a lone African American woman.

Hill's and Thomas's life stories offer coded testimonial accounts of the racial past and present in the United States. Together, they referenced the submerged legality of slavery and Jim Crow's legacy as well as the emergent legal framework of sexual harassment law. They reveal again that testimonial networks are never neutral. They represent contact zones within which clashing claims to credibility and competing methods for judging them circulate. Witnesses often struggle to regain sense and establish contexts necessary for their testimony to be recognized as legitimate once formal and vernacular judgments attach negatively to them. Testimonial acts often expose the limits of the jurisdictions in which they initially emerge. Anita Hill's testimony exposed the limits of the confirmation hearings when she disrupted the carefully managed construction of Clarence Thomas as Justice Thurgood Marshall's postracial replacement. When Thomas responded to Hill's testimony by calling the nomination process "a high tech lynching for uppity blacks," he exposed the false representation of racial history as "over" that he and his handlers had worked so hard to construct.

The expressive and affective structures of the hearing had been used initially to bind the power of racism from tainting Thomas until Hill testified and racism was unleashed on both of them in a dominant display of senatorial, white power. Through this display, the sexual degradation Anita Hill experienced in a governmental workplace not only was put on stage in the form of testimony but was reenacted and amplified by the legal setting. There, she was accused of pornographic revenge fantasies and punished for bearing witness as the Senate Judiciary Committee enacted the spectacle of exerting power over an African American woman who dared to demand a hearing for her sexual mistreatment. The response exposed the stark rejection that such a demand would be heard by the committee, even as her testimony found an adequate witness nationwide and was lodged in the testimonial network until new witnesses could emerge.

2

JURISDICTIONS AND
TESTIMONIAL NETWORKS

Rigoberta Menchú

*Everything that is done today, is done in memory of those
who have passed on.*

—RIGOBERTA MENCHÚ, *I, RIGOBERTA MENCHÚ:
AN INDIAN WOMAN IN GUATEMALA*

Rigoberta Menchú is back in the news following the verdict in January 2015 convicting the former police chief of Guatemala City of crimes against humanity for his role in the Spanish Embassy fire in which Menchú's father died. The verdict demands a new framing of Rigoberta Menchú's testimony to counter its labeling as scandal. As the slow pace of adjudicating human rights in national courts finally overtakes the frenzy of scandal, *I, Rigoberta Menchú* ought to relocate from the archive of the hoax to the record of authentic testimony, and her notoriety as a tainted witness be replaced with the more accurate name of witness.[1] Offered initially to a large international audience as a *testimonio*, a personal account based on an interview Menchú gave rather than a book she wrote, this genre would play a key role in debates about how Menchú was subject to doubt. John Beverly defines *testimonio* as "a narrative . . . told in the first person by a narrator who is also the real protagonist or witness of the events he or she recounts."[2] That it also carries assumptions about the narrator's responsibility to offer a plural perspective on community events, and to take on the role of witness for those who might otherwise be endangered by taking that position themselves, made genre into a term of debate in the 1980s and 1990s. As interesting as these earlier debates were, the news of the verdict does not simply open a new chapter in Menchú's career as a contested author of *testimonio*; instead, it prompts another look at testimonial culture in the Americas and the global jurisdiction in which testimonial practices circulate. As we trace her testimony from scandal to vindication in court, we anatomize the testimonial network in which her account was not only thwarted as scandal but also continuously mobilized through a range of media, political organizing, and community projects to bear witness to genocide in Guatemala.

To think of the testimonial network as a circulatory system within which life story and testimony encounter conflicting ideologies, politics, and judgments as they move in search of a hearing is also to engage with how the people who bear witness travel. Whether in flight or stealth, through clandestine migration, or with and without documentation, women who bear witness face judgments embedded in the original contexts of harm, which are translated to new jurisdictions in which women testify, where they also encounter new judgments. As much as there is hope that new audiences will take up their testimony, in new venues and with new witnesses, witnesses also discover that the terms through which they will be known may not be within their power to alter. Menchú's testimony was mobilized along distinct pathways, those of scandal and testimony, and these parallel paths demonstrate how routinely repressed or ignored histories circulate within testimonial networks. When they reach adequate witnesses, responsibilities to the buried past can be awakened by contemporary trauma.

The slow pursuit of justice began in the past century. On January 31, 1980, a group of protesters including Menchú's father Vicente occupied the Spanish Embassy in Guatemala City to protest the abuses committed by security forces against indigenous communities in the Guatemalan highlands. Guatemalan security forces surrounded the building, sealed the exits, and set it on fire. In the ensuing conflagration, thirty-seven protesters and hostages, including embassy staff, died. Four years later the publication of Rigoberta Menchú's *testimonio* in English claimed the security forces were responsible for the deaths of her father and the others they locked into the embassy. In 1999 Rigoberta Menchú filed a criminal complaint in Spain accusing former government officials of responsibility for the incident. The protestors had chosen the Spanish Embassy because Spain was sympathetic to their cause, and the suit in Spain represented an effort to press a claim in a viable jurisdiction. In 2005 a Spanish judge issued an arrest warrant holding former Guatemalan Interior Minister Donaldo Álvarez responsible for the incident, but the case did not advance. On January 30, 2009, twenty-nine years after the incident, the Guatemalan government filed 3,350 criminal complaints against former soldiers and paramilitaries alleging human rights violations. Rigoberta Menchú was a party to the suit. On January 20, 2015, former police chief Pedro García Arredondo was sentenced to forty years in prison for murder and crimes against humanity stemming from the embassy massacre. He was sentenced to fifty additional years for killing two students at the funeral for the embassy fire victims. Judge Jeannette Valdés, the president of the three-judge tribunal, acknowledged the long-unresolved case and expressed the court's hope that the judgment would be "water that will extinguish the flames."[3]

TARGETING THE WITNESS

Readers already aware of Menchú's transformation from indigenous rights activist to tainted witness may recall a different set of key events crowded into this time frame. Menchú's *testimonio* was received as an authentic and powerful claim for indigenous rights and social justice on behalf of the Quiché people when it was translated into English by Ann Wright and began to circulate in college and university courses in

1984. It was adopted as a text in the revised Stanford University core curriculum in 1988 and subsequently cast in a major role in the culture wars inflamed by conservatives in the United States who saw universities as newly volatile and vulnerable sites for political activism. As the *Wall Street Journal* commented in late 1988, Dante's *Inferno* "is out" and *I, Rigoberta Menchú* "is in." Stanford's decision to include third-world authors in its required curriculum struck conservatives in the United States as an attack on Western values and civilization, a perilous recasting of "the evolution of such ideas as faith and justice" as a legacy of "sexism, racism and the faults of its ruling classes."[4] Menchú's appearance in the *Wall Street Journal* isolated her as a target for a conservative movement in search of an example of the excesses of the multicultural left. Promoting Menchú's text was represented as an affront to the processes of canon formation solidified in Stanford's original Western Civilization syllabus. "Undergraduates do not read about Rigoberta," opined the American Enterprise Institute's Dinesh D'Souza in 1991, "because she has written a great and immortal book, or performed a great deed, or invented something useful. She simply happened to be in the right place and the right time."[5] Being in the right place at the right time, we should remember, is precisely one definition of a witness.

The "right place" was Guatemala's Western Highlands, home to almost four million people, the majority of whom were indigenous peoples living in remote villages like Menchú's hometown of Chimel.[6] The "right time" was the late 1970s, when the Guatemalan military government was waging a murderous pacification campaign against the population rivaling the Spanish conquest in genocidal impact. By the time the campaign ended, Menchú's mother and father, two brothers, and 200,000 other Guatemalans had been murdered.[7] According to D'Souza, although this campaign may have been "unfortunate for her personal happiness," it was "indispensable for her academic reputation," transforming Menchú into a "fetish object" onto which "minority students" could affirm their "victim status" and professors could project their "Marxist and feminist views onto South American Indian culture."[8] For D'Souza, Menchú's significance as a witness to the genocide in Guatemala was less significant than the role he assigned her in the culture wars.

Menchú was awarded the Nobel Peace Prize in 1992 for her work on human and indigenous rights. David Stoll, an anthropology professor at Middlebury College, attacked the veracity of Menchú's representation of Guatemala in his 1998 exposé of her *testimonio*. Stoll offered a perspective on Menchú's involvement with the Marxist EGP (Ejército Guerrillero de los Pobres—the guerrilla army of the people). He thought Menchú's self-representation as a simple, indigenous woman disguised her role as a mouthpiece for the EGP. For Stoll, also interested in Guatemalan culture and politics, though supportive of different elements, Menchú and her comrades' political agitation prolonged the thirty-six years of brutal repression in Guatemala. Although Stoll's account was motivated by a political stance toward resistance movements in Guatemala and not many scholars share his analysis of its politics, his views were replaced by a critique of Menchú; namely, the assertion of a binary of truth versus lies to describe some specific elements in her account rather than a wholesale disagreement with her politics within an otherwise accurate representation of the struggle of the indigenous in Guatemala.[9] In the context of what became a one-sided ideological battle (one-sided because Menchú would lack access to the same news venues and would not be able to supply adequate context for her life), the particulars through which Stoll established his case dominated how Menchú was presented in conservative media as well as global news outlets, including the *New York Times*. Stoll's most troubling claims included the following: (1) the land dispute between indigenous Quiché people and *ladinos*, landowners with Spanish surnames, was a family fight between her father and some relatives, (2) the Spanish Embassy fire in Guatemala City was started by those trapped inside, (3) Menchú was better educated than she admitted, (4) she falsely placed herself at the scene of the immolation of her brother, Petrocinio, by paramilitaries in Chajul, and (5) no younger brother named Nicolás Tum died of malnutrition.[10] Although Menchú responded to these claims at the time and all these accusations can also now be placed in contexts in which Menchú's choices replace the "truth versus lies" judgment with context and interpretation, many argued from within the temporality of scandal that Menchú was already herself supplying context, as were scholars, activists, and people living in Guatemala who knew the events she narrated. Dante Liano called the *Times* article a "classic campaign to rewrite history" that follows the strategy used to discredit survivors of the Holocaust: "but you just said you were in that camp, whereas the documents prove you were in another camp; and if that concentration camp did not exist, perhaps no concentration camps ever existed at all."[11] The terms necessary to understand her *testimonio*, including genre, testimony about trauma, and the power imbalance between Menchú and her antagonists, were being replaced by a campaign to transform her into a tainted witness.

Well-funded conservatives like David Horowitz and D'Souza, regrouping after successes during the Reagan years and newly savvy in exploiting college curricula and the book market for their purposes, attacked Menchú and demanded that she be stripped of her Nobel Prize for lying. The *New York Times* swiftly picked up Stoll's accusations and in 1998 ran a center-column, above-the-fold, front-page story by Latin American bureau chief Larry Rohter entitled "Tarnished Laureate."[12] As with Anita Hill's tainting, the language of dirt and shame attached to Menchú in an attack framed as whether she told the truth. The imputation was that she was both personally unscrupulous and ideologically motivated. As with Anita Hill's testimony, a fuller context for understanding how Stoll misrepresented Menchú's testimony was suppressed. "Tarnished Laureate" simply repeated Stoll's accusations that Menchú had not witnessed her brother's torture and public immolation by paramilitaries in Chajul (though Rohter confirms the factuality of the Chajul event), that a young brother died of starvation while the family worked in the coastal plantations, that the embassy fire victims were to blame for their deaths, and that Menchú had received some education. Rohter, Liano argues, "might be forgiven for confusing 'autobiography,' the term he uses exclusively to refer to Rigoberta's edited statements and '*testimonio*,'" but his repetition of it nonetheless represents a "reinvention" of testimonial literature as flawed evidence.[13] Stoll's reinvention stuck and, combined with a defamation campaign "led by Guatemala's oligarchy and its foreign supporters," was recycled through a global media in such a way that Stoll's claims were reported as truth, quoted as such, and generally lost the specificity of his method through repetition of his assertion that her *testimonio* was false testimony.[14]

Although the concerns were exaggerated as if the text were riddled with inconsistencies, and as if they had no other explanation than deception, fact checking turned up very few disputed facts. Menchú received some education from the Belgian nuns when she worked as a servant in a convent, her young brother's death from starvation has been confirmed, the Guatemalan court disproved Stoll's accusation of a suicide pact as the source of the embassy fire, her brother Petrocinio's torture and immolation has been confirmed, and although Rigoberta Menchú was not an eyewitness to the murder, her mother was: "My mother saw it. And she can no longer speak about it. And how could I have possibly placed my mother as the number one witness, when they killed so many witnesses so they can't speak?"[15] Similarly, her choice to downplay her education was prompted by the need to protect those who would have been endangered had she named them. A more detailed account of the Chajul executions, including the names of witnesses, or her experience with the Belgian nuns in whose convent she was a servant would have risked their lives. All the events she recounted occurred during the brutal Guatemalan dirty war. Half of the total atrocities of that war took place during eighteen months in 1982–83 when General Riós Montt was in power; this was the time frame in which Menchú was beginning to speak out. During 1982 alone, "In the Ixil region, between 70 and 90 percent of the community were wiped out."[16] Riós Montt's reach and punitive zeal offer a context for Menchú's choices. Yet Menchú's *testimonio* came to emblematize the concerns about the unreliability of testimony, and she was stigmatized as a tainted witness. Menchú's own account of this tactic is crucial. By undermining her credibility on small points but endorsing her version of events overall, Stoll stuck doubt not only to Menchú but to the people in whose name she bore witness: "all poor Guatemalans."

TESTIMONY ON THE MOVE

In light of what historian Greg Grandin calls Menchú's "vindication" by the courts, we can return to these archives and ponder two key questions: First, questions of gender, which enable us to focus on the swiftness with which women and those in positions of relative vulnerability who challenge both illegal and legal forms of violence can be discredited as tainted witnesses, how judgments that smear and tarnish them are made to stick, and the ensuing vulnerability of testimonial discourse to charges of female lying. Second, questions of how narratives of scandal overtake testimonial narratives and displace them in the court of public opinion while testimony continues to travel to courts of law in search of an adequate witness. This case, sprawling as it is, reveals the incommensurability of the time of scandal in the court of public opinion and the time of legal processes in national courts. A new framing of *I, Rigoberta Menchú* can measure the slow pace of adjudicating human rights in national courts and the rapid uptake of scandal. By focusing on testimony's movements in both cultural and legal processes, we might better understand testimonial agency as distinct from individual agency: how it moves in search of a hearing, how it bears witness to trauma, seeks justice, and engages with institutions in ways that disrupt a neoliberal framing of the individual, and, finally, how, while scandal consigns its targets and critics to the archives of tainted witness, testimony can still carve a track within networks in order to bear witness. However, when the scandal story is repeated, even after it has been discredited as false accusation, then that story, in a sense, fastens onto testimony, weighs it down, and continues to feed off the legitimacy of testimony. It takes parasitic life from the body of testimony, and old, illegitimate stories have long half-lives in testimonial networks.

Cycles of testimony continue to revive events, which emerge and recede in relation not only to the evidence that can be brought forward and the access to a public those who bear witness can claim but also to the changing interests and variable investments and attention of those who form witnessing publics. In these cycles, the defining tempo of scandal is acceleration. Judgment produced in an instant relies less on truth or an ample factual record than on the capacity to control the message. In contrast to scandal's giddy tempo, the temporality of justice is protraction, often enacted in courts, tribunals, and trials, and even outlasts witnesses' life spans, though it can, in their absence, give them voice. Timelines are not only chronologies. They carry and compress historical, legal, and narrative claims about social reality and human value. What counts as testimonial truth or empirical evidence in each enactment about events and persons—in history, law, and literary genres—is not stable. Testimony about mass killing in Guatemala and Rigoberta Menchú's role in bringing this to international, public awareness form two histories: first, the history of scandal, which unfolds within a U.S. culture war over conservative ideologies and multiculturalism. Some of its key fights targeted curriculum reform and the hiring of new faculty. Second, the history of testimony about genocide in Guatemala. The histories of scandal and testimony can overlap, but scandal seizes the dominant historical narrative in order to distract, derail, discredit, and deny testimony. When the timelines run in parallel, we can see a persistent tactic of scandal: the promotion of empirical evidence over testimonial truth, the recasting of the complexities of testimony into a purposefully and often meaninglessly narrow notion of truth and lies in order to seize a legal and moral advantage, and the strategic use of lying masking as the revelation of lies, the fraudulent attribution of fraud, the assertion or imputation of a hoax where none exists, and the extent to which the script for this in the U.S. context features the gendered figure of the tainted witness. The public smearing of Anita Hill in many ways provided the playbook for how conservatives like D'Souza and Horowitz would bash Menchú. The funding was from the same sources, and the methods similar in two ways; they were enacted by Reagan supporters, supporters of a president (1981–89) who had legally and illegally provided arms and U.S. military training to dictatorships in Central America, and their targets were similarly credible women. As with Anita Hill, the binary rubric of truth and lies as evaluative criteria for life story did not simply arise from those narratives themselves.

Instead, it gained traction as a critical metric, in part, through conservative-funded campaigns against women of color who brought forward accounts of harm in the public sphere.

By separating the histories of scandal and testimony, and tracking them both, we see how testimonial networks carry life story about genocide to distant publics within a globally conceived jurisdiction. But to do so requires telling multiple narratives, plotting their enactments alongside each other, and highlighting how they participate in a testimonial network. Rigoberta Menchú's narrative, as she memorably asserted, is not her story alone but the story of a people. She was born in 1959 in Guatemala, five years after Jacobo Árbenz was deposed as president in a CIA-lead coup and well into the looting of Guatemalan resources and exploitation of land and labor by United Fruit, with the United States extending diplomacy with strings attached. President Árbenz, who had been politicized during his own participation in exploiting agrarian workers when he was in the military, advocated land reform. More comprehensively, the context broadens to include the five-hundred-year aftermath of the Spanish conquest of the Maya. Menchú evokes the Spanish conquest as well as the Guatemalan dirty war as the context of her family's suffering. She is forced into exile in Mexico for a year, before she goes to Paris in January 1982 to meet with Venezuelan-born anthropologist Elisabeth Burgos-Debray and Arturo Taracena, a Guatemalan historian and EGP representative in Paris, to record an interview.

Elisabeth Burgos-Debray, who was working toward a doctorate in ethnopsychiatry at the time of the interview, put out a call to interview a generic "Guatemalan Mayan woman," not Menchú in particular.[17] She interviewed Menchú in Paris over the course of several days, transcribed the tapes, edited the manuscript, and published the result as Menchú's *testimonio*.[18] Aside from supplying the testimony, Menchú was not involved in the transcription, editing, revision, or translation of the book. The two principals responsible for those tasks, Burgos-Debray and Taracena, confirm that Menchú took control of the interview, "speaking in a strong, certain voice."[19] They suggested topics to be covered, but they had to "rethink the outline" as Menchú's "narrative capacity" exceeded "what we had originally conceived. . . . There was a profound literary quality to Rigoberta Menchú's voice."[20] The editors corrected Menchú's poor Spanish grammar and syntax and arranged her account chronologically, but the "book is a narration only by Rigoberta, with her own rhythm, with her own inventions, if there are any, with her own emotions."[21]

When Rigoberta Menchú gave the interview that would produce *I, Rigoberta Menchú*, she was twenty-three years old. Her parents were dead, she had spent a year in exile in Mexico, and she was just beginning to speak out about the genocide in Guatemala. Yet with General Ríos Montt assuming the presidency, an unprecedented eighteen-month intensification in repression began. Menchú arrived in Paris traumatized by what she had survived and motivated as a living representative of a people undergoing genocide to "tell a compelling story."[22] As scholars have explained, Menchú came from a society in which most information was transmitted orally but also from immediate conditions of extraordinary repression around speech, where people were tortured in order to compel them to give up the names of anyone involved in labor organizing. During the year she spent hiding in exile in Mexico, she had not been able to talk about her experience without risking the safety of those still in Guatemala or connected with the resistance. However, her "experience speaking to reporters and solidarity delegations before her Paris interviews had led her to realize the value audiences place on eyewitness accounts. [She wanted to] draw attention to Guatemala, which, compared to neighboring Nicaragua and El Salvador, was being ignored by the international press."[23]

When we think of the conditions in which Menchú bore witness, the image of an apartment in Paris obscures the history she carried with her to that place. Two important contexts inform her testimony: Mayan culture and its practices around orality and disclosure and the layered histories of conquest, colonization, and genocide breaking over the Maya for five hundred years. She mobilizes her witness in the joint context of history and trauma. This context helps to clarify the two clashing histories unfolding in the contact zone the testimonial network became: the story of Menchú's life and the story of her *testimonio*. Reshaped as scandal, Menchú's tarnishing is perhaps better understood as Stoll's story rather than hers. While the scandal story is his, Menchú continues to testify and to search for an adequate witness for her testimony outside that construction.

The story of her interview, its travels and controversies, represents a detachable aspect of Menchú's life. How we consider the fate of this interview is shaped in part by how we think about genre. Denounced as propaganda, promoted as primary source, read as memoir, and recontextualized by scholars who defended *I, Rigoberta Menchú* as *testimonio*,[24] Menchú's first-person account was propelled across multiple publics by the literary quality of her political testimony. It crossed geographical, institutional, and political frames. Taracena and Burgos-Debray expected a generic representative, but they recorded the voice of a poet. Menchú surprised her interviewers as the eloquent voice of traumatized exile poured out over several days. What publics can a literary witness mobilize to bear witness? This is a question I will take up in chapters 3 and 5 more fully, but I raise it here to identify the significance of the literary to testimony.

PARALLEL PATHS: SCANDAL OR TESTIMONY

Almost a decade after the scandal, interest in Menchú revived. Greg Grandin's reevaluation in 2010 in a long article in the *Nation*, and a subsequent series of books he and others wrote that coincided with trials of Riós Montt, showed that the charges against Menchú along with the political analysis Stoll asserted about Guatemala were untrue in some cases and distortions in others. This new activity revealed more importantly that her testimony, immured as it was in scandal, had not stopped its search for an adequate witness. After Menchú's *testimonio* was published, circulated and taught, and denounced, it relocated to documentary film, human rights activism, and court. More specifically, Menchú's *testimonio* traveled down two parallel paths, one in which she became a tainted witness in a whipped-up scandal and another, which was more cohesive with the purposes of her testimony, in which she became a human rights activist with an international platform, a collaborator in a series of documentary films, and part of the legal prosecution of war crimes in Guatemala, including the trial of General Ríos Montt, the first prosecution of a war crime in the Americas in the nation in which the crimes occurred. While the second path illuminates how documentary, human rights, and national and international courts are part of a testimonial network through which Menchú's witness has been able to circulate, only the first path commanded front-page *New York Times* coverage and has all but substituted for knowledge of Menchú's subsequent life and work for many.

Menchú collaborated with documentary filmmaker and human rights activist Pamela Yates at Skylight Productions on a documentary, *When the Mountain Trembles*. Yates and her team were filming in Guatemala during 1982, when Ríos Montt was in power and paramilitaries were kidnapping and murdering those suspected of organizing or participating in any resistance. From Catholic priests who preached a gospel of liberation theology, to labor organizers, to journalists, to the entire civilian population, anyone could be killed with impunity. Kidnappings were commonplace, and the bodies of those tortured were dumped publicly. The footage in the documentary shows such kidnappings by groups of men who roll through city streets in military vehicles and abduct their victims in crowded public places in full daylight. Armed soldiers and police are everywhere; they patrol in search of "revolutionaries." When Yates asks them why, the soldiers shrug and smile: this is the machinery of genocide.

The documentary uses footage gathered in both the cities and the countryside. It includes interviews with a lawyer in Guatemala who describes the persecution of the labor movement, and also with a corrupt priest who says that he is well taken care of by the government and informs to maintain his position. There are two effective reenactments to show what Yates could not film, including a scene in which Árbenz tries to persuade a U.S. government official that a democratic Guatemala is a stronger regional partner. Yates also intercuts actual footage of Ríos

Montt saying that peasants need to be crushed with a State of the Union speech by Ronald Reagan about the urgent need to support the governments in Central America so they might simply defend themselves against communist insurgencies. Yates juxtaposes Reagan's speech with footage of U.S. Army personnel training Guatemalan security forces. She threads Menchú's testimony throughout the film. In a bare studio, Menchú is seated in front of a black background, looks directly into the camera, and describes the deaths of her family members. When she describes the Spanish Embassy massacre, Yates's footage from the event rolls. Menchú seems at first to be narrating the event in voiceover because what she says describes what the film shows. However, it becomes clear that Menchú's testimony derives from memory, and the footage of the embassy fire is proof of her original version of the events. The footage supplies the proof that was present from the beginning, despite claims that the rebels had locked themselves into the embassy and set themselves on fire, as Stoll asserted. The film shows security forces forming a barrier around the building and preventing people from reaching it. A man in the street stares at the embassy and calls out, "They are in there." The sequence concludes with footage of the burned bodies carried in sheets from the embassy and dumped on the ground.

In January 2015, as Pamela Yates filmed the trial of police involved in the embassy fire, she reflected on filming Menchú's previous account of the fire:

> In 1983, the now-Nobel Peace Prize winner Rigoberta Menchú and I collaborated on the film *When the Mountains Tremble*. She told the story of the Spanish Embassy massacre where her father Vicente Menchú died, directly to camera. . . . You see a profound sadness in her eyes, but also the determination to tell the world what had happened, what the significance of the attack on the Spanish Embassy was really about, all with the hope that international pressure could help to stop the violence in Guatemala. Watching it today, I see that even that early on in her political career, Rigoberta was a strong analyst of the political situation, and prescient about the response of state and security forces that was soon to follow.[25]

Yates's choice to frame Menchú as the sole focus of her camera represents a visual technique that amplifies the witness position. Yates triangulated her documentarian voice, footage of the fire, and Menchú's testimony to create an adequate witness.

Rigoberta Menchú went from Guatemala to Mexico to Paris; her *testimonio* went around the world and turned into a scandal. Yet after the suspension of her testimony as scandal, Menchú continued to travel and to collaborate with Yates, as her testimony was mobilized from written account to documentary films, and from films to court in the trial of Riós Montt, where Menchú also participated in developing the case against him. Following *When the Mountain Trembles* in 1983, Yates made another documentary film for Skylight Productions about Riós Montt, *Granito: How to Nail a Dictator*, which premiered in 2012, and both films were submitted as forensic evidence in his trial for crimes against humanity.

Granito, as Yates describes it, "is a story of destinies joined by Guatemala's past, and how a documentary film intertwined with a nation's turbulent history emerges as an active player in the present. In *Granito* our characters sift for clues buried in archives of mind and place and historical memory, seeking to uncover a narrative that could unlock the past and settle matters of life and death in the present." The film follows five main characters connected by Guatemala's past and highlights 1982, the year Menchú goes to Paris, Riós Montt takes power, and Guatemala is engulfed in an armed conflict during which a genocidal "scorched earth" campaign by the military kills nearly 200,000 Maya people, including 45,000 disappeared. The documentary seeks to restore memory of the violent past, "weaving back together threads of a story unraveled by the passage of time, forgotten by most."[26]

In 2013 Yates followed *Granito* with *Dictator in the Dock*, an inside-the-courtroom documentary of the entire trial of Riós Montt for genocide and crimes against humanity in Guatemala. This historic case marked the first time, anywhere in the world, that a former head of state was tried for genocide in a national court, in the country where the crimes were committed. Yates writes, "It is also the first time in the history of South or North America, that the genocide of indigenous peoples was tried in a court of law, significantly in a country of the Americas with a majority indigenous population."[27] The camera captures testimony by victims of rape, witnesses to murder, and survivors of torture, as well as the reaction in the gallery of witnesses, and of Riós Montt and his legal team, as they sit a few steps away from those who testify.[28] As with the historical context of slavery and Jim Crow that haunted Clarence Thomas's nomination hearings until Anita Hill testified and Thomas uttered the word, "lynching," that exposed that history's presence, the historical context of Spanish conquest, colonization, and the implication of the United States in the ongoing exploitation of Guatemala as a source of foreign capital was onstage in the war crimes trial. As Francisco Soto, legal representative of the Maya victims, said in his concluding statement at the trial, "Justice is poised to play an important role in the historical memory of our country. For the first time in five hundred years we are able to judge genocide."[29] Soto insists that the relevant testimonial time frame defining the search for a hearing in this case is five hundred years. Yates echoes the time frame and references, too, and reterritorializes the colonized globe as indigenous space: "The symbolic and precedent setting nature of this trial for all indigenous peoples and all national justice systems cannot be overestimated."[30] In Yates, Rigoberta Menchú finds an adequate witness who amplifies Menchú's testimony; mobilizes it in legal networks, through various media, and to new audiences; and facilitates its renewal and return to a new generation of Guatemalans as Menchú and her testimony continue to seek new witnesses.

TESTIMONIAL CYCLES AND CROSSINGS

Perhaps it is no surprise that the discourse of judgment with the monitory categories of truth and lies infiltrates testimonial networks. The terms are both technical and vernacular. They mediate the distance between the institutional complexities of the law and "my truth," between what one can say and what can be done with it. Testimony crosses the boundary between life and death, but it also tarries at that border and inhabits it as an extracorporeal entity. The testimonial body both is a surrogate for those who cannot testify and possesses a life of its own. It persists across jurisdictions and can travel the globe. Its future is defined by its capacity to communicate about the past. It exceeds the bodies of the dead, but it carries their voice where it cannot go. Testimony constantly traverses the boundary of the living and the dead and derives its affective charge from its disembodied and authentic location. Testimony is haunted: by the dead to whom it bears witness, as well as the living who offer and hear it. It carries histories of the past that are difficult to narrate, and it makes a claim on the present about current situations. And here we come to another paradox of testimony: testimonial cycles embed histories of violence, including slavery, conquest, and genocide, and current crises alike. No single act of testimony can fully bear the weight, but we can chart how, as Sidonie Smith and Kay Schaeffer have shown, testimony operates in humanitarian storytelling, and how it moves around the globe through creative, legal, and literary transactions, as Gillian Whitlock has described.[31]

As it moves, testimony generates affect and attracts judgment. This becomes clearer as we trace legal testimony's imbrication with coerced confession and torture, as well as the proximity of judgment in the presence of testimony. One of the byproducts of histories of coercion in both sites is testimonial affect, a sense that the truth is present in the speech of the person, but that to destroy the truth, one can attack the body of the person. Perhaps it is this detachment of body and speech that lets us see how testimony moves beyond the individual. In *The Social Life of Things*, Arjun Appadurai calls attention to how "things-in-motion . . . illuminate their human and social context."[32] We are not used to calling testimony a thing, especially when that sounds like we are detaching it from the persons who give it and from the events to which it bears witness, but I want to undertake the thought experiment this locution implies in order to attribute agency to testimony and its movements, so that we may follow as it goes where a person is barred from going yet persists in carrying traces of the human with it, sometimes amplifying voices silenced by death or muting their force by conforming to rules of evidence in court. Testimony as a thing in motion illuminates the human and social contexts of war and helps us to understand how women's testimony in particular traverses literary and legal domains, twinning narratives about atrocities and legal trials, in the complexities of transnational witness. And what testimony illuminates as it moves is both the testimonial network of courts and tribunals—international and national courts and the routes that connect them—but also the testimonial network's shadow—the carceral network of black sites and sites of illegal detention where bodies are broken into vehicles for coerced confessions. The detachment of body and speech lets us see how testimony moves beyond the individual.

Testimonial cycles return us to cases and remind us that testimonial agency moves in search of an adequate witness beyond the speeded up life cycle and death spiral of scandal. As these cycles call us to attend again to archives from which we may have temporarily moved on, we can review our own critical histories by engaging anew with the methodologies of our previous encounters. Scandal distorts the testimonial signal. It produces an echo in which when one generates the name Menchú, one hears back the echo of a recycled story of scandal. Scandal sticks to testimony and we get stuck with the weight it imposes. Scandal represents a diversion from larger political issues. It masks the truth by making testimony seem to be about an individual rather than a people. This, I would argue, was the real hoax. Scandal distracted attention from the movement of testimony, falsely asserting that Menchú was effectively compromised and silenced, when in fact her testimony was traveling in various forms, on different platforms, and in new jurisdictions. Instead of ceasing its movements and its capacity to move witnesses, Menchú's testimony continued to trace a path through a global testimonial network: from Guatemala to Mexico to Paris in its initial movement, and from the Spanish to the Guatemalan legal systems. As her testimony moved, it gathered new technologies—documentary film, for example—opened new archives of evidence, and coevolved with forensic methodologies designed by the International Criminal Court to hear the testimony of the victims of mass killing.

JURISDICTIONS: INTIMATE PUBLICS,
PURE VICTIMS

While the haunting historical context is the Spanish conquest and colonization, the Menchú case reveals how disparate histories and contexts circulate in testimonial networks. For Anita Hill's testimony, women's increasing professionalization and the feminist movement's exposure of sexual harassment provide further context. Singly and together, these historical transformations functioned as obstacles within the conservative Washington networks that propelled Clarence Thomas's nomination process. The context for Rigoberta Menchú's testimony is similarly layered and, in addition to the history and politics of Guatemala and U.S. imperialism, includes the surge in memoir publication that began around the time *I, Rigoberta Menchú* was circulating in North America. As I argue in chapter 3, personal accounts of trauma reached new, broad audiences beginning in the 1980s, and we can see how scandals like the one surrounding Menchú function as jurisdictions.[33] To historicize the Menchú scandal is to return to memoir publishing's rise in the late 1990s, when Menchú's text and others were caught up in scandals animated by cultural anxieties related to gender, trauma, and testimony.

Life writing (here, in the forms of memoir and *testimonio*) represents another jurisdiction, or forum of judgment.[34] Both the text itself and the public sphere it enters can be understood as jurisdictions; indeed, thinking of the public sphere in this way elucidates the mechanisms of judgment that pervade it, the contest of authorities that can arise around oppositional texts, and the levering forward of ethics, truth telling, and scandal as the language through which such extrajudicial "trials" unfold. Thinking of life narrative as a jurisdiction also helps to clarify the kind of agency a text can exert and the quasi-legal authority it possesses for its advocates and detractors. Jurisdictions share some informal characteristics with what Lauren Berlant calls "intimate publics,"[35] although members of a jurisdiction assemble in relation to judgment to create a shared sense of belonging and comprise dominant and nondominant members, both of whom seek to make their opinions stick but need not "feel in common" as they produce judgment. Indeed, they may feel as if they are acting alone, even righteously, on behalf of or in relation to a higher moral standard. Authorities within courts of public opinion are dispersed. Additional actants include the press and online venues for weighing in, where participants are bound more by admonitory than by affiliative energies, and membership is shifting and temporary. While a jurisdiction may contain an intimate public, it also includes agents opposed to the development of collectivity and for this reason better resembles an assemblage,[36] which depends on conflictual energies in order to form. The appeal of testimony to those who bear witness as well as those who taint it constitutes part of its force. Within a jurisdiction, agency attaches to testimony and the judgments that stick to it, even as testimony continues to move in search of an adequate witness.

Jurisdictional conflicts over how to represent trauma and gender, and who may do so and with what limits, may occur whenever personal accounts are introduced into the public sphere, but particularly when those accounts concern the relation between individual injury and collective politics and make a claim for the representativeness of one person's experience of, or perspective on, violence.[37] When an individual who speaks of injury emerges as the subject of a testimonial practice and makes a claim on public attention through the dissemination of that practice, a jurisdiction may form. Both subject to a jurisdiction and engaged in an act of critical articulation, memoir and *testimonio* themselves offer a forum of judgment in which the subject may achieve a control over her story that she would not hold in court. Jurisdiction is a legal term that borrows from Michel Foucault's notion of the juridical (here, involving the whole discursive arsenal of law, judgment, punishment, and the "regimes of truth")[38] in order to point toward culture more broadly and to indicate that scandals are historically specific rather than isolated or aberrant in their functioning. Legal protocols that seek to contain antagonists, evidence, and outcomes within territorially defined jurisdictions do not strictly apply to testimonial speech or its reception; however, an examination of scandals within the public sphere will reveal the tendency to substitute a deceptively neutral line of inquiry; namely, "Who did what, to whom, and where?" for the more binding "Who has the authority to judge its meaning?"

Conceptual issues in jurisdiction are indissoluble from jurisdiction's materiality and territoriality. Although we typically think of jurisdiction in terms of territory and the hold it has on the movements of persons and objects, we must also recognize its symbolic power to mark an inside and an outside to national affiliation and identity. The hold jurisdiction has on a person produces something less flexible and geographically mutable, and more akin to status and identity. Jurisdiction binds citizens to the laws of their home nations when they travel, for example, and therefore exceeds its geographical boundaries to become a property of persons: "Jurisdictions define the identity of the people that occupy them."[39] Jurisdictions also mark temporal boundaries: we think of testimony as bounded by time and finite, and therefore as static. Its credibility is tied to its stability. Simply to suggest that someone's story changed over time is to raise doubt, even when that change represents the addition or clarification of information that was suppressed or supplies previously absent context necessary to understanding.

When Rigoberta Menchú left Guatemala for Mexico and then France, she and her testimony were set loose in a shifting jurisdictional landscape. Borders delimit, but they also hold the promise of transformation. Dreams of crossing over, and crossing back, of carrying meaning across jurisdictional lines, or suspending some meanings altogether, apply to witness accounts as well as persons. The work of jurisdiction is to make the central practices and modes of judgment in a particular context meaningful. How do moving witnesses gain or retain credibility? Why are witnesses credible in some settings and not others? If the forum of judgment is so consequential, how can we speak of truth as the basis of judgment?

Is the bar to giving credible testimony too high to meet for those who have experienced trauma? Those who seek to represent trauma often say they feel compromised by or implicated in the degradation of the experience; few feel confident that anything like purity or innocence will emerge as they bear witness. Legal discourse requires some traumatized subjects to endure a secondary traumatization by testifying, to be sure, but also to constrain their stories of harm within the law's protocols and thereby limit the capacity of those stories to develop new terms for understanding and addressing that harm (in its complexity) outside the law. By bringing predominantly legalistic models of testimony to bear on life narrative, and thereby importing the universalizing tendencies of law, we foreclose the alternative knowledge that emerges in dissonant narratives. When the standard of credibility for bearing witness is measured against an escalating demand for testimonial purity that virtually no one can meet when trauma is involved, those standards ought to be inspected for ideological bias rather than permitted to stand solely as an ethical norm worthy of endorsement.

Instead of viewing practices that organize painful and sometimes conflictual materials through an "I" as merely personal and therefore limited political acts or versions of historical events, consider how self-representational practices bear on history, politics, and subjectivity in my analysis of the judgments that circulate around trauma and gender in the public sphere. Life narratives, no less than jurisdiction, concern "the production of political subjectivity."[40] While autobiographical self-representation offers a means by which to position personal history within the public sphere, any potentially disruptive performance in that location is freighted with risk. Dissident versions of personal and collective histories are in a dialectical relation to dominant notions of legitimacy and as such are more likely to elicit skepticism or condemnation than to invite sympathy or vindication, form a resistant discourse, or secure alternative meanings about contested events.[41]

While it is often easy to understand why any particular memoir or *testimonio* becomes scandalous after the scandal has flared, those retroactive constructions attribute the air of inevitability to events and the forces animating them that are often far less distinct in "real time." To transform credible women like Anita Hill and Rigoberta Menchú, notably women to whom unsubstantiated and inaccurate accusations stuck only through bias and repetition, the seemingly ethical question "Who is telling the truth?" moves to the fore and displaces the context necessary for an adequate witness to assemble.

Both memoir and *testimonio* are engaged in a process through which personal history gains interpretive leverage on dominant history and are thereby laid bare to a kind of scrutiny that characterizes the politics of truth telling. Such scrutiny is central to the emergence of scandal and serves to inhibit the "I" of memoir from achieving its politicization or, equally, to short-circuit the emergence of a "we" politicized in its response to the "I." *Testimonio* makes political claims insofar as those who have witnessed violence are authorized to speak truth to power. Memoir makes a claim on history even if, in the assertion of subjective privilege, it seems to align more with the fluidity of imagination and memory. Nancy K. Miller captures memoir's dual and antigeneric position in this way: "By its roots, memoir encompasses both acts of memory and acts of recording—personal reminiscences and documentation."[42] We are often, and appropriately, willing to let memoir and *testimonio* have it both ways. That is, as long as autobiographical self-representation is neither libelous nor slanderous, it can be maintained easily within a liberal discourse in which individuals may offer various, and even conflicting, accounts of experience. Even the more explicitly resistant form of *testimonio* can be conscripted into a pluralistic canon of multicultural difference. When the claims of the private (or prepoliticized) person impinge on dominant cultural narratives, however, or when the witnessing "I" politicizes a "we," then memoir and *testimonio* exceed the tolerance they are accorded and become something more influential, hence subject to judgment.

An accusation of lying proves especially sticky judgment within a testimonial network.[43] It not only taints specific witnesses but also spreads doubt and represents a form of destabilization to which the testimonial "I" is especially vulnerable. Lying is purposeful and malign. Sworn witnesses promise to tell the truth. Tainted witnesses are compromised as truth tellers: even if some aspects of their account might stand scrutiny, they don't. Lying defines an ethical limit: legal, cultural, and intimate formations rely on trust to function. D'Souza, Horowitz, Stoll, and Rohter accused Menchú of propagandizing, which suggests willful conduct, but also of being a mouthpiece and a dupe of Marxist resistance movements, which strips her of agency and thought. They could have suggested that she misremembered some of the details they found to be inaccurate. After all, she was certainly traumatized by what she had seen and experienced. Instead, they accused her of lying, which shifted the grid of evaluation to truth versus lies and placed Menchú and Stoll into the familiar coupling of he said/she said. Within the jurisdiction that assembled to judge Menchú, scandal represented an indexical sign of gender. Gender animates scandal, in part, because critical and popular notions of truth telling are gendered. The epithet "liar" hangs in the air less as a provable accusation than as a metonymic symptom of a woman falling under public scrutiny and censure.

When Menchú was accused of lying because her text "cannot be the eyewitness account it purports to be" as she describes as her own "experiences she never had herself,"[44] Stoll remobilized her testimony as a lie. As this new name traveled, her testimony's status as scandal superseded the story of genocide in Guatemala. In Larry Rohter's *New York Times* article, the scandal—whether she lied—was the story, not the crisis in Guatemala. Why was this substitution persuasive? Why didn't Rohter tell a different story about Guatemala? Pamela Yates certainly had a different story to offer, as well as corroborating film supporting Menchú's testimony. As the depth and diversity of scholarship assembled to contextualize Menchú's *testimonio* in the aftermath of the controversy demonstrates, there were other stories to tell.

Menchú's text offers an explicitly politicized "I" who calls for the politicization of a "we" that includes both indigenous peoples and multiple and diverse publics galvanized to bear witness. Little of her text resembles political dogma; instead, its testimonial "I" lyrically evokes life in the Guatemalan highlands of her birth. An elegiac picture of home contrasts life in Chimel with labor in the *fincas* where her family worked for most of the year. Her pastoral depiction of Chimel links the integrity and specificity of the Quiché to indigeneity and land rights. Memory for her is a supple, politicizable instrument through which a contemporary situation can be contextualized. When the issue is narrowed to the legalistic "Did she lie?" almost none of the complexity of representing the self in the context of representing histories of violence and contemporary trauma can be retained without seeming to sink into ethical relativism and equivocation.[45] The charge of lying reorganizes the value and authority of her account retroactively: it imposes new rules that Menchú is accused of violating instead of elaborating the context from which her testimony emerged. The jurisdiction of scandal was organized to obscure how the standard of "truth or lies" led swiftly to the charge of lying for women and stripped context from Menchú's highly defensible and ultimately vindicated testimony.

When Menchú is asked to comment on oppression, she often answers by linking racism and sexism. Although Arturo Arias points out that "there is no simplistic leftist or feminist rhetoric" in the *testimonio*,[46] Menchú emphasizes the centrality of gender in her experience of trauma, memory, culture, and rights. For her, gender produces the sharpest negative reactions to her political work. Voices critical of her often link bias against indigenous activists to notions about women's proper and subordinate roles in dominant and traditional cultures. Because various feminist commentators have spoken to the presumptive saturation of contemporary culture in an identity-based rhetoric of victimization and have noted the irony in feminists seeking redress from the state for state-sponsored violence against women,[47] notice that Menchú does not adopt the language of legal plaint in her testimony. Instead, she presses her claims through testimonial speech that welds the personal to the collective and posits an international, ethical "you" and "we" who will listen and respond. In other words, she seeks to mobilize her testimony in search of an adequate witness. As a target of tainting, her *testimonio* is stuck in the jurisdiction of scandal and suffers the fate of dragging forward that story with subsequent efforts to bear witness to ongoing political crises around indigenous, women's, and human rights. Yet as a testimonial subject who was able to bear witness in the multiple jurisdictions of text, documentary film, and court, Menchú mobilized testimony through life story.

Scandal's characteristic mode is to reject the terms in which the author casts her project and introduce hostile ones in their place. This taints her as a witness. The popular caveat that what transpired between Anita Hill and Clarence Thomas at the EEOC in 1981 was unknowable and undecidable was a purposeful construction designed to render women incapable of providing credible witness about sexual harassment. The thoroughness of the public campaign to discredit Hill's testimony showcased strategies that would be taken up in various ways over the next decades. Although these strategies were not new, they were displayed in public, in a setting with legal elements, at a new level of visibility. When conservative Washington pundits attacked Rigoberta Menchú's *testimonio*, their campaigns dovetailed with Stoll's effort to discredit Menchú. In an echo of the strategy Thomas used to taint Hill, Menchú was represented as a political pawn rather than a subject in her own right. That diminishment stuck, too, so that even when new information came to light, Menchú's new status as "vindicated" did not fully circulate within the jurisdictions that pronounced her "tarnished." There has been no apology in response to the verdicts in Guatemala, no front-page follow-up in the *New York Times*, and an online search of Menchú's name foregrounds the controversy as one in which she was implicated rather than the concerted political attack it was. The afterlife of tainting, and the persistence of its attachment to reputation, forms a microcosm of the delegitimization caused by the compounding of histories of violence and contemporary trauma.

3

NEOLIBERAL LIFE NARRATIVE

From Testimony to Self-Help

Perhaps we get, not what we deserve, but what we demand.

—EMMA DONOGHUE, *KISSING THE WITCH:*
OLD TALES IN NEW SKINS

THE MEMOIR BOOM/LASH

The surge in life narratives published in the late twentieth century has been described as a memoir boom.[1] In this expanding market, women's life stories gained new prominence. They were published by commercial presses, were circulated to broad audiences, garnered reviews, were widely adopted in resurgent book clubs, and were consumed within the dynamics of "compassionate liberalism" that Lauren Berlant has described as an "intimate public." As Berlant notes, popular forms like memoir, where audiences experience reading together as emotional connection to others, participated in and themselves represented a form of politics: a sentimental citizenship that promoted feelings of attachment to the ideals of democracy that the objects themselves could not guarantee.[2]

Unlike the boom-bust cycle suggested by the analogy to a boom, memoir publishing remains strong. However, the boom now incorporates a full-blown backlash against memoir itself and women's memoir in particular, in the form of a *boom/lash*.[3] The boom/lash describes how the discrediting of the genre of memoir is now routinely included in reviews of specific texts. The stigma attached to memoir represents a form of witness tainting that can be mobilized as a ready-made judgment against any particular text. What accounts for the simultaneous popularity and denunciation of this form of testimony? How does the act of publishing a memoir provide material for further judgment that can stick to women witnesses? How do the transits of specific memoirs enable us to view the range of judgments circulating within testimonial networks now?

If we focus on the rise of neoliberal life narratives less as the periodization of a boom followed by a bust and more as the attachment of backlash to first-person nonfiction, we gain a new perspective on the investments in tainting witnesses during this period of testimony, as well as an alternative historicization of its time frame.[4] We notice two key features here: first, a different historicization of the boom recognizes that the popularity of memoirs published in the mid-1990s—like *Girl, Interrupted*, by Susanna Kaysen (1993); *The Liar's Club*, by Mary Karr (1995); and *Angela's Ashes*, by Frank McCourt (1996)[5]—is preceded and prepared for by Anita Hill's testimony, as well as the rise in the publication and circulation of first-person literature by women of color, including Rigoberta Menchú, and queer writers. And, second, a focus on Oprah Winfrey's media empire and its relation to testimonial networks reveals how representations of trauma and gender migrated from memoir to self-help through her television show, book club, magazine, network, and live tours at a particular moment in the boom/lash and provided a structure for preserving the redemption narrative's popularity by relocating to self-help from its proximity to doubt.

The memoir boom/lash represents a neoliberal formation in which the potency, and threat, of nonnormative witnesses and narratives that catalyzed this period of vitality in life writing were absorbed and neutralized by a newly ascendant redemption narrative. Although memoir was initially welcomed as it reached broader audiences, writers like Kathryn Harrison, whose memoir, *The Kiss* (1998), focused on adult daughter–father incest, were subsequently tainted: first, as rule breakers of public decorum, and second, as potential liars and frauds. Within an earlier moment of openness to such confessional accounts, testimony seemed almost welcome. It drew new audiences to memoir through popular and critically acclaimed texts, enabled a politics of identity to come into view, and demonstrated the persistent cultural authority of a first-person account. This openness would prove brief, but that it was displaced so rapidly by more traditional notions of social, human, and literary value indicates that the jurisdiction of memoir already contained the sticky judgments that would amend doubt to women's testimony.

TRUTH OR LIES

There are some tales not for telling, whether because they are too long, too precious, too laughable, too painful, too easy to need telling or too hard to explain. After all, after years and travels my secrets are all I have left to chew on in the night.

—EMMA DONOGHUE, *KISSING THE WITCH:
OLD TALES IN NEW SKINS*

In the decades after highly charged jurisdictions coalesced around Anita Hill and Rigoberta Menchú's testimony, life stories by women with compelling literary voices and stories to tell about everyday violence circulated to broad audiences. Publishing houses added memoirs to existing lists and created new imprints, booksellers reorganized displays to create profiles for these narratives, and editors and agents focused new attention on memoir, which often meant shifting away from the autobiographical first novel to marketing a first book as memoir.[6] A marketplace emerged for writers whose personal accounts emphasized aspects of experience and consciousness that differed from those typically featured in memoirs by famous men with public careers or by distinguished figures writing retrospectively later in life. Perhaps surprisingly, the market showed considerable interest in these new narratives and they claimed memoir's distinction as being the literary eyewitness to history, capturing the experience of complex lives not characterized by privilege and status.[7] Many of the texts brimmed with formal innovation that experimented with or exposed the limits of genre.[8] Some revealed the limits of genre to contain their testimony: they were often hybrid in combining poetry with essays, memoir, and autobiographical fiction; occasionally bilingual; and innovative in drawing life story into new media, like graphic memoirs and blogs.[9]

Yet as these narratives gained in prominence enough to become representative of life writing, readers, reviewers, and some scholars began to greet these stories with censure.[10] They were tagged as both lies and inconvenient truths, and their authors were shamed, sidelined, and turned into examples of the excesses of identity politics, and increasingly of the pitfalls of memoir itself. Women's testimonial narratives in the last decades of the twentieth century were displaced by a new influx of neoliberal life narratives. At the same time, the capacity to criticize any memoirist as potentially untrustworthy through association with memoir as an incubator for tainted testimonial witnesses and potential liars became increasingly routine. How was this accomplished? The application of a binary test of whether or not a witness was telling the truth migrated to autobiographical literature. The strategy of preempting the formation of an adequate context to contain the testimony of complex lives had been used to discredit both Anita Hill and Rigoberta Menchú. It now attached to memoirists and to memoir, a form whose testimonial energies test the limits of genre to contain them. Through an increasing hostility to innovation and invention in life writing associated with women of color, queer writers, and white writers who expose violence within the family, self-representational texts about lives in crisis were absorbed within neoliberalism.

OTHER "I'S": NEOLIBERAL LIFE
NARRATIVE'S DISPLACEMENTS

What is a neoliberal life narrative? Like the life story offered by Clarence Thomas in his Pin Point strategy, the neoliberal life narrative features an "I" who overcomes hardship and recasts historical and systemic harm as something an individual alone can, and should, manage through pluck, perseverance, and enterprise. The individual transforms disadvantage into value.[11] The message frames the narrative and also shapes the self and its career, as the narrative becomes a platform to launch new ventures, from Supreme Court justice to motivational speaker. Neoliberal life narrative conditions readers to affirm and accept the redemption story as natural and desirable, and to embrace life stories that absolve readers of the requirement to do anything other than follow the writer's advice in their own lives because the writer has relieved readers of history's ethical claims on us.[12]

The best-selling memoir *The Glass Castle* by Jeanette Walls offers an example of neoliberal life narrative.[13] The memoir has been extraordinarily popular since its publication in 2005. It spent 216 weeks on the *New York Times* best seller list, was adopted in middle and high school curricula for young readers, and, in a nod to this new market, won an American Library Association Alex Award in 2006.[14] In *The Glass Castle*, Walls maintains that she was able to overcome poverty in Appalachia, one of the most persistently impoverished areas in the United States, by doing well in school, going to college, and marrying up. Her parents, she claims, made a personal decision to be homeless and she, as an individual, chose differently. Following the success of the memoir, Walls became a popular speaker, who focuses on the theme of leadership for young, female audiences. A blurb by Keppler Speakers, which manages Walls's speaking events, succinctly captures the key features of her brand: "Walls shares an inspiring message of triumph over obstacles and encourages audiences to face their fears, confront their past, and understand that our flaws can be our greatest assets."[15]

Walls's successful book follows years in which autobiographical narratives by women of color transformed nonfiction. These texts paved the way for the surge in memoir publishing by establishing it as a newly important form for a civil rights era. Although the texts most often associated with the memoir boom are written by white authors (Mary Karr, Frank McCourt, and Tobias Wolff, among them), this limits the frame of reference to a moment in the mid-1990s when memoir's prominence seemed to rise out of nowhere and obscures the pathbreaking cultural and literary precursors: Maya Angelou's *I Know Why the Caged Bird Sings* (1969); Maxine Hong Kingston's *The Woman Warrior* (1976); Audre Lorde's biomythography *Zami: A New Spelling of My Name* (1982); Cherrie Moraga's formally and bilingual hybrid *Loving in the War Years* (1983); Sandra Cisneros's *The House on Mango Street* (1984); the collection coedited by Cherríe Moraga and Gloria Anzaldúa that included personal essays, *This Bridge Called My Back* (1984); and Gloria Anzaldúa's *Borderlands: La Frontera* (1987).[16] Allied with and energized by these first-person texts, scholars in the academic fields of women's studies and ethnic studies included these texts in college curricula, often alongside *I, Rigoberta Menchú*, to theorize a range of issues from self-representational texts. Authors and texts with a range of investments in feminist inquiry and aesthetics, including Carolyn Steedman's *Landscape for a Good Woman* (1986) and Monique Wittig's *Lesbian Body* (translated in 1975), and a host of formally diverse autobiographical texts presented multiple feminist "I's" characterized by intellect, creativity, and political critique.[17] Through their place in college curricula, feminist reviewing, and interdisciplinary scholarship, they circulated to knowing and new audiences alike. In contrast to the conservative voices of Clarence Thomas and Jeanette Walls, these texts were fueled by a "feminist killjoy" affect and a profound commitment to building resilient communities.[18] They abided by no set trajectory of narrative resolution or closure. Verging into autobiographical fiction, the essay and manifesto, and graphic memoir and comics, they connected submerged histories of violence to contemporary trauma and brought both into view.

Neoliberalism has gained traction as a critical term in the humanities after being imported from the fields of political science and economics, where it specifies the capitalist ideology associated with economist Milton Friedman's promotion of individuals as beneficiaries of free markets, and the effective masking of this unrestrained activity's tendency to produce inequality by concentrating wealth narrowly. It is used in globalization studies to describe how financial regulators like the International Monetary Fund and World Bank use policies including structural adjustment to undermine national sovereignty and the structure of local communities. The disastrous consequences of austerity measures—in the absence of other forms of support to address poverty—are on view in multiple nations who are the laboratories for neoliberal financial policies. The narrative that underwrites neoliberalism promotes personal responsibility. It places both the blame for structural problems and the responsibility for their solution on individuals. Within neoliberalism, the individual is endowed with the appearance of personal choice (Pepsi or Coke?), while the asymmetries of actual power, vulnerability, and reward are continuously suppressed through the language of self-striving. If we think of the Pin Point strategy in this context, it exemplifies neoliberal life narrative because it pits Clarence Thomas as an individual against structural racism and poverty, which he is said to overcome in order to rise to the Supreme Court. His largest obstacle in this narrative is affirmative action and the conspiracy to punish him for his conservative politics that allegedly used Anita Hill to destroy him. And while neoliberalism trades in persecutorial fantasy and falsifies who disproportionately benefits from the deregulation of financial markets and the removal of workplace and labor protections, it does so by attaching itself to the rhetoric of self-improvement and the rags-to-riches life story that functions as a vernacular corollary to democracy in the United States.

In the aftermath of the financial crisis in 2008 and the bursting of the housing and tech bubbles, a narrative of blame was readily applied to individuals in the absence of a narrative of responsibility for creditors who were excused as "too big too fail." Neoliberalism's need for a robust discourse of individual choice and responsibility points to the cultural work the popularity of memoir performs. The pervasiveness of the redemption narrative preserves the hope that neoliberal policies and ideologies mock. Specifically, the transformations that occurred within the memoir boom in order to promote neoliberal life narrative included the shift from a politicized "I" of self-representation—a hard-won space carved out by feminism, critical race theory, and queer studies—to a type of the resilient and redeemed individual, including the postracial nominee, the self-made man, and the empowered woman. These generic selves offer self-help, which turns out to be "merely personal" rather than critical or revelatory of the functions of power.[19] Yet this move buried emotions now bursting the seams of neoliberal life narrative, which are often characterized by intense and sometimes inchoate pain[20]—the kind of engulfing pain that indicates, in the context of this book's focus, the presence of painful pasts but nothing that cannot, in neoliberal narrative, be overcome and redeemed.[21] My alternative periodization of neoliberal life narrative acknowledges the actual breakthroughs in publishing that characterized the run-up to the memoir boom, highlights the later ascendancy of popular redemption stories, and contextualizes the danger of disaffiliation: of being called out as a liar, fake, or hoax.[22]

Memoir in the late 1980s was less characterized by trauma per se, although that became the narrative associated with the boom, than by the self-representation of complex lives that included it. In other words, trauma consisted in exposure to the everyday violence of poverty, racism, homophobia, and misogyny. Rather than falling "outside the range" of experience, it was chronic, systemic, and ordinary. Indeed, feminist clinicians and scholars shifted the definition of trauma during the memoir surge from the Freudian notion of the event that breaks the frame to feminist theorizing about chronic exposure to vulnerability and everyday violence.[23] Exemplified by autobiographical texts like *Bastard Out of Carolina*, by Dorothy Allison (1992), and, including the critical essays and poetry of Audre Lorde, Adrienne Rich, and other poets, as well as writing from the AIDS epidemic, like David Wojnarowicz's *Close to the Knives* (1991),[24] these texts drew both acclaim and censure, and generated new strategies for writers who sought alternative jurisdictions to the genre of memoir, which was increasingly policed by reviewers sniffing out "impropriety" and calling out public disclosures of family violence as unethical because family members did not have a reciprocal opportunity to respond. Such disciplinary responses represent how the feminist use of memoir to expose violence came to be depoliticized and folded into the juridical framework of "he said/she said."

As I have argued elsewhere, writers such as Dorothy Allison, Jeanette Winterson, and Jamaica Kincaid sought the freedom of self-representation and a public forum but avoided the genre of memoir rather than see their innovative and nuanced presentations of trauma reduced to "he said/she said."[25] Because the radical potential of memoir consists in the public platform it offers to newly visible writers and the social and literary transformations they seek, its potential had to be absorbed into neoliberalism by emptying the form of its challenging and politicized content and replacing its aesthetic challenges with the closure of the redemption narrative. Memoir became a tainted witness, certain kinds of texts were substituted as its representative, and authors were dismissed as self-indulgent or disreputable.

Testimony travels along the same pathways as neoliberal life narrative, to similar audiences, and can also reinforce judgment. Although testimony is rooted in specific contexts of contemporary harm for which witnesses seek a hearing and relief, neoliberal life narratives adapt this form toward other ends. Neoliberal life narratives, like *The Glass Castle*, are better understood as neoconfessional rather than testimonial insofar as they promote individual life experiences as examples of a generic humanity and eschew historical or political analysis or contextualization. The engrossing examples within this pattern scale up such that the rise and fall of specific narratives reproduces the narrative template of redemption writ large. The cycle of praise and blame is gendered, to be sure, with women often standing to lose the most by being too closely associated with testimonial forms that carry with them the taint of scandal.

Neoliberal life narrative does more than play out endless versions of down and outers who make good: it displaces other life narratives, including those that commanded attention in the early years of a memoir boom stretching into the twenty-first century. These memoirs identified the systemic nature of disenfranchisement, unmasked middle-class pieties about privacy and sexual violence, linked suffering and violence to poverty and state indifference, and challenged dominant reading practices around testimony. Kathryn Harrison's *The Kiss*, for example, challenged expectations around incest in white, middle-class families and literary self-representation, while *I, Rigoberta Menchú* raised questions about translation and collaboration, eyewitness testimony, and the gender politics of indigenous activism. As Gillian Harkins argues, neoliberalism emerges to counter social movements as they gain traction, including feminism, racial recognition, and LGBTQ movements.[26] The brief period of openness that greeted memoirs about violence within families, addiction, and illness gave critics a new target and helped them to hone the message that not only an individual and her memoir were tainted, but the entire genre was spoiled.

We see here how markets and jurisdictions overlap conceptually and materially to promote certain kinds of life stories. In contrast to counter-confessional and redemption-wary self-representation, neoconfessional life narrative is situated at the crossroads of self-help, travel narrative, and memoir. These texts now construct the conditions in which testimony by insufficiently redeemed narrators is denigrated and drops out of view. Neoliberal life narratives diminish other witnesses as they are mobilized within the testimonial network they cohabit. As redemption narratives become increasingly generic, tolerance for other life narrative decreases. How, then, do we keep the feminist witness in view?

KISSING (OFF) THE MEMOIR BOOM

Sometimes you must shed your skin to save it.

—EMMA DONOGHUE, *KISSING THE WITCH:
OLD TALES IN NEW SKINS*

In *The Kiss*, Kathryn Harrison restores the representation of incest to its statistically normative locale—the white, middle-class family—and bears witness to an adult experience of incest with her father that she expects no one to find particularly sympathetic. Harrison does not file suit, it is important to note, nor does she name names explicitly.[27]

Instead she writes a memoir. Like testimony, memoir seeks a hearing, can be oppositional, and, in its elicitation of a forum of judgment in which to air its claims, creates the possibilities around which to form politicized energies. Memoir need not be confessional, as Harrison's is not, in the sense that it need not promote a victimized identity as its subject or seek relief from or offer penance to any authorities. Memoir is often written from a position wholly unlike that configured via the embrace of injury-as-identity.[28] As an anticonfessional subject, Harrison refuses to behave like a victim or a criminal, and attempts instead to present herself as a subject coming to terms more with the mystery of her agency than her injury.

Harrison's mother divorced Harrison's father when Harrison was six months old. Her mother moved out of her parents' home and into an apartment when Harrison was six years old but left Harrison behind to be raised by her grandparents. When Harrison is twenty and a college sophomore, her father returns for the kind of visit of which apocalypses are made. He devours her with "hungry eyes" and obsesses over her body, all of which creepily foreshadows his violation of their roles and her integrity. It is both surprising and horribly predicted that on the morning of her father's departure, he will betray her mother by telling Harrison he slept with her because "she asked me" and violate his daughter by turning their goodbye into a bewitching straight out of the unexpurgated Brothers Grimm: "My father pushes his tongue deep into my mouth: wet, insistent, exploring, then withdrawn. . . . In years to come, I'll think of the kiss as a kind of transforming sting, like that of a scorpion: a narcotic that spreads from my mouth to my brain. The kiss is the point at which I begin, slowly, inexorably, to fall asleep, to surrender volition, to become paralyzed."[29]

Harrison's memoir places this four-year adult incest experience in the context of her relationship with her mother. The writing is elliptical and etches brief scenes focused on images of entrapment, violation, and inertia. The memoir's refusal of a conventional rhetoric of blame, judgment, and expiation persuaded many readers that Harrison was implicated ethically in both the incest and its retelling. At fault, stained by having a secret and for exposing it, Harrison's capacity to bear witness was derailed into scandal. Yet what was lost in this shift from attending to Harrison's account to blaming her for it was an engagement with an ethically allusive representation of incest that seemed to call for a chorus from Greek tragedy as its adequate witness. How else to encounter the evocation of mythic precursors, particularly the figures of Oedipus and Antigone, fused into Harrison, and the doomed familial relations in which damage, debt, and agency develop? As the tragic daughter, she is a stranger to herself and within her family, estranged from custom and law, and speaking as if she could bear public witness to her grief. She has not buried a brother in defiance of an edict; she has buried herself. Harrison achieves a condensation of Greek tragedy and fairy tales through her figure of the violated daughter for whom the primary locus of injury cannot be limited to childhood or even to gender.

Harrison withholds the language of blame in order to explore her curiosity and participation. Both are conditioned by bargains the adults in her life have made, and embodied by the secrets and silences Harrison must navigate. Harrison enlists the iconography of enchantment in fairy tales, initially through her use of the kiss as a trope, but also in the deathly and inert slumber of fairy tale heroines, if slumber is the right word for figures so profoundly immobilized in nightmarish inaction. Immured in glass coffins, towers, and overgrown forests, they are, like Harrison, spellbound for a time. We witness how Harrison is caught in this state. What redemption is possible for this subject? Exile or suicide? Martyrdom, perhaps? Ultimately, the spell is broken when Harrison embraces her mother's dead body at the end of the memoir and saves herself by kissing the estranged beloved's cold lips. Her blending of fairy tales and classical myth into a new literature of incest exposes the violence that haunts those sources.

FINDING FAULT

I looked in my mirror and saw, not myself, but every place
I'd never been.

—EMMA DONOGHUE, *KISSING THE WITCH:*
OLD TALES IN NEW SKINS

Upon publication, *The Kiss* was greeted with some reviews that praised its literary achievement, as one might expect from a contemporary memoir by an established author and characterized by skillful allusions to fairy tales and Greek tragedy, as well as Harrison's courage.[30] However, psychologist and author of *The Moral Life of Children* (1986) Robert Coles withdrew his blurb for the book when he was told the author had young children.[31] Soon, other critics worried that Harrison's artfulness confused the boundary between fiction and memoir and undermined her credibility. Christopher Lehmann-Haupt in particular wondered "whether a memoir can ring too artistic for truth" and concluded that "the mystery of her survival is a flaw in the memoir."[32] For him and others, Harrison's success as a writer and her achievement of marriage and motherhood discredited her claim to harm. If she could marry, have children, and write the book, they asked, how bad could the incest have been? On one hand, the claim seems to be that trauma is unrepresentable, so Harrison should have been silent, too; on the other, that injury is transparent with no art or interpretation needed to represent it, so Harrison should have said it all rather less artfully. The irreconcilable demands (to be silent, to be transparent) implied in this judgment mark the place where the woman witness is made to vanish.

The injunction not to tell this tale took many forms but emerged most succinctly in Cynthia Crossen's concluding words to her *Wall Street Journal* review: "Hush up."[33] "The Naked Literary Come-On," an article in the *New York Times* about sex and sales, featured a photo of Candace Bushnell, author of *Sex and the City*, sprawled on a bed and described how publicists use sex to market authors and, to a lesser degree, their books. It assessed Harrison's marketability: "If an unattractive woman were to write a book about sleeping with her father, it would not command the same media real estate as an attractive woman sleeping with her father."[34] The claim that women's testimony about incest is best contextualized as one commodity among others related to feminine appeal, and that one text by a woman is interchangeable with any other, highlights the merging of women's testimony into a neoliberal marketplace. Just as capital is regulated to protect global finance,[35] life narrative is regulated to protect testimonial speech about the family. As Gillian Harkins observes, the critical response is a market strategy that merges an "excitation of moral disapproval as an incitement to buy the book."[36]

In the negative reviews and the controversy generally, the complicated terms through which Harrison represents incest were manipulated, flattened, and misrepresented. Those manipulations were then debated as if they were hers. In other words, the scandal operates here as it did in Stoll's attack on Menchú; namely, the author's terms were mischaracterized and the substitute terms were recycled via media, and then taken up in debates. In this case, because of her age at the time and her physical appearance, incest was turned into one more version of sexiness. In this reformulation, Harrison becomes the greedy purveyor who attaches her own sexiness and story, and therefore the exploiter of her experience for profit. The market's prurience catachrestically becomes Harrison's come-on. When Harrison appeared as an interview subject in newspaper and magazine articles, her attractiveness rendered her unintelligible as one who had suffered harm. The copresence of past sexual violation and current vitality suggests something of the atemporality associated with trauma and its survival: the wound of trauma injures not only the person but also the person's sense of time, splitting it into before and after, hypostatizing the traumatic contents of the past in flashbacks, and disordering memory. In this case, many of Harrison's readers seem themselves to be caught in the delayed effect of trauma. That Harrison can tell this story and not have it be her suicide note, can appear in photographs in which she holds the camera's gaze without shielding her face or her body, and can give interviews in which she embraces her sexuality are disturbing in a jurisdiction that requires Harrison to appear as a proper victim

Harrison's memoir is more troubling to many readers than the narratives by women who suffered sexual abuse as children. Harrison was an adult when her father's incestuous demand wiped out her precarious sense of self. Surely, some critics want to say (and did), she was an adult, she was protected by her majority status, by the law, by her independence. If there were ever a time for just saying no, this was it: Why couldn't she? Why wouldn't she? Isn't she responsible? Isn't she at fault? Cast as indictments of her personal judgment rather than her father's actions, these questions go to the construction of privacy in law, the family, and memoir and also to the legacy of disbelief and censure that greets women's representations of sexual trauma. They point to a familiar pattern in which radically different material and psychic formations from the ones in which many women live are fervently wished for. Those wishes are then promoted into phantasms of substance and endowed with legitimacy such that those phantasmic constructions of some other "reality" for women (one in which women do not experience incest, for example) may then be invoked as a standard of behavior that women have violated. That is, the "reality" behind sexualized violence is represented as the phantasm. While Harrison expands an analysis of incest, sex, and the family beyond the courts of family law and beyond debates about recovered childhood memory, judgments that fetishize incest as the sex that dares not speak its name circulate in various admonitory responses to her memoir. Although a very different reading of *The Kiss* is certainly possible, the scandalous one obscured the harm initiated by her father and brought out the daughter to stand trial.

The critical response to *The Kiss* caps a developing anxiety about the proliferation of trauma narratives. When judgment about women and memoir itself overlap, the boom fuses with its backlash. Memoirs of sexual trauma by women particularize the anonymous statistics of sexual violence. Thus the prevalence of trauma narratives threatens to rewrite the meaning of autobiography as a genre of representative individualism. Can such inappropriate victims really be representative? The politics of representative individualism as they are staged in life narrative hold both threat and promise. In the U.S. context, the cultural work done around the autobiographies of Frederick Douglass, Harriet Jacobs, and Malcolm X, as well as those by Benjamin Franklin, Ralph Waldo Emerson, and Henry David Thoreau, provides a discourse through which to understand political status, or the linking of citizenship and identity. Not as fully constrained as legal testimony, these self-representational antecedents offer a way to think about the nexus of trauma, gender, and race. This is the material of testimonial life narrative. In this jurisdiction, an alternative to the sovereign subject or the confessional subject as producer of meaning emerges to offer a testimonial account that risks censure, to be sure, but also opens up the possibility for other authorities and advocates to engage in the production of meaning with regard to trauma and gender.

In choosing *testimonio* and memoir, Menchú and Harrison forgo instruments of the state (including the courts) in order both to construct an alternative jurisdiction and to enter the jurisdiction of the public sphere through the language of self-representation rather than legal petition. That scandal erupts confirms the necessity of producing texts such as memoir and *testimonio* that challenge prevailing notions of gender and trauma in the public sphere, even if the scandals threaten oppositional speech by women *for a time*. The time of scandal and the time of adequate witness mark different durational economies, as the case of Rigoberta Menchú demonstrates. To keep the woman witness in view as her testimonial life narrative is tainted by judgments that distort it, we need to slow down the temporality of scandal in order to see how judgment becomes sticky. Menchú, as indigenous and political witness, and Harrison, as participant witness, offer two different examples through which to chart how judgments about women's credibility operate across legal and cultural courts of public opinion.

OPRAH WINFREY, JURISDICTION OF TASTE: FROM TESTIMONY TO SELF HELP

The underlying message of redemption in James Frey's
memoir still resonates with me.

—OPRAH WINFREY

I will look at four texts—James Frey's *A Million Little Pieces*, Elizabeth Gilbert's *Eat, Pray, Love: One Woman's Search for Everything Across Italy, India and Indonesia*, Eckhart Tolle's *The Power of Now*, and Cheryl Strayed's *Wild: From Lost to Found on the Pacific Crest Trail*—in order to chart the movement from testimony to self-help, and to highlight Oprah Winfrey's Book Club's force within the testimonial network.[37] Eva Illouz describes the "tentacular structure" of Winfrey's media empire, but also the boundary-crossing movements within it, as Winfrey's own personal story magnetizes to the stories of others, to experts, and to products.[38] The force of this structure draws together the market of book publishing with the activity of reading in intimate publics and forms a jurisdiction of taste that has shaped life writing in the history I am describing.

"A million little pieces" is precisely what many predicted the market for memoir would shatter into with the revelation in 2006 that James Frey's narrative of the same name was not the true story of addiction and recovery its author claimed it to be. Yet because the publication and sales of memoir remain robust, we see how scandal is less an anomaly than an integrated feature of how life narrative is consumed during the boom/lash. The popularity of redemption is important here because it names the preferred theme of life narrative and also describes the structure of participation in scandal: when readers consume narratives and throw out the fakers, then tastemakers and readers participate in a ritual cleanse of the category and the redemption narrative is redeemed for future use. The predominance of redemption narratives helps to discredit other life narratives, often written by women and exposing sexual violence, as well as memoirs written by authors who do not resemble majority book-buying audiences, and whose personal stories rely on a critique of the nation for its subjects' legibility. As Patricia Williams points out, without the context of slavery and generations of family and community experience in its long shadow, as well as the contemporary complexities of post–civil rights racism, an African American woman—herself—who expresses anger does not make sense; instead, she looks crazy.[39] It is precisely the evacuation of specific histories of harm that has enabled a series of shifts in the literary marketplace.

Unlike testimonials that bear witness to human rights abuses and are more directly political in their aims, the neoconfessional primarily bears witness to personal pain that can be overcome and redeemed. By locating the cause, experience, and end of suffering within the framework of the individual rather than in histories of violence that require political critique and legal and social remedies, and that compel readers to negotiate acts of witnessing, neoliberal life narratives displace the analysis of wrongdoing away from questions of justice. Instead, they focus on a personal subject whose particularities are smoothed to fit the amorphous and general shape of a generic self. Even as the market expands in volume, neoliberalism narrows and norms permissible accounts. To secure dominance, this market formation recruits new audiences and pressures all life narratives to enter the mass market through the narrow gate of the redemption narrative. In the packaging of the redemption narrative in neoliberal times, the individual becomes tasked with her own redemption.

The consumption of popular memoirs promotes a practice of reading in public focused on the mass circulation of life narratives, especially those with a redemption plot whose authors become the target of potent judgmental energies. In response to the presence of hoaxes, these energies are mediated and negotiated through the intertwining strands of memoir and self-help discourse represented by *A Million Little Pieces*; *The Power of Now*; *Eat, Pray, Love*; and *Wild*. The normalizing effect of self-help narratives that offer stories of personal trauma with happy endings directs the sympathy that autobiography can mobilize away from nonnormative life narrative and toward life writing that allows readers to experience compassion for similar others. Yet neoconfessional voices, like the confessional voices that Foucault famously warned were not simply speaking of truth, have an enigmatic force beyond the universals they propound. Instead, as Foucault suggests, "silence itself—the things one declines to say, or is forbidden to name, the discretion that is required between different speakers—is less the absolute limit of discourse, the other side from which it is separated by a strict boundary, than an element that functions alongside the things said, with them and in relation to them."[40] Although neoconfessional speech has been read as communicating an enhanced, even robust, form of civic engagement[41]— namely, that as it pours forth from voices too numerous to count, it represents a democratization of the public sphere—unspoken norms and explicit market formulas shape the dynamics of reading and limit whose lives may claim attention, for how long, and with what capacity to challenge the norms of reception. Neoconfessional speech that successfully hails an audience primed to expect certain conventions cannot by itself provide the materials for an analysis of its own truth claims, ethical investments, and identificatory desires. Indeed, what is not being currently discussed includes the value of autobiographical accounts that fail in public without harming the neoconfessional brand.

For many readers, the bedrock of autobiographical narrative is confessional in the sense that the writer and reader can be taken to be in a particular relation to each other, bound by a demand on the writer to render a transparent truth taken as ethical norm.[42] Compounding the confessional compact between reader and writer, and in fact reinforcing its confessional core, is the theoretical claim that the writer may be so bound and judged precisely because she or he has already assented to this quasi-juridical relation via the choice of genre (memoir and its variants) and is now obligated as if by contractual agreement. Legal contract and ethical relation reinforce each other within the confessional compact. The benefit of a verifiable relation between life writing and the events it narrates is hard to argue against, yet the ethical issues here are vexed in the mass market for life narrative. If the confessional compact is part of what generates the coercions and distortions within self-representation— constitutively and not merely facetiously so—then current controversies around memoirs are unlikely to be further illuminated by calls for more properly confessional (i.e., "truthful") autobiographical performances.

Yet if the histories consumed in neoliberal life narratives have been emptied of vexed realities, economic inequalities, and hierarchies of human value, then what grounds the ethical contract audiences claim to have had violated by memoirists like Frey? When experience is displaced by the requirements of the redemption narrative, then who is contracting with whom, and in what terms? It seems that the privileged relation autobiography relies on now is less one between writer and biographical events (the referential contract), or even between the writer as guarantor of the meaning of these events and the reader who believes them (the autobiographical contract/pact). If what memoir offers now is largely sentimental—an opportunity to feel together with/as a reading community—then can history only haunt neoliberal life narrative? And what does this haunting look like?

WITNESSING OPRAH, WITNESSING FREY: REDEMPTION ON TRIAL

Oprah Winfrey may be described as both media/market assemblage and a jurisdiction of taste when it comes to the reach and diversity of her brand and the centrality of personal life story within the talk and writing she promotes so successfully. Acts of witness emerge as Oprah interviews authors of redemption memoirs, positions these writers more as guides and sages than literary authors, advocates for self-improvement, and promotes and sells many, many books.[43] Her position as a reader who is also a platform marks the public that forms around her with differing affective and economic interests. When Oprah picked Frey's faux rehab memoir, she endorsed his book, his message, and him. When its exaggerations were discovered, she had to negotiate how best to walk away from book and author without discrediting the message so closely tied to her brand. When memoir itself became a target of criticism during the boom/lash, memoir's most public promoter and consumer became a tainted witness.

Many of the issues about shareable life story, including the critical narratives produced about them, have been raised on Oprah's couch, a site that blends therapy with commerce in the production of "talk."[44] Winfrey has presided over the fall of celebrity autobiographers and the compensatory rise of self-help. She is a complex witness, however, and also subject to the forms of discrediting that attach to women's life narratives because in the 1980s she was instrumental in opening a public discussion about sexual violence against women. Indeed, in the unlikely forum of the single-host, daytime TV talk show, she sponsored a counterdiscourse to the sensationalized accounts that revictimized survivors on other talk shows. Winfrey's intervention in the production of knowledge about sexual abuse helped to create a market for nonfiction and fiction *by* women that featured sophisticated critiques of the limits of privacy *for* women. Winfrey herself participated publicly in the production of a therapeutic narrative of female suffering by telling her own story of abuse, and by modeling a form of public listening in the mode of empathy rather than judgment. She became a dual witness to trauma: she told her story and she provided an adequate witness for the stories of others.

Although Winfrey has been able to capitalize in her Book Club on the market for first-person accounts of suffering and redemption that her talk show taught women to consume as a means of belonging, she has hardly done so from the imperious distance of a Rupert Murdoch. Instead, she immersed herself as an active subject in the production of this community, whose complexities exceed her. It is important to underscore, as a generation of intensive scholarship on Winfrey has ably demonstrated, that Oprah is complicated. Among the currents that swirl around her are racializing discourses and stereotypes, her own considerable rhetorical skills drawn from Southern Baptist preaching experience and her years in Chicago television, and the proliferation of her lifestyle brand with its investment in reading as self-improvement. Winfrey's overwhelming success and popularity, however, often create a perplexing effect: although she empathizes with survivor speech, and recognizes the realities of suffering that redemption narratives include, her public modeling of how to consume the current neoconfessionals consistently directs audiences away from the racist and sexist histories such discourses carry.[45]

Winfrey's preference for the redemption narrative predicts her promotion of self-help discourse, which I trace here through her handling of the wildly popular memoirs *A Million Little Pieces* and *Eat, Pray, Love*, and her subsequent promotion of *A New Earth: Awakening to Your Life's Purpose* and *The Power of Now*,[46] as well as her return to *Wild*, a book that successfully merges self-help and memoir in a potent narrative of a daughter's struggle following her mother's death. *Wild* prompted Winfrey to revive her moribund Book Club in 2012. The first three books were published between 1996 and 2006 during the height of memoir's popularity and notoriety when boom had become boom/lash. They trace a tight spiral around the themes of judgment and sentimentality, celebrity and self-help, and gender, race, and redemption so vivid in the neoconfessional. Yet long before a notable number of discredited memoirists found their way to celebrity on Oprah, critiques of Winfrey already presented her as an emblem of what would be censured in memoir. Like these memoirs, Winfrey fuses "public issues and private problems" without political analysis.[47] Like Winfrey and her guests, these memoirs are part of "the explosion in the 1980's of the 'recovery movement'—an amalgam of therapeutic practices, self-help groups, publications, mental health policies, and treatment programs."[48] Like Winfrey, they prefer confession and redemption to the messier histories and subjects with which testimony engages.

As critics and fans alike note, Winfrey engages in emotional displays, invites and performs confessions about sexual trauma, and seeks to coproduce with her guests a therapeutic narrative that takes pain as material for self-transformation[49] rather than an adequate politics. Lauren Berlant agrees with Janice Peck and Eva Illouz that these therapeutic narratives lack political analysis, even as they teem with political material. For Berlant, talk shows, the recovery movement, and even memoirs are "juxtapolitical": they are proximate to politics but represent a space that seems more available for participation—and even civic engagement—"because the political is deemed an elsewhere managed by elites who are . . . not [interested] in the well-being of ordinary people or life-worlds."[50] Part of Winfrey's canny appeal to popular markets and women readers depends on traveling a neoliberal path of personal redemption that does not lead to political analysis or action.

Winfrey's status as dual witness depends on how her own story conjoins two classical autobiographical storylines—the rise and the redemption narrative—and sutures them to the stories she promotes. Winfrey's biography includes her rise from poverty in Mississippi and sexual abuse to become *Forbes*'s richest woman and the most powerful woman in media. At the same time, she showcases redemption narratives through her ongoing and public search for spiritual meaning, and her promotion of writers who produce them. These two storylines are complicated by Winfrey's transformation of the presentation of survivor speech for a female audience in the 1980s. In those early shows, Winfrey altered the dynamics in which women had previously spoken about incest, rape, and sexual assault on daytime TV. Instead of having experts on such shows tell the audience what this violence meant, the women themselves were given the authority to interpret as well as narrate their experience.

Winfrey spoke openly about her own experience of sexual violence, and in so doing radically realigned power on her couch. Trauma and survival became material for a new market for memoirs through the production of personal stories and the promotion of nonexperts as consumers and authenticators of these performances. Winfrey shifted the "us-them" status of expert and witness, thereby opening a gendered and seemingly democratic realm of transaction. Her Book Club continues this realignment as it taps into the gendered emotion of belonging, which Berlant astutely limns as "community." It achieves this through the infinitely renewable experience of finding a new best self, a new "I," through a new "you" with whom to identify. Aspirations for a democratization of the public sphere, however, are constrained by Winfrey's pedagogy of reading in public, in which the community consumes spectacle and participates in rituals of shaming. The community is tutored by the pedagogy of Oprah's couch to succumb to the lure of the redemption narrative, and to preserve it as a privileged mode of self-representation, even if continuing to resonate with this message means sacrificing authors who confound its formulas as one of the pleasures of its consumption.

Winfrey's temptation by the redemption narrative suggests an angel/devil tableau. On one shoulder, the blonde-haired, blue-eyed, radiant Elizabeth Gilbert whispers of true goodness as birthright and destiny, toward which the journey of self-discovery and acceptance proceeds. On the other, the bearded bad boy of privileged white masculinity, James Frey, glowers. Each represents resonant aspects of the redemption narrative, in which, through a combination of unfortunate choices and circumstances, the narrator finds him- or herself in a world of hurt and struggles not only to rise but, through suffering, to transform damage into self-knowledge and reap the rewards that follow. Although as exemplars of living through, these narratives corroborate an optimistic set of principles consistent with the self-help discourse Winfrey prefers, their authors' suffering, if compelling, is thin. Both have received their hard knocks while standing fully in the social and psychic space of white privilege. Well-educated, with supportive and materially comfortable families, Gilbert and Frey drift away from happiness and become miserable. Oprah's couch became a forum of judgment first for acknowledging the worthiness of their pain and endorsing their programs for self-improvement, and later for testing the tolerances around scandal and the celebrity that such memoirs generated—most spectacularly in the exposé of Frey.

Before Winfrey became acquainted with Frey, he had shopped a novel manuscript and received numerous rejections. Frey presented the same project as a memoir to Random House, which published it in 2003. After being selected in 2005 for Oprah's Book Club, *A Million Little Pieces* spent fifteen straight weeks as the number one best-selling nonfiction paperback on the *New York Times* best seller list, selling 1.77 million copies. In September 2006 The Smoking Gun exposed exaggeration in Frey's rehab narrative. Details about his criminal, drug, and rehab history were challenged by factual evidence, which The Smoking Gun publicized on its website, and determined to be invented or exaggerated. For example, in the memoir, Frey relates crashing into a police car after a crack-fueled rampage and claims to have done hard time for his crime; however, as his mug shot, intake information, and interviews with police make clear, Frey instead spent a couple of hours in the public waiting area of a Granville, Ohio, police station following his citation for an open container violation. He was never restrained during the time he was booked and posted bail. In another embellishment, he claimed to have refused novocaine for root canals that were performed in rehab, a claim that was flatly denied by the staff at the facility where the procedure was said to have happened.

Frey created a persona—a hard-core addict—who refused AA or any twelve-step program because surrender to a higher power was effeminate. Both persona and his white-knuckle recovery plan were revealed to be largely fictional, and, because other details also conformed more to the genre in which Frey originally crafted the tale, he and his publisher entered into a legal agreement that required Frey to acknowledge the claims established by his critics in an "Author's Note" that would accompany future printings of the book. Readers could also ask for a refund. Frey made a few public appearances as the scandal broke but did little to reduce its damage. While he tried to shift the discussion to a more literary distinction between "writing from memory" and "writing from fact," the shift asked audiences who knew only the tough guy persona Frey had gone on the road as for two and a half years of interviews to encounter him as a literary writer debating the elasticity granted by creative license.

The failure of this strategy to replace the persona of *A Million Little Pieces* with Frey the author was clear in his appearance on *Larry King Live*, during which Oprah Winfrey called in to defend the message of the book. She also sought to reposition herself within the affective community of readers who were disavowing Frey. Winfrey had been Frey's champion—Frey the recovered addict not Frey the fiction writer—and was drawing fire for it. To maneuver out of the position of tainted witness she was quickly sharing with Frey, Winfrey invited him back to her show, more to redeem her authority and salvage the redemption narrative's appeal than to engage in a discussion about memoir's use of narrative devices in its representation of history. Although Frey claimed his book possessed emotional if not historical truth, Winfrey held him and his editor to account for what she pronounced "the lie of it, James, the lie of it." In Berlantian terms, the elements that had previously created the possibility of an affective transaction included not only the redemption narrative but also the prospect of rescuing Frey's bad boy persona from self-destruction. The dynamics that underpinned community within this jurisdiction were highly mobile. Judgment flowed over Frey and stuck to Winfrey. Within this economy, her best move as the scandal unfolded was to model how condemning him would offer a salutary form of belonging.

Winfrey was exposed to the dynamics of judgment surrounding Frey. She was defamed as his promoter but was not hailed as his discreditor. Following his second seating on Oprah's couch, Frey let it be known that he felt ill-used by Winfrey. In comments on websites and in blogs, the tide turned against her: she was assailed not only for being gullible but for overreaching, and, in a surprising turn, sympathy shifted to Frey.

The spectacle of Winfrey calling Frey to account offered another scene for possible affective transaction. One need not to have read the memoir to participate but only to sense in Frey's shaming the opportunity to join in the judgment. What was lost was an encounter with all that the neoconfessional cannot offer—namely, a critical engagement with historic, systemic inequalities and violence that exceed the neoliberal focus on the individual—and the substitution, in its place, of certainties about truth that life narrative should provide. In the scandal, the assertion of moral outrage at Frey was coupled with an enigmatic anger at Winfrey for taking her community into a real experience of sympathy with a memoirist they were beginning to see, to some extent, as a fake. The collective spectacle of punishment preserved the private realm of identification that life narratives offer. Ever the canny boundary-crosser of the boom/lash, Frey tried to shift the blame, first, onto the genre of memoir itself and then onto Winfrey.

In the shiftiness of judgment that took place and the affective currents Frey identified as he tried to preserve his career, the racism that stalks Winfrey's authority but is typically held in check by her skillful self-presentation flared. Throughout the show featuring Frey, his editor, and other experts (all white), the racialized currents of punishment were present. The representative of white masculinity sat with hands folded as Winfrey pressured him to own up in a manner unselfconsciously referred to by many commentators as "taking him behind the woodshed"—a site of physical punishment that evokes racial violence. The representative of African American femininity sought to bring Frey and an expert panel of white publishers, editors, and reviewers to account. They largely refused to engage. They parried her effort to gain the upper hand as the one who would judge rather than the leader of those who had been duped. She did not escape her positioning as the tainted witness. Frey withdrew into a legal agreement that seems to have cost Random House little, deflected some of the criticism directed at him onto memoir itself and Winfrey as its popular purveyor, and achieved notoriety.

THE RISE OF SELF-HELP AS NEOLIBERAL LIFE NARRATIVE

Elizabeth Gilbert's *Eat, Pray, Love* began its spectacular rise squarely in the shadow of Frey's fall. In 2007 alone, the first year of publication and the year following Frey's decline, readers bought 4,274,804 copies of *Eat, Pray, Love*. Book clubs were provided not only sample discussion topics but theme party planning tips. Gilbert's memoir claimed the number 1 spot on the *Chronicle of Higher Education*'s list of "What They're Reading on College Campuses" in 2008, and continues to perch high atop the *New York Times* paperback best seller list. Ubiquitous in print interviews and radio and television appearances, including two visits to *Oprah*, Gilbert has translated success in memoir to success on the motivational speaker circuit. Acting as an anti—James Frey, Gilbert provided Winfrey and legions of readers, many if not most of them women, a new heroine for neoliberal times. Gilbert's success offers a case study in how contemporary literary markets operate within neoliberalism, how they shift away from problematic subjects by directing readers elsewhere, and how they create value and determine what stories and lives are worth attention. But the story we should not miss is how well poised Gilbert was to abandon the unsteady ship of memoir and catch the rising wave of self-help discourse, and how swiftly Oprah maneuvered to a new form of redemption narrative and away from the mud thrown at Frey that struck memoir and her.

Once a market has been created, as with memoir, something interesting happens: the texts themselves are secondary to the possibility of identification and belonging they offer. Thus any such intimate public would not be defined by genre alone but could, in its own interests, preserve the promise of absorption by broadening the domain of texts to include, for example, self-help. When Gilbert slipped to the number 8 spot on "What They're Reading on College Campuses" on May 23, 2008, the number 1 position was held by self-help guru Eckhart Tolle's *A New Earth*, Oprah's sixty-first pick for her Book Club and the first self-help book chosen. The shift to self-help preserves the possibility of affective transaction at a time it was rendered less available in memoir. Berlant's model provides insight into how self-help, with its autobiographical roots in its authors' traumatic experiences, could become memoir's sunny twin, absorbing the singularity of autobiography and reshaping suffering as remediable to improvement. Indeed, where memoirs focused on wrenching human trauma obligate readers to witness injustice for which remedies must be crafted, self-help discourse urges readers to lay aside injustice by changing their view of the past, and to address happiness, pleasure, and contentment as their birthright, objective, and mission. Self-help speech differs from survivor speech in that it does not cry out for justice; instead, it offers the end of crying out and asks, who would not want that?

Self-help gurus like Eckhart Tolle, Byron Katie (author of *Loving What Is* and creator of a therapy program called "The Work"), Wayne Dyer, Louise Hay, and the cast of *The Secret* advertise themselves as the first selves helped by their methods. Self-help discourse succeeds by producing a celebrity guru identity that draws on but is never bogged down by autobiographical history, then streamlines this identity toward the construction of a new self. No longer exemplary by virtue of a striking particularity and historical grounding, the self in self-help is universal by virtue of its nonspecificity. A generic humanity replaces the specific subjects who might offer testimony or engage ethical witnessing. Readers who might have turned to autobiography to learn about someone else, a "you," may find affective transaction barred by shifts in reception—like memoir's discrediting—that magnify vexed specificity. This frustration in engaging with "you" finds relief in the consumption of an alternative capacious, undifferentiated, and universal "me" that smoothes over the complexities of injustice, racial dynamics of address, and gender politics. By providing such structures for identification, self-help discourse taps fantasies of belonging in which consumers feel that before any such market existed, they were already part of a web of strangers who intimately understood and sympathized with each other's "compassionate liberalism."[51]

The overriding message of self-help discourse literalizes those longings. The ease with which consumers absorb such texts is enabled by the autobiographical pretexts with which many begin and which audiences have been trained to consume. In self-help discourse a guru briefly presents an autobiography that condenses elements of the conversion and redemption narratives. These mini-memoirs provide a portal through which consumers of memoir might enter but quickly redirect their identification from the guru to the imagined community of self-help. In many of these autobiographical sketches, the guru briefly offers a retrospective account of a conventional life filled with inexplicable unhappiness, condensed for maximum ease of sympathetic consumption. Byron Katie, for example, briefly notes a severe depression that struck in her early thirties and lasted over a decade, until one February morning in 1986 she "woke up." In "The Origin of this Book" section in *The Power of Now*, Eckhart Tolle, too, describes experiencing years of depression before waking up "one night not long after my twenty-ninth birthday." He clearly flags the pedagogic use of life story: "I have little use for the past and rarely think about it," and, indeed, he is disconnected from the histories or contexts from which he has departed: "It feels now as if I am talking about some past lifetime or somebody else's life." He characterizes waking up with a terrible sense of dread as a familiar experience. He describes suicidal ideation: "I could feel that a deep longing for annihilation, for nonexistence, was now becoming much stronger than the instinctive desire to continue to live." Two thoughts arise in succession, neither of which feels as much like thought as some other experience of consciousness. First, " 'I cannot live with myself any longer,' " followed by, " 'If I cannot live with myself, there must be two of me: the 'I' and the 'self' that 'I' cannot live with.' 'Maybe,' I thought, 'only one of them is real.' "[52]

Tolle awakens from this episode a new man. The remainder of the introduction, however, begins to untether the narrative from the self who tells it. Filled with self-knowledge, Tolle is awakened but not fully fledged. He spends several subsequent years studying spiritual writings and sitting on park benches but offers no description of where he lived or how he supported himself—only these words: "no relationships, no job, no home, no socially defined identity."[53] What Tolle loses in his crisis is a false, suffering self, which he previously identified simply as himself.

The self that emerges has a hard time continuing in the autobiographical mode. Indeed, whenever Tolle begins to observe himself, to reflect, or to dwell on autobiographical singularity, he falls into time, anxiety, and the multiform qualities of the "I" with which autobiographers grapple. He advises his readers against this. The autobiographical sketch, marked by trauma, history, and the burden to narrate it, concludes, cannot be reengaged without risk, and is abandoned. As a witness to history, Tolle counsels not looking back.

Tolle provides an example of how self-help autobiographical pretexts are pervasively traumatic, without being described as such. In fact, these accounts of lives, careers, relationships, and families disrupted (even spectacularly so) are presented as fortunate steps along a preordained path. Memoirists are under less generic pressure to present the chaos of life as purposeful than self-help writers. Indeed, memoir admits chaos as a goad to self-reflection; unruly events make writers square the demands of narration with the resistance of history. In self-help texts, however, this tension is unsustainable and would undermine a program that presents personal choice as part of an inevitable universal mandate.

Self-help authors offer a kind of witness. The author repackages pain, sorrow, and blank dissatisfaction in such a way that his or her personal narrative comes to sound a lot like everyone else's. It offers readers a generic language of personal growth to call their own. Although the opportunity to tell one's story differently constitutes the ongoing appeal of self-representation for many, the influences of self-help and the redemption narrative steer toward normativity. The self at the center of these texts is adumbrated in the autobiographical pretext in which trauma begets awakening, cut loose from the material conditions in which this begetting occurs. The rhetorical program of self-help replaces a wounded self—anxious, depressed, suicidal—with a generic "I."

As I have been arguing, such homogeneity developed out of greater diversity in life writing. In the 1980s and 1990s self-representation— mostly by women, people of color, and queer people—explored themes of wounding, vulnerability, and recovery and resisted the confessional compact. These texts circulated within testimonial networks as new forms of judgment were emerging and the redemption narrative was rising.

Although all these accounts have been lumped together as "confessional" in order to disparage them as pathography or self-exploitation, taken as a whole this eruption of grief and grievance in the public sphere had the effect of recalibrating norms for a time. These memoirs were anticonfessional because they refused shame and judgment. They also represented life writing as a form of ethical engagement.

NEOLIBERALISM AND ETHICS

Neoliberal life narratives do not impose an ethical demand on readers. They focus on one's relation to one's self rather than to others. They focus on what one person can do, and they distill politics and social change to an *n* of one. They suggest, as Clarence Thomas's narrative did, that it is the work of the individual to overcome hardship. The ethical engagement a generic "I" elicits is too general to translate to action on another's behalf. It does not prepare readers to engage with life writing that represents histories that exceed this framing. Critical here is the legacy of the Anita Hill and Rigoberta Menchú controversies. As witnesses, they demanded action in response to contemporary harm.

The clashing demands of entertainment and education offered by a genre that purports, in part, to teach us how to live, taxes our capacities to hold open the narrow portal of the "I," and the singularities and histories it represents, even as the expansive market offered by O magazine and the interchangeability of the self-help "I" promise absorption in a fantasy of belonging. Even as readers' investments in the redemption narrative expose them to a range of traumatic materials, the preference for stories that can be unmoored from specific historical conditions to become "everybody's" story is currently edging out narratives that take readers into the anxious realm of nonnormativity and the lack of clear moral guidelines they associate with culturally protected privacies.

What are the obligations of citizens to national narrative forms that reproduce normativity as life story, eviscerate histories of harm, and urge women readers to follow Elizabeth Gilbert on personal journeys that lead more often to the purchase of O magazine than to the international travel few can afford, or acts to benefit others? In other words, what narratives will we get more of and be more conditioned to norm once the ethical work of veiling all the inappropriate exposures has occurred? In this context, consider, finally, *Wild*, by Cheryl Strayed, the memoir of her 1,100-mile hike along the Pacific Crest Trail as personal redemption program, an American version of the *Camino* without the religious history of pilgrimage. As if to concede that readers seek specific outcomes from an array of interchangeable experiences, the subtitle declares its true destination: *From Lost to Found on the Pacific Crest Trail*. Strayed depicts her effort to cope with her mother's death when Strayed was twenty-two years old. In the aftermath of this loss, Strayed's marriage and life fall apart and she conceives the plan to hike in order to redeem her mother's faith in her.

Strayed's project differs from Gilbert's: Gilbert is a successful writer whose trips were undertaken on assignment; Strayed, an accomplished professional writer at the time she wrote her memoir, took the trip on her own. *Wild* moves the personal redemption story to the wilderness, where it has often been located, and tests herself. Like Frey, her program is self-styled; unlike Frey, she does not present herself as winging it. She has a guide to the PCT, and although she has an overloaded pack and ill-fitting boots, she has prepared by mailing herself provisions and cash to post offices along her intended route. Unlike Tolle, who abjures reflection on personal history, *Wild* is saturated in Strayed's plaintive grief for her dead mother.

Wild represents a shift and renewal in the market for life narratives by women. Strayed's persona as a nurturing, sincere, and down-to-earth advice columnist in her *Dear Sugar* columns at the online site *The Rumpus*, published in book form as *Tiny Beautiful Things: Advice on Love and Life from Dear Sugar* in 2012,[54] rolls over the self-help message expressed by Tolle from her successful advice column to her memoir and sets the travel narrative of *Eat, Pray, Love* on a rough track of wilderness hiking trail. In 2010 Oprah Winfrey launched her Book Club 2.0 to embrace *Wild*, endorsing for the first time both print and e-book, and championing Strayed, as she had Elizabeth Gilbert, as both a fine writer and a life mentor. Reese Witherspoon bought the film rights to *Wild* and won an Oscar nomination for her portrayal of Strayed. Cheryl Strayed has become a popular speaker, she and writer Steve Almond are featured in a *Dear Sugar* podcast where they give life advice, and Strayed published *Brave Enough* in 2015, which Amazon.com describes thus: "From the best-selling author of *Wild*, a collection of quotes—drawn from the wide range of her writings—that capture her wisdom, courage, and outspoken humor, presented in a gift-sized package that's as irresistible to give as it is to receive."[55] Elizabeth Gilbert was featured as a lead player in Oprah's worldwide "The Life You Want" tour and has followed a big and successful novel, *The Signature of All Things*, with *Big Magic*, a guide for incorporating creativity into daily life.[56]

Unlike Tolle and Byron Katie, who repress personal story and are not literary authors, Gilbert and Strayed illuminate new pathways in testimonial networks that reveal the power of markets to monetize misery and norm self-help as the "responsibilizing" solution when structural solutions don't exist. They also testify to the continuing potency of the literary voice: both are skilled and compelling writers whose progress reveals the energies—literary and market-driven—that propel life story now. They offer examples of the fusion of women's witness within a testimonial network and the canny marketing of feminist empowerment redeemed from earlier women's writing about trauma combined with the heroic survivor of self-help.

Within neoliberal life narrative, trauma is survived and redeemed. Those who thrive in this brand may use life story as a platform from which to launch careers in offering advice in personal appearances, via social media, and in popular TED Talks, and to continue as professional and accomplished authors, like Gilbert and Strayed. Or they can flame out, like Frey, and regroup elsewhere.[57] In chapter 4 I examine how the dual emphasis on *self* and *help* migrates to humanitarian storytelling where a reading public trained to associate feelings with help and to consume life story as something to learn from, enjoy, and judge finds a sufficiently familiar and generic human subject at the center of stories of overcoming and resilience.

4

WITNESS BY PROXY

Girls in Humanitarian Storytelling

"ONE MAN'S MISSION"

In 2006 Greg Mortenson published *Three Cups of Tea: One Man's Mission to Promote Peace . . . One School at a Time*, an account cowritten with David Oliver Relin about Mortenson's rise as a humanitarian hero. Told in third person and skillfully blending interviews, photographs, and narration, *Three Cups of Tea* promotes a "schools not bombs" program of humanitarian engagement to counter the rise of the Taliban in Afghanistan and Pakistan. Propelled by the power of his personal story, Mortenson and the book shot to international fame during the years in which the U.S.-led invasions of Iraq and Afghanistan following the terrorist attacks of September 11, 2001, were expanding into a global war on terror. Mortenson's pitch for saving girls dovetailed with the Bush administration's humanitarian rationale for regime change[1] and appealed, as did other life narratives published in this time frame, to liberal antiwar sentiments circulating within intimate publics eager to learn about central Asia.[2] Mortenson secured donations to his nongovernmental organization, the Central Asia Initiative (CAI), became an adviser to U.S. elected representatives, and entered the pantheon of internationally known celebrity humanitarians. His book became required reading in some units in the U.S. military, and he served as an advisor on training in the region.[3] Mortenson was shortlisted for the Nobel Peace Prize for three consecutive years.[4]

The personal story that he crafted with his cowriter was riveting: In 1993, after a failed attempt to climb K2, Mortenson became separated from his companions on the descent and, disoriented and ill, stumbled into the mountain village of Korphe in the rugged Karakoram Range where Pakistan borders China. He was embraced by the village elder, Haji Ali, and nursed back to health. When he departed, Mortenson promised he would return to the village where the people saved his life and build them a school. The story is sharp and compact. From the vivid descriptions of a mountain rescue to the domestic details of being cared for in a Balti home, *Three Cups of Tea*'s origin story delivers maximum emotional impact.

Mortenson spent five years honing his personal story for Western audiences in letters and lectures soliciting support for his plan to build schools. By the time he collaborated with professional author David Oliver Relin, Mortenson had shaped a potent life narrative that concocted elements of travel, adventure, saving girls, and individual pluck into a vehicle for eliciting sympathy from his audience and extracting donations. In its savvy combination of adventure and exoticism and featuring a compelling action figure at its center, *Three Cups* provided a way for Western audiences to connect with a part of the world in which their government was pursuing an endless war. By the time Relin and Mortenson collaborated, the origin story of *Three Cups of Tea* had become a pitch masquerading as testimony.[5]

As late as 2010 and 2011 Mortenson was a fundraising dynamo and popular figure. He was championed by *New York Times* op-ed writers Thomas Friedman and Nicholas Kristof, who praised his ability to build schools in Taliban territory and promoted his "guidance" for Afghanistan.[6] Yet in 2011 Jon Krakauer, the author himself of several iterations of the boys' adventure genre that combine mountaineering, wilderness adventure, and young men in the throes of coming of age, smelled a rat.[7] Krakauer, an early supporter of Mortenson, had been mightily moved by Mortenson's story and donated $75,000 to CAI. Based in part on his sense that there was something wrong with Mortenson's chronology and topography, Krakauer investigated. The result was an exposé entitled *Three Cups of Deceit: How Greg Mortenson, Humanitarian Hero, Lost His Way*.[8] According to Krakauer, Mortenson was using his nonprofit as a "personal ATM." Krakauer debunked the Korphe narrative, claiming that Mortenson may have spent a couple of hours there on the K2 descent, but it is more likely he went to Korphe later. Thus the gripping tale of a fateful wrong turn on the descent from K2, the treacherous crossing of a swollen river, and the experience of tender care that brought Mortenson through a life-threatening illness and inspired his promise to build a school were all invented. Krakauer disputes that Mortenson could have crossed the river, as it had no bridge the year he attempted to climb K2, and alleges that the narrative that follows is a fable. In addition to the financial mismanagement and fictional adventure story, Krakauer revealed that many of Mortenson's schools stand empty, and that what Mortenson described as his abduction by the Taliban consisted of a few days of hospitality by Waziri hosts.[9] Krakauer contended that Mortenson had a bullied and complicit board of directors who refused to fire him and continued to pay his salary. Krakauer was featured in an interview on *60 Minutes*, the attorney general of Montana opened an investigation into Mortenson's misuse of CAI's nonprofit status, and Mortenson, pleading ill health, retired from public view.

Recently, Mortenson has begun to venture into public. He steadfastly refuses to acknowledge any intentional wrongdoing; instead, he demurs about financial mismanagement: "I always have operated from my heart. I'm not a really head person." Mortenson calls himself a "storyteller" who is not much interested in "accountability, transparency." He leans on the privilege of "poetic license" and suggests that what Krakauer identified as deceit consisted mainly of compressions in the timeline that resulted from Mortenson and Relin's collaboration: "I stand by the stories. The stories happened, but . . . not in the sequence or the timing." When pressed to express regret for his actions, tellingly, Mortenson talks about life writing rather than life: "What I regret is that we were under tremendous pressure to bring about a million words down to 300,000 words."[10] For Mortenson, the "stories happened" even if the events to which they testify did not.[11]

Relin, too, found Mortenson's sense of time to be fluid and the details tricky to pin down. But as Relin traveled with Mortenson in the course of preparing the book, he became a convert and an advocate. "So this is a confession," Relin writes at the end of his introduction to the book: "Rather than simply reporting on his progress, I want to see Greg Mortenson succeed. I wish him success because he is fighting the war on terror the way I think it should be conducted." Relin amplified the literary voice that characterized Mortenson's narration of the Korphe origin story, and it proved crucial in speeding Mortenson's message through the testimonial network: "Working on this book was a true collaboration. I wrote the story. But Greg Mortenson lived it."[12] Life and writing came to represent separate domains for Relin, but not for Mortenson, who claims lead author status in the byline.[13]

NEOLIBERAL HUMANITARIANISM

Mortenson's comments about Relin's role go beyond mere deflection of shared responsibility. They indicate the appeal of the neoliberal humanitarian narrative Mortenson developed over five years of pitching and that Relin successfully transposed into print. Mortenson's account combines familiar elements of individual overcoming with distant locales newly pertinent to Western book buyers. More important, it presents a new figure in what Gillian Whitlock describes as the "soft weapons" armory: the humanitarian hero, whose testimony on behalf of education and girls, in particular, will offer a proxy witness to their experience.[14] Mortenson's new role as spokesperson for girls, global advocate for building schools, and valued cultural advisor to the U.S. military in Central Asia all arise from the power of a highly developed personal story. As with Clarence Thomas's Pin Point strategy, the story would provide access its narrator's life alone could not.

Life writing as a testimonial art evolves alongside the novel, law, and human rights discourse and shares with them an investment in an "I" that is endowed with a unique and communicable perspective and is capable of bearing witness. Less a bounded genre with unifying stylistic features than a flexible discourse in which one can say "I," life writing in the context of neoliberal humanitarianism can become the means through which to offer proxy witness, as Mortenson and Relin's text demonstrates. Mortenson and Relin adapt the boys' adventure story to enable a man to represent the needs of girls. In so doing, they capitalize on the capacity of the personal story to contribute to humanitarianism a face and a form through which to see and touch the suffering of distant others, and they borrow, too, from the novel in their crafting of a testimonial and literary "I."[15] Mortenson offers a conduit through which to channel feelings of responsiveness in others. He uses girls as proxies to perform a gendered and colonialist ventriloquism through which the voices of women and girls are occluded. Stories like those created by Greg Mortenson do a particular kind of work in testimonial networks: they simultaneously indicate an openness to and even a demand for the personal stories of girls and women and yet attach credibility to a white, Western, and male spokesperson who amplifies his significance as an intermediary in understanding and engaging with them and their needs.[16] Mortenson's exposure in 2011, like the exposure of James Frey in 2006, taints the circuits through which all testimony travels. Yet *Three Cups of Tea*, published in the same year as Frey was exposed, made its way for five years without challenge. Mortenson's case shows how the stigma of doubt attaches to testimony differentially based on gender, race, and nationality, and also how the market for narratives from Afghanistan provided cover, as Gillian Whitlock argues, for deceit.[17]

Three Cups sits squarely within the context of neoliberal storytelling, an ascendant subgenre that grows out of the surge in memoir publishing and displaces feminist life stories that combine creative innovation and the representation of, among other things, trauma, as I argued in chapter 3. By the time Mortenson published *Three Cups of Tea* in 2006, the canon of neoliberal life narrative had gelled. Published in the same year as *Eat, Pray, Love* and with a similar non-Western setting as the "Love" section of Gilbert's text, and following the 2005 publication of Jeanette Walls's *The Glass Castle*, personal stories of redemption hit a high-water mark. Mortenson added a twist: adventure philanthropy.

The neoliberal life narrative offers such a familiar script that Mortenson's account fit neatly within its contours: rule-governed to the point of formula and resistant to complexity, it shrunk a global crisis to the scale of manageable, individual response. The key features of Mortenson's neoliberal humanitarianism include the use of an individual's story in the service of a cause, the capacity of a compelling story to carry and cover deceit, and the strategic use of girls and young women to justify intervention. Frey's *A Million Little Pieces* likewise made use of the redemption story as Frey faced addiction and forged a recovery. Mortenson's *Three Cups of Tea* offered a "failure," as he called himself, who was determined to do something meaningful with his life.

More significant are the ethical and political claims Mortenson makes through the expression of his personal life plan. Through his intervention, the lives of girls and women from the global South are transformed into vehicles for Western audiences to feel in particular ways: to experience themselves as caring and philanthropic, to have, in the ghostly embodiment of this discourse, their eyes opened and hearts touched. The actual life stories of women and girls are proxy lives that advance Mortenson's agenda.[18] Mortenson uses third world girls' life stories to construct a humanitarian heroism that enables him to travel undetected and authoritatively within the testimonial network. He grounds ethics in empathy elicited in response to his neoliberal life narrative in ways that limit the formation of an ethical response to insufficiently pure or sympathetic victims.

Neoliberal humanitarian narratives claim to benefit others by basing an ethics of engagement in the development of sympathy for those whose stories the hero tells. Gillian Whitlock suggests "fair trade" as a useful model for how Westerners should consume life stories; that is, that they should recognize that it is in "their own ethical interest to ask questions"[19] about the sources of such stories. That readers prefer the story even after such due diligence has been undertaken highlights the potency of genre. Despite the generic quality of Mortenson and Relin's tale, this account sped through testimonial networks for five years without attracting doubt. In a network that already harbored the mechanisms for tainting women's life stories and memoir, Mortenson's gender, race, and timing combined to represent the story a hungry Western audience wanted about U.S. involvement in Afghanistan and Pakistan. For some, the astonishing durability of Mortenson's appeal exceeds Krakauer's criticism. Unlike Lance Armstrong, who was let go by the Livestrong Foundation after the full range of his doping came to light, Mortenson's CAI has not gone forward without him, and Mortenson remains on the payroll.

IMAGES IN THE TESTIMONIAL NETWORK

Visual representations of Muslim girls and young women were enlisted in the marketing of books like *Three Cups of Tea*. As Gillian Whitlock notes, an explosion of images of veiled girls appeared on books marketed to Western audiences after 2001. Featured in block displays in bookstores, book covers highlighted veiled girls and women in a canny marketing strategy that offers up images to a colonial gaze.[20] Hillary Chute points to the homogenizing effect of this visual strategy and how it obscures the differences between texts like Azar Nafisi's *Reading Lolita in Tehran*, for example, and Marjane Satrapi's *Persepolis*, both published in 2003.[21] Elizabeth Marshall and Özlem Sensoy chart the rise in narratives about saving global girls directed at young Western readers and accompanying the more adult-directed *Three Cups of Tea* and *Reading Lolita* and the welding of an ascendant missionary project to save Muslim girls.[22] The marketing of humanitarian narratives relies on images and narratives that reference the veil as a form of oppression and in so doing reinstitute a colonial gaze.[23]

The cover photo of *Three Cups of Tea* features three young girls, their heads bent over books and covered in white hijabs. A young adult version of *Three Cups* repeats the image but reduces the girls to two. The images echo the cover of the best-selling memoir *Reading Lolita in Tehran* that features a closely cropped photograph of the faces of young women presumably reading the Western classics that are the focus of the memoir. Hamid Dabashi has shown that the original photo serving as the cover image for *Reading Lolita in Tehran* was cropped to remove the newspaper the women were reading and their public location.[24] The incorporation of specific visuals in the peritexts exemplifies a moment in which the iconography of the veil as shorthand for "in need of saving" and the neoliberal life narrative coincide to represent and encourage humanitarian witnessing about the global South for Western audiences.

Images make crucial contributions to the testimonial network.[25] As recent studies in visual culture that focus on witnessing underscore, images create relationships between viewers and objects. In so doing, they rely on the appearance of transparency, and the fiction that what is framed in the image is simply captured from life.[26] For Wendy Kozol, visuality is a primary mode of engaging with distant suffering. Looking at images of distant conflicts is structured through ambiguity because of the ways in which spectatorship blends with ethical witnessing: "Without visuality, and without spectacle," she asks, "how can representations acknowledge the ways in which trauma is not a universal experience but rather occurs in historically specific contexts that mobilize gender, race, sexual, religious, and other factors to produce differences foundational to such violences?" Images, like the ones above, bear witness as they "mobilize gender, race, sexual, religious, and other factors" in complex ways.[27] The images that represent credibility and truth in the visual matrix Kozol describes play on gender, as well as expectations of cultural similarity and difference, to span distances of knowledge and affect. But the attribution of Western norms to interpret the needs and aspirations of distant women and girls narrows the pathways along which witnesses may travel.

Images of veiled schoolgirls and young women that repeat the association of books as a symbol of beneficial Western intervention also shape views of the complex societies women and girls inhabit. What life stories may women and girls tell about their complex lives in relation to their association with certain visual images? How are their stories conditioned by the visual preference for young, pure female victims as the worthy focus of ethical engagement? At risk here is the promotion of an ethics built on sympathy for those who can become knowable in particular ways: for example, by desiring education, or needing protection from religious fundamentalism. Thus the Mortenson case reveals two key features conditioning how the benevolence of humanitarian witness compromises women's credibility: First, their voices are presented through the "I" of the humanitarian hero, as his experience and valor supplant her perspective, further centralizing, in a subtle way, the credible voice as his and the authenticator of testimony as the humanitarian. Second, the visual iconography of veiled girls and young women reading further strengthens Mortenson's argument about what they need, a commonsense appeal that enabled the Central Asia Institute to mismanage funds for years before detection. More than that, the first world audiences believed they were hearing girls' stories and responding to their call for attention and action when what they were hearing was the compelling "I" of human rights heroes and the neoliberal life narrative, and what they were seeing was an illustration of this discourse.

The "I" of neoliberal humanitarian narrative offers a stock figure—the humanitarian hero who helps or makes it possible for the girl to be courageous—honed to deliver a message of transformation and uplift. This figure connects with audiences to promote the fellow feeling of an intimate public and to draw together the discourse of humanitarianism and ethical witnessing by evoking the testimonial "I" central to both. The testimonial "I" carries the burden of hope, but it has limits. It *can* bear witness, elicit testimony, and provide a framework for understanding how human rights emerge in specific contexts.[28] It *cannot*, however, "guarantee the ethical and political conditions that secure an appropriate response."[29] Even as the "I" bears witness, its uptake is "unpredictable."[30] In memoir, the desire for "forensic truth" (the verifiable facts) must give way to an acceptance of "narrative truth" (the personal and subjective truths of storytelling).[31] The truth of testimony is ambiguous,[32] is affectively insecure,[33] is difficult to interpret, and cannot guarantee satisfying conclusions. Ultimately, as Gillian Whitlock notes, its use has purposes that exceed the conditions from which it arises: the "management of testimony is almost always strategic."[34]

HALF THE SKY: GENRE, AFFECT, AND GENDER IN HUMANITARIAN STORYTELLING

In a project related to *Three Cups of Tea*, the husband and wife team of *New York Times* columnist Nicholas Kristof and journalist/investment banker Sheryl WuDunn share the view that humanitarianism ought to focus particular energies on girls and women. To Mortenson's political vision of "books not bombs" and conflict resolution, Kristof and WuDunn add an economic argument for helping girls and women: they represent an economic resource the world cannot stand to lose. In their best-selling book *Half the Sky: Turning Oppression into Opportunity for Women Worldwide* (2009), foundation, and two-part PBS television special, Kristof and WuDunn chronicle the exploitation of third world women and girls as the moral stain of the twentieth and twenty-first centuries. Equivalent to slavery in the eighteenth century, they argue, exploitation based on gender throws away massive human capital. Like Mortenson, they advocate for education, practical programs such as microlending and microfinancing of women-led, community-based projects, and IMF and World Bank projects that extend credit to poor women because all these show comparable or better results than other loans to men.

Kristof and Wu Dunn launched an essay contest in the *New York Times* as part of the rollout of *Half the Sky*, their book and "movement to end oppression of women worldwide."[35] The contest called for stories of survival and hope by women in extreme conditions. Kristof and WuDunn invited readers to share stories that would build their case for "fighting poverty and extremism globally by educating and empowering girls through tales of suffering and overcoming."[36] The choice of "tale" is important here: it evokes a genre that blends entertainment with moralism.[37] These stories, "as powerful as they are heartbreaking," offer rescue and redemption narratives in which all the victims have suffered greatly, are worthy of compassion from Western readers, and show resilience in the face of overwhelming hardship. They endure and they rise. And because they are young, they are credible witnesses. Kristof and

WuDunn's preferred narrative grounds sympathy in the victim's blame-lessness and resilience. Their contest to find the best stories of "suffering and overcoming" recognizes the power of this story and promotes it into a genre via Kristof's storytelling in his *New York Times* column, and also across the media and platforms promoted by the Half the Sky Movement. The preferred story circulates broadly, influences human rights reporting, and presents a model for what testimony should sound like. Through the emotional appeal of genre, Kristof and WuDunn declare: "We hope to recruit you to join an incipient movement to emancipate women and fight global poverty by unlocking women's power as economic catalysts. That is the process under way—not a drama of victimization but of empowerment, the kind that transforms bubbly teenage girls from brothel slaves into successful businesswomen. This is a story of transformation. It is change that is already taking place, and change that can accelerate if you'll just open your heart and join in."[38] Winning stories open hearts.

The book was followed by a film of the same name in 2012 that featured "A List celebrities" touching down around a deterritorialized globe in search of women of color overcoming poverty and exploitation through courage (and the benefits of microlending). The film offered celebrity empathy as a model of engagement with the women and girls depicted in it. Half the Sky also offers teaching tools and a Facebook game though its website, Kristof and WuDunn have given TED Talks, and Half the Sky has branded itself as a movement. The Half the Sky Movement, formed as a nonprofit in 1998, is but one example of how such a cause expands by remediating the experiences and stories of girls and women of color. The template has been so successful that a network of foundations uses women's life narrative to elicit empathy for deserving victims and promote various humanitarian and economic causes.

Yet who's "I" and whose image sustain and motivate the empathy and ethical model that underwrite these projects? Kristof and WuDunn's work raises questions about the relation of empathy and ethics. Like Mortenson, Kristof and WuDunn blend the pitch (e.g., "here's the problem and here's how to solve it") with their own enactment of witness by proxy. As an example of humanitarian discourse, *Half the Sky* also mediates the voices of women and girls by scripting how their testimonial "I" will bear witness. In this shaping of their life stories, we hear the humanitarian voice, even as audiences feel they are hearing and seeing otherwise. When Kristof and WuDunn seek to show Western audiences what it feels like for a young woman to emerge from enslavement in a brothel to become a valued economic resource for her family, they use life narrative to compel empathy and elicit humanitarian action independent of political or historical understanding or cultural specificity.[39]

Mortenson and Kristof advance humanitarian aims through storytelling. They aim at the heart, they say, and use the stories of vulnerable girls and women to carry forward their messages about global citizenship. Mortenson is initially in Pakistan for adventure. He is a tourist who returns to help. Kristof is a journalist who travels the globe to facilitate Western intervention in disparate locales. Neither Mortenson nor Kristof relies on a structure of testimony to ground projects ethically, to establish processes or goals, or to produce over time anything like the national narratives of truth and reconciliation that would hold Western donors accountable for how the governments' activities contribute to structural problems outside the United States.[40] Instead, with the heart as their target, they rely on neoliberal storytelling, with its compelling cast of two-dimensional figures, its redemption and rescue plots, and its substitution of political action for the cash nexus of philanthropy.

The representation of catastrophic events in words and images has the capacity to elicit empathy. For many, the possibility of this emotional response—just, spontaneous, and reliable—represents the redemptive core of suffering and elicits the commonality of feeling that unites sentient beings. It carries the hope that, in the presence of a witness, violence can be survived. How first-person narratives by survivors of trauma elicit empathy in testimonial networks, as I have been arguing, cannot be predicted. Because gender and race stick to witnesses in the form of doubt, their testimony is often shaped strategically to evade aversion and apathy. When empathy fails, doubt and discrediting emerge. Neoliberal storytelling may well represent a canny intervention in the testimonial network to ensure that witnesses who would otherwise languish are heard. If the presence of doubt and its attachment to women witnesses, in particular, motivates the ventriloquization of increasingly formulaic life stories to elicit empathy, should we embrace the neoliberal life story valorized by Kristof and WuDunn strategically, as Gayatri Spivak previously invited feminists to embrace a strategic essentialism as a way for postcolonial subjects to maneuver within available discourses of self-representation?[41]

Given the strategic use of a proxy testimonial "I" in humanitarian storytelling, in what resides the power of Mortenson's witness? What does the focus on his story as the vehicle for their stories contribute to the power of Western intervention on behalf of the health and education of communities, including girls? The choice of a shifting focus for empathy—Mortenson *and* girls *and* villagers in Korphe *and* Muslims in Afghanistan and Pakistan—propels a story that is so powerful, its generic witness so compelling, that it dispenses with the doubts that would attach to this tale had it come from a different spokesperson. We see in this case how whiteness and maleness speed what would otherwise be the sticky progress of his account through testimonial networks because Mortenson was not greeted with adequate credulity. The moving witness here is Mortenson, whose voice is crafted by Relin to emphasize his valor, vision, and value. Thus the intolerance for women's accounts of harm is created alongside the acceptance of a male spokesman as the sponsor of women's accounts.

In terms of understanding the copresence of narratives of harm about and by women and girls and the means to discredit them, we see how Kristof's benign humanitarian contest narrows the portal through which testimony must pass and makes what counts as legitimate speech about harm into what will win a contest. Yet what precisely is the evidentiary standard for *tale* as distinct from *testimony*? The former privileges "story"; the latter seeks justice. Stories are shaped, and in this case shaped self-consciously to convey messages about resilience that induce empathy for the distant suffering of "similar others." This is hardly the genre of deposition, a species of testimony that emerges through multiple interviews conducted by police and district attorneys in U.S. criminal courts and presented to grand juries. Yet as surely as legal protocols define how human rights claims can be pursued in distinct national locations, humanitarianism shapes courts of public opinion as stories circulated in the form of tales.

As Carole S. Vance argues about the infusion of melodrama in the form of documentary, "the outrage it evokes on behalf of the innocent victim reaffirm[s] a single intervention and 'dream justice': rescue and return to home, which is not the justice most women [who are trafficked into prostitution] want." The problem is that "the larger structure of an increasingly globalized world economy is missing from [personal] accounts."[42] It is not simply that Mortenson and Relin are missing the point about how girls and women suffer and might be helped, but that the life stories they prefer are too limited. Structured as melodrama, in Vance's reading, or as rescue and redemption narratives, or in the service of Mortenson's and Kristof's own heroic narratives of decent white men intervening with brown men on behalf of brown girls and women,[43] neoliberal tales invite identification with a Westerner who models empathy and action. This is proxy compassion, safer than an engagement with the complexities beyond saving an individual from abuse, and it generates a proxy politics of humanitarian neoliberalism.

These accounts narrow and norm women's testimony. They create a context that motivates the use of witness by proxy. In the case of the stories sought and circulated by Kristof, the genre of the redemption narrative communicates what actual women are not allowed to: agentic speech about experiences of injury in order to access forms of redress. It is strategic: it represents a proxy politics of gender within the constraints of tainted witness. To offset the limited "education of the heart" in which such narratives school audiences, we must continue to engage with unsympathetic women witnesses, follow the arc of their testimony as it seeks a hearing, and learn to disentangle doubt from the discourses that construct it. Learning to read the testimony of tainted witness does more than broaden our sense of harm, agency, and justice, it restores the demand on the witness to cross a boundary in herself or himself, to move from sympathy as a form of ethics to something more fraught but more suited to the broken world from which testimony arises.

5

TAINTED WITNESS IN
LAW AND LITERATURE

Nafissatou Diallo and Jamaica Kincaid

*The past is a fixed point, the future is open-ended; for me
the future must remain capable of casting a light on the past
such that in my defeat lies the seed of my great victory, in
my defeat lies the beginning of my great revenge.*

—JAMAICA KINCAID, *AUTOBIOGRAPHY OF MY MOTHER*

Humanitarian storytelling creates a normative scale on which testimonial narrative is weighed and valued. To understand the complex admixture of sympathy and hostility that women's testimony about sexual violence engenders, it is helpful to recall the contradiction between the invitation to offer testimony and bear witness and the often precipitous discrediting of speech before an adequate witness can emerge. This contradiction fuels the coalescence of a forum of judgment for women's testimony that is characterized by doubt. Here, the coordinates of time, in the form of multiple and entangled histories, and space, in the transits of those who cross boundaries by choice and force, are prevented from emerging, and testimony is judged, instead, by the prevailing biases that may stick to witnesses and their complex accounts of coercion and harm. In addition to verbal accounts, the body, too, occupies this geographical, narrative, and temporal intersection: as the locus of evidence collection in sexual assault, the scene of a crime that one inhabits, and the sign that is read for its capacity to seduce despite verbal evidence testifying to harm.

Rape culture forms a jurisdiction within which testimony about sexual violence is judged. Coined in the 1970s by feminist scholars and activists working on violence against women, *rape culture* designates a pervasive cultural formation that includes the real threats of sexual violence women face alongside the construction of women's sexuality as something that men can control and, specifically, women cannot.[1] Rape culture distorts notions of women's sexuality, violence against women, and women's agency; it fosters hyperawareness of risk while obscuring the actual conditions in which it typically arises. Either a woman's body is taken to offer a duplicitous witness in rape culture or her verbal and nonverbal behavior is ignored or overridden. "Her words said no, but her eyes said yes" is a less crude version of what the Yale frat boys chanted, "No means yes, yes means anal," but it distills the right to disregard women's autonomy; moreover, it is learned behavior tolerated by institutions and encouraged by peers.[2] And it is ubiquitous, which enables this extreme formation of thought and action to appear as if it were an inevitable and immutable part of everyday life.[3] The demand for women's testimony and the venues, authorities, rhetoric, and judgments that taint it are coevolving. Against the backdrop of humanitarian storytelling with its reliance on ever purer victims to elicit sympathy, and in the context of rape culture, this chapter examines two cases of women's witness, one legal, the other literary, in order to bring together insights into how women's testimonial agency seeks a hearing in the context of histories of colonialism.

Here two unsympathetic women witnesses of color articulate complex accounts of harm, precarity, and agency. The first case presents a crime and its search for a hearing. The crime, which occurred at the Sofitel in New York City in 2011, was the rape of a West African immigrant woman, Nafissatou Diallo, by Dominique Strauss-Kahn, who, at the time, was the head of the International Monetary Fund and a French presidential hopeful. Her accusation traveled through different legal, public, and popular contexts in search of an adequate witness, and this entire transit constitutes Diallo's testimony. My second example moves from an examination of sympathy and gendered witness in courts of law and the court of public opinion to take up a literary account of an unsympathetic woman witness in *Autobiography of My Mother* by Jamaica Kincaid, and the mode of reading it enables. While at first glance it may seem odd to pair the diverse stories together, literary witness challenges the sufficiency of sympathy as the basis of ethical engagement. Literary witness, while not free from the kinds of judgment that attach to actual women, offers an alternative, imaginative jurisdiction in which elements of doubt, sympathy, judgment, agency, harm, and vulnerability are untethered from the demands of courts and may, through its suspension of the demand to inspire sympathy, redeem harm, and emerge resilient and victorious, interrupt and reorient what we think we know about "what really happened."

LEGAL WITNESS ON THE MOVE: NAFISSATOU DIALLO

On May 14, 2011, Nafissatou Diallo went to her job at the Sofitel in Manhattan where she worked as a housekeeper. When Diallo entered room 2806 in order to clean it, a room she understood to be vacated by its guest, she encountered Dominique Strauss-Kahn, then head of the International Monetary Fund. He was wearing only a towel, and he attacked her violently and sexually.[4] All physical evidence from the scene and Diallo's body confirm this description of the attack. What happened as this event was transformed into testimony in criminal court, the court of public opinion, and, finally, civil court reveals the entanglement of testimony and life story with rape discourse and neoliberal storytelling. Moreover, it offers a concrete example of how the outcome is shaped by the rules of evidence within a jurisdiction, rules that are not shared across forums of judgment. As I have argued, in the presence of doubt as a judgment that sticks to women's testimonial accounts, truth is hardly a neutral value or reliable measurement of what happened.

Although the Manhattan district attorney dropped charges against Strauss-Kahn in criminal court, Diallo pressed her case in civil court in the Bronx. The change in jurisdiction resulted in a different outcome; yet the verdict registered minimally in the same media outlets that had so energetically prosecuted the case as scandal. In fact, the only verdict rendered for this crime confirmed Strauss-Kahn's guilt. However Diallo's discrediting as a witness was not reversed. I use this case study to examine how Nafissatou Diallo's life stories were mobilized in and crossed the frames among criminal court, civil court, and the court of public opinion. By following the movement of her testimony, we see how rape discourse was tapped to maximize doubt about Diallo's capacity to tell the truth, to constrain her testimony within a "he said/she said" binary, and to transform her from sympathetic victim to tainted witness.

The discourses about rape that circulate within rape culture undermine women's testimony. Rape discourse casts doubt on women as credible witnesses to their own harm, and on claims of rape in general.[5] Through rape discourse, women who bring forward accounts of sexual violence are turned into tainted witnesses before the law and in courts of public opinion. Rape discourse is structured in such a way that it produces and holds up to public view women as tainted witnesses to crimes against them and, in the case of women who have offered accounts of their lives to other authorities, have filed requests for immigration or asylum, and have otherwise given rule-governed testimony in order to achieve specific outcomes, uses life story as part of its means to cast doubt on testimony about sexual violence. Rape discourse is about misperceiving risk, harm, and accountability. It does not educate about law and justice, it does not inform about real and perceived risk, and it does not favor fairness and due process.[6] Instead, it produces general, default notions of women's unreliability.

Women witnesses, especially women of color articulating complex accounts of harm and agency, represent a hard case in the neoliberal circuits of sympathy that rule public opinion. For instance, images of smiling brown girls in classrooms juxtaposed with images in which they are threatened in their homes or environment promote the idea that Western-style institutions such as schools and the law provide safe haven from gender violence. Yet this visual storytelling and the narratives of rescue that accompany it avoid hard questions about what happens when women turn to courts of law to tell stories about rape and sexual assault that occur with the iconography of women's rightful place (either in the home or in specific occupations), stories that often include histories of immigration and asylum seeking. Invitations for women and girls of color to tell stories of survival and redemption may bolster the kinds of humanitarian projects I described in chapter 4, but they also sidestep questions of how such storytelling can backfire. In contrast, feminist analyses of the complexities of women's stories about transnational migration, sexual harm, and justice better acknowledge the complex networks that shape the production and reception of life narrative.[7]

In the separate locations of immigration and naturalization services, police stations, and criminal and civil courts, we find that "unequal human agency, unequal human impacts, and unequal human vulnerabilities"[8] travel with the narrative demand to tell one's story. How, then, do we attend to the recurrent stories of sexual violence in relation to the large story of women's and girls' inequalities before the law without making every story seem like a reiteration of the general story? How can feminist readings recognize the force of specific stories as well as their often illuminating idiosyncrasies? How do we follow the transit of testimony in and out of the varying locations in which it will be elicited? How do we connect the very different affective and concrete responses life story generates on the move?[9] How do we keep women witnesses in view as their testimony travels in search of an adequate witness?

In criminal court it took less than two months for the charge of rape brought by Diallo, then a thirty-two-year-old Guinean immigrant, against Strauss-Kahn to collapse. From mid-May to the end of June 2011, Diallo was transformed from an initially sympathetic victim of rape to a witness who lacked credibility, while Strauss-Kahn was exposed as an aggressive serial sexual predator, was replaced as head of the IMF by Christine Lagarde, and lost his position as presumed presidential challenger in France. No major shift in the accounts by Diallo and Strauss-Kahn emerged during this time; in fact, the legal core of the dispute remained intact: whether the acts had been consensual (Strauss-Kahn's view) or assaultive and hence criminal (the position Diallo maintained). During the period in which the case fell apart, no new evidence from the crime scene was discovered or disputed, and no exculpatory information about Strauss-Kahn emerged. Testimony by women who had suffered Strauss-Kahn's sexual predation poured forth. In the "he said/she said" theater of credibility, he initially appeared to be the compromised party and sympathy was hers. This reveals the power of the he said/she said binary: even in the absence of a credible "he said" testimonial account to offset what "she said," whatever "she said" is necessarily diminished when forced into this formula. In other words, it is not the case that the credibility of what "he said" outweighs the evidence of what "she said." The form works in the absence of compelling content.

Because the core disagreement about what happened in the hotel room between Strauss-Kahn and Diallo focused on consent, the issue became whether Diallo could testify "credibly." It did not mean whether she had been raped, nor whether the evidence could bear the charge. Yet when the legal criterion of credibility broadened beyond Diallo's capacity to speak to the crime itself and attached, instead, to her capacity to speak about her life as an immigrant West African woman with a specific history, the mechanisms that turn women in the public sphere into tainted witnesses were set on their course. In inexorable slow motion, the case fell apart: not because Strauss-Kahn seemed innocent but because his accuser did not seem innocent enough; not because of what happened in the hotel room but, in part, because numerous commentators asserted that she had previously "testified" about sexual violence in her application for asylum. Prosecutors feared that Diallo the immigration applicant compromised the credibility of Diallo the rape victim because both, it was reported, had testified to sexual assault. Her testimonies as an immigration applicant, an asylum seeker, and a sexual assault victim flared into conflict largely through false reporting about her immigration application. The conflicts among her life narratives rather than the evidence against Strauss-Kahn became central.

Two important issues emerge here in relation to law, shifting testimonial venues, and women's capacity to offer credible witness about sexual violence: (1) the centrality of life narrative and the proliferating venues

in which they are elicited and judged; and (2), the increasing likeli-
hood that life accounts—including applications for political asylum,
legal testimony in national courts and international tribunals, personal
stories showcased in humanitarian campaigns, and memoirs and
autobiography—all of which are produced in accordance with different
rules and for different purposes and audiences—will come into conflict.
When this happens, women's credibility will be adjudicated on the basis
of the relation of the narratives to each other rather than in relation to
specific events under scrutiny, such as a claim of sexual violence.

Further, this recontextualization of life narratives in relation to each
other fails to remark that such narratives are produced according to specific rules of genre and protocols of reporting, that different things "count"
in these narratives, and that authorities other than the women themselves are empowered to judge women's veracity. The de-agentic place
of women within the framework of witness presents a stark challenge to
claims that life narrative can provide an ethical basis for engagement in
any simple way, as claimed by Kristof and WuDunn. Indeed it exposes a
contradiction playing out in multiple locations in which first-person
accounts by girls and young women of color are increasingly featured as
a centerpiece of humanitarian and human rights campaigns directed at
Western audiences, which seems to suggest an unprecedented openness
to the accounts of inequalities they might bring forward at the same time
as the mechanisms that discredit them are highly mobile, strident, and
multiform. It is important to talk about credibility and discrediting as
cultural practices that produce doubt and taint witnesses in the context
of the circulation and even what we might call the popularity of witness
accounts. Not only is it inadequate to call for stories as a spur to empathy, as if once a story is told, compassion spills forth automatically, it can
be dangerous to the women telling the stories.[10]

Here is where witnesses can learn to suspend the automatic association of credibility with innocence, and empathy with justice.[11] These
coordinates do not well serve the unsympathetic witness, whom almost
any woman may become, as her testimony travels. Instead, something of
Kincaid's willingness to regard the fictional Xuela as an unsympathetic
witness deserving of attention models the epistemological challenge of

reading the dense textuality of harm before coming to judgment. There is more here than whether a reviewer or a reader can relate to Xuela. It is that she can be described as "inhuman" because she is "pitiless," as many readers would agree. Yet why ought the one who does not feel pity, and fails to engender it in others, be cast outside the bounds of the human? Such judgments happen quickly, mobilize into doubt, obscure the colonial history of slavery in which such judgment is bound up, and swiftly produce the conclusion that this particular subject is a bad witness, a tainted witness, one whose account it is too difficult to read.

LEARNING TO DOUBT

The figure of the woman witness in first-person narratives is an example of superposition with respect to truth; that is, at any point in her testimony, she is present as both reliable and unreliable witness.[12] It is impossible to know whether a woman will ultimately emerge as a reliable witness because the standard of truthfulness exists not simply in relation to her experience but also within the testimonial limits circumscribing gendered speech about trauma. Formulations such as "nobody really knows what happened" in the cases of sexual assault and rape, for example, work to discredit victims before they speak. They represent a free-floating form of collective judgment that attaches to testimony in the form of doubt. Instead of applying a meaningful brake on wrongful accusations, such skepticism tends to foster underreporting of sexual assault. Moreover, it is part of a pattern of response woven through institutions and bolstered by training and habit that diminishes our capacity (and the capacity of institutions) to engage meaningfully and justly with the prevalence of gendered violence.

As soon as Nafissatou Diallo reported the alleged rape, Dominique Strauss-Kahn was detained at JFK Airport as he was boarding a flight to France and charged in Manhattan with sexual assault. He hired a cadre of attorneys and private investigators who immediately went to work attacking Diallo's reputation. Diallo, too, had legal counsel, but immediately after the police questioned her, information regarding the contents of that deposition was leaked to the press. As it turned out, Strauss-Kahn's team was feeding false information about her immigration application to the press and bloggers. In all these storytelling processes, stories of sexual violence were central. Yet the rules governing the elicitation and circulation of Diallo's multiple testimonies were blurred. For example, during her interview with detectives, Diallo was asked questions that would be inadmissible in a rape trial in criminal court. Namely, she was asked if she had previously been a victim of sexual assault. Because this question sought information about "sexual history," it is likely to have been ruled out of order and never answered in criminal court. Yet, in a surprising twist that remains unexplained, Diallo answered in the affirmative. She narrated a vivid scene in which she claimed soldiers had broken into her home in Guinea and raped her in front of her two-year-old daughter. Detectives initially believed this story, which turned out to be false. It did not happen, nor did she ever say it did in her immigration application. It was, however, widely reported she had told this story as part of her immigration application and prompted many to call for her to be deported. Whose testimony was this, or, how was this Diallo's testimony? Why did she tell it in the police station, and why was it so easy to believe she lied in her immigration application? The distance between what happened and the narratives Diallo offered, all of which circulate in a testimonial network with incommensurable standards of evidence, further highlights the problem with tying such narratives to truth. This is a difficult point because truth has the capacity to unmake complexity and reduce judgment to the discovery of error. Testimonial narratives, as I have shown, are produced strategically, can be taken up capriciously, are sometimes persuasive but subject to doubt and discrediting, and do the work of permitting persons to pass through checkpoints of many kinds. To say that Diallo's narrative in any of the contexts that reward persuasive speech is not true when it is placed in a different context deceptively ties truth to narrative instead of the authorities, often multiple, within a jurisdiction. To insinuate doubt about truth is to amplify the asymmetries that structure how testimonial narratives circulate and persuade.

Doubt is a commonsense word for a gendered formation that is produced over time. Doubt is also a legal term entwined with burdens of proof and rules of evidence. It may be initially withheld as one hears an account of sexual harassment, for example, but creep in as evidence is presented. Although it is a public feeling that readily and demonstrably attaches to speech by women about harm, it feels personal. It is my doubt. Yet in cases of rape and sexual assault, the benefit of the doubt often migrates to the accused when the accuser is female. Doubt represents the limit of basing an ethical response on feelings. When doubting women is constructed as a commonsense and rational response, doubt feels righteous. These political feelings, including sympathy and doubt, do not offer an unproblematic ethical basis for attending to suffering, even if they can be elicited to do good. The locution "no one knows what really happened" is less a position of reasoned and reasonable skepticism than an active, reflexive, and ultimately political feeling that women cannot be trusted to say what harm has befallen them. All too often, a short-circuiting of credibility appears as the unique fault of specific women rather than a predictable product of rape discourse; that is, of many cultural mechanisms working together to produce doubt. Thus the Diallo "story" is not only one she herself told multiple times but one that we must retell in order to disentangle the canny construction of shifting credibility created by the interactions of life narrative and rape discourse.

The theme of her unreliability rapidly became "the" Diallo story. Reporters in a range of media claim that the gang rape story was one she was coached to perform by someone she paid to prepare her for her asylum hearing. Gang rape in Guinea is one of the crimes that Immigration and Naturalization Services officials recognize as grounds for asylum. Knowledge of which stories succeed circulates in immigrant communities, and there is a business in coaching applicants in how to tell these stories. Diallo had a tape of a gang rape narrative and memorized it. This is the story she told detectives. She did not, as reported, use it in her asylum application. The district attorney declined to press criminal charges against Strauss-Kahn because he found Diallo unreliable, ironically, because she had been so persuasive about something that did not happen.

Patricia Williams, the author of *The Alchemy of Race and Rights*, wrote in the *Nation* that Diallo's allegedly conflicting accounts of past violence were not, on their own, enough to derail prosecution: "The fact that she falsely claimed to have been gang-raped in Guinea probably wasn't enough to doom the case—she might still have presented herself quite sympathetically as a desperate refugee fleeing a war zone."[13] Williams recognized that the problem lay in the proliferation of speech: the more Diallo talked, the more she exposed gaps in the sequence of her account of the hotel room attack. Through exposure and repetition, Diallo was rendered an insufficiently pure victim for criminal proceedings despite the physical evidence, despite Strauss-Kahn's lengthy history of what he preferred to call "rough sex," which would find its way into court in another, unrelated trial.[14] Narrative inconsistency stuck to Diallo in ways that made the crime of rape slide off Strauss-Kahn and into undecidability. At that moment, it appeared Diallo would not have her day in court.

Yet Diallo's testimony continued to seek a hearing: in the court of public opinion, and in civil court. Diallo pleaded her case on television, on the steps of the courthouse, on behalf of women hotel workers, and, as she said, for her daughter so she would not learn to be afraid. Finally her moving testimony came to rest within a jurisdiction in which it could be heard: Diallo sued Strauss-Kahn in her home borough of the Bronx. This change in jurisdiction meant that the burden of proof would shift from "beyond a reasonable doubt" to "by a preponderance of the evidence." When this case succeeded, it also exposed the extent to which the "rational doubt" embedded in the phrase "nobody knows what happened" in cases of rape is catalyzed by the standard of evidence in criminal cases. When the burden of proof is "beyond a reasonable doubt," and doubt is the reasonable judgment for accounts of rape and sexual assault, then "nobody knows what really happened" is produced as a rhetorical gesture in relation to rationality and law. It is not, nor need it be, a response to the facts in a case, or to any specific woman's testimony about rape as much as it is part of legal rhetoric: "nobody knows what really happened" emerges in relation to the standard of evidence required in criminal court. It represents political rhetoric masking as common sense and crystallizes in everyday language the claim that women cannot tell the truth about sexual assault. Because civil courts have a different standard of evidence, Diallo's testimony did not automatically catalyze doubt.

Interestingly, a changed Diallo emerged in this jurisdiction. Justice Douglas McKeon of the Bronx County Supreme Court heard the case and ruled in Diallo's favor. Strauss-Kahn did not attend the final court date. There were no tense scenes on courthouse steps with attorney and client fielding a barrage of questions from the press, few cameras, and no spectacle. Diallo, who settled for an undisclosed amount, simply left the courtroom smiling and said: "I thank everyone who supported me all over the world. I want to thank everybody, thank God. God bless you all." Her attorney lauded his client: "Ms. Diallo is a strong and courageous woman who has never lost faith in our system of justice. With this resolution behind her she can now move on with her life." The judge issued a statement in which he praised her courage.

Recalling Wai Chee Dimock's observation that "no mileage can tell us how far authors are from each other,"[15] I would observe that in a story that featured a Muslim woman from the former French colony of Guinea in West Africa currently living in New York and the former head of the International Monetary Fund Frenchman Dominique Strauss-Kahn, the greatest distance was not between his status and hers, or the geographical locations of their homes of origin, but between the criminal court in Manhattan and the civil court in the Bronx. In these two venues, Nafissatou Diallo's testimony, which came to stand in for what had transpired between her and Strauss-Kahn, produced very different outcomes. Her story told through the Manhattan criminal court repeats the violations of the hotel room in eerie ways. Her testimony in civil court in the Bronx offers an example of justice served. In the context of a criminal charge of rape, the standard of proof animated the "no one knows what happened" judgment, mooting Diallo's ability to present a story of enduring and rising. Neither sympathetic nor credible, freighted with stories, she sank, the transit of her testimony at an end in the jurisdiction of criminal court and the court of public opinion.

Yet testimony seeks a witness, and she found hers in civil court where she proved her claim by a preponderance of the evidence. No new story rose from this outcome. She did not lie on her asylum application, as alleged, thus calls for her to be deported were not based in facts and ceased. Nor did she ever explain why she referred to the rape story in her interview with police investigators. We step outside this moment to observe the seeming agency of rape discourse itself, its perplexing and disturbing animacy, how it was the "right story" for the moment and venue for Diallo, and yet was not her story. She spoke the story convincingly with the perverse effect that the attorney general concluded she would be unconvincing before a jury telling her own story. Stories have achieved a kind of disembodied agency. They speak through us even when they are not ours, they conjure events that happened somewhere to persons not present, they record harms in the voices of those who cannot properly witness. Patricia Williams returns to provide crucial insight. When faced with the case of Tawana Brawley, a young African American woman who emerged after a brief absence with the letters KKK scratched into her skin, smeared in feces, falsely claiming an attack by three white men, Williams refused to dismiss even this obdurate an example of unreadable testimony: Brawley "has been the victim of some unspeakable crime. No matter how she got there. No matter who did it to her and even if she did it to herself."[16] Williams holds open the possibility in the face of rape discourse and racism that we must do something other than discredit this testimony, which was never able to move to another public location for a hearing. Williams's capacity to attend to the ruptures in testimony performs a way of transforming silence into listening and hence into meaning, even if that meaning lies in challenging the general condition of doubt that greets women who bring forward accounts of rape.

LITERARY WITNESS: JAMAICA KINCAID

Legal witnesses, humanitarian storytelling, and literary testimony travel together. Their copresence shapes how audiences respond to the ethical claims in each. As I have shown, first-person accounts are a central feature of humanitarian campaigns that seek to free political prisoners, educate about and end human rights abuses, and hold governments accountable, in an international forum of judgment, for their abusive practices. Audiences with differing degrees of distance (spatial, political, cultural, economic, and so on) are enjoined to act—to write letters or participate online, to donate money and time—in order to help the actual people offering first-person accounts as well as others who are similarly in need and whom such testimony represents. The power of the first-person witness thus rests on both the singularity and the wider representative capacity of the witness. In speaking to and for many, first-person accounts expand human rights beyond the frame of the individual. They speak to state-sponsored violence, environmental degradation, and extraordinary need. Increasingly, they also speak of resilience, optimism, and overcoming as part of the production of an autobiographical subject with whom Western readers can identify. In this context I examine how the figure of the literary witness is lodged in the testimonial archive and why this figure's resistance to an emerging norm in humanitarian and philanthropic discourse matters in the broader project of social justice. I take Jamaica Kincaid's *Autobiography of My Mother*, an entry in her serial autobiographical fiction about her family and the decolonization in Antigua and Dominica, as an example of literary witness in order to argue that we should read across genres of witness narrative as part of the ethical project such accounts demand. When histories and contexts for understanding witnesses have been destroyed by slavery and colonialism, displaced by migration, and reshaped by the demands to shape one's story according to bureaucratic and legal requirements, literature offers a density of affect beyond sympathy or suspicion, suspends judgment, and permits undecidability as a value.

Literary witness challenges current formations of which stories have currency, a formation crystallized in a *New York Times Magazine* cover story by Nicholas Kristof and Sheryl WuDunn discussed in chapter 4.[17] In that piece, drawn from and promoting their book, *Half the Sky: Turning Oppression into Opportunity for Women Worldwide*, Kristof and WuDunn build their case for "fighting poverty and extremism globally by educating and empowering girls through tales of suffering and overcoming."[18] How can girls be empowered by the circulation of specific kinds of stories? The claim seems to rest on the belief that stories permit an affective transaction in readers; specifically, one in which feelings substitute for other forms of knowing about history, culture, policy, and local activism. The rescue and redemption narratives teach readers how to engage with pure and worthy victims. Diallo's testimony and Kincaid's literary autobiographical works fail the Kristof and WuDunn litmus test for redemptive suffering. However, Kincaid's use of autobiographical narrative helpfully contextualizes Kristof and WuDunn's popular work in important ways that hold open the forms in which stories about experiences of gendered violence are brought forward.

In interviews, Kincaid describes her work as "very autobiographical."[19] She welds the testimonial and witnessing dimensions of autobiography to an imaginative and transformative project associated more typically with fiction than with nonfiction. She seizes on the expansive potential of autobiography, including its abilities to carry truth claims and to speak for many in the voice of one, to transform the text of history through the entry of a nonnormative speaking subject. Most specifically, she uses autobiographical fiction in a project of witnessing the impact of colonial violence and decolonization on gendered family relationships. Yet obviously Kincaid's work does not meet the evidentiary requirements of documentary testimony or human rights discourse; nor can it function without mediation to intervene for social justice, seek reparation, or plead for sanctions. It stakes no legal claim, and it does not appeal for donor support. Its complicated female protagonists, modeled on Kincaid, do not open hearts according to any predictable plot. Her work does, however, display the layering and occlusions testimony cannot escape, and in that respect it can become part of the critical practice of attending to trauma narratives. Kincaid's autobiographical fiction and her nonfiction highlight the overlay of histories of colonial violence on the quotidian; the legacies of postcolonial structures in education, government, commerce, and land development; and their force in intimate life. They are not narrowed to a script of suffering and overcoming, and the female protagonists do not conform to Western ideological (and, increasingly, narrative) requirements in humanitarian discourse about gender norms, including selfless mothering, heterosexual virtue, and faith in and desire for Western-style education and empowerment. She shows what structures and obstructs testimony, what prevents sympathetic victims from arising, and the ambivalences with which testimony can be met.

In many testimonial archives, how the stories are brought out involves intermediaries and their methodological differences, forensic and philanthropic others, danger, belatedness, randomness—all of which together create a matrix in which testimony and witnessing might emerge. The project of bringing out other people's stories is an important activity in the making of a testimonial archive. If we think of a life as what a person must offer up without translation or other form of facilitation in order to testify compellingly and authentically, then we draw a sharp generic line between fact and fiction and name the management of that line, by the writer and others, in terms of ethics. But if we say that a life both equips and disables our tellings of it (our stories) and that others might tell stories and thereby carry lives with them to other audiences, might be faithful to and ethical in relation to others by telling these stories, then authenticity is still a criterion, but fidelity to others and to the stories of others needs a language different from what is currently available through a strictly individualistic notion of the "I." Accounts like Kincaid's use the literary to perform the work of translating, or of bringing out, life narrative as a way to ensure the expansiveness of the human instead of narrowing it through genre.

Reviewers greeted *The Autobiography of My Mother* (1996), Kincaid's third work of autobiographical fiction, as "shocking" in its lyrical rendering of a pitiless world by a first-person narrator.[20] Xuela's perspective, described as "inhuman," took a determinedly bleak view not only of Dominican society but of humanity, including the narrator herself. This was an unsympathetic witness not because of what she had done but because of how she understood the world. *The Autobiography of My Mother* recounts Xuela's life story: her birth and upbringing, her lovers, her refusal to have children, and, by the death of her mother, her overwhelming sense of exposure to fate: "no one between me and the black room of the world."[21]

Kincaid's literary oeuvre concerns the Caribbean islands of her and her family's birth, Antigua and Dominica. In her early autobiographical fiction, *Annie John* (1985) and *Lucy* (1990), Kincaid's first-person narrator's subject is her larger-than-life mother. In *Lucy*, she asks why her mother is "not an ordinary human being but something from an ancient book."[22] I have described Kincaid's work elsewhere as serial autobiography to account for how the mutating first-person narrators of Kincaid's work share Kincaid's life story, especially the relationship of mother and daughter at the center of her work. In *Autobiography of My Mother*, readers seem to greet this mother who, because her own mother dies in childbirth, comes into the world as if by the manifestation of her own will. "My mother died at the moment I was born," is the first sentence of the book, "and so for my whole life there was nothing standing between myself and eternity; at my back was always a bleak, black wind" (3). This new "I" is a sojourner on earth who wanders without attachment to or comfort from kin or home. She experiences a neglect of her personhood that evolves from generations of enslavement: "brutality is the only real inheritance and cruelty is sometimes the only thing freely given" (5). She is immersed in physicality as menstrual blood, the smell of sex, and perspiration evoke a sticky cloud of sensuality, as do repeated descriptions of lush island vegetation barely this side of rot. The condition the "I" is born into entwines shame and shamelessness: she is unashamed of her embodiment, indeed, she revels in it, but shame delimits her horizon of becoming from birth and she can do no more than name it. Consistently, she names it as "black." The recurrence of black as the color of the sea, ink, hair, and eyes also names the black wind that brings her into the world and carries her mother away, and the black room of the world she enters unprotected by a mother's love. Blackness twins existential condition with skin color and status on Dominica where Xuela, daughter of a Carib woman and half-Scottish, half-African father, inhabits an archipelagan society saturated in colonial history, commerce, and law. For most of the text, the narrator is unnamed. When she offers it, Xuela Claudette Richardson, it is in the context of learning what names mean in school and encountering genealogies of colonial pain: "Who are these people Claudette . . . and

Richardson? To look into it, to look at it . . . could only make you intox-
icated with self-hatred" (79).

Kincaid has the narrator of *The Autobiography of My Mother*, Xuela,
contemplate the perverse circuits of desire and damage that characterize
life for the powerless under colonial rule and the perplexity of her own
suffering and survival. In a retrospective passage near the end of the
text and her narrated life, she asks, "What was I?" (225). As with many
narratives of trauma as well as human rights testimonials, her account
hovers around a traumatic moment embedded in a history of trauma it
labors to comprehend. From her position in the aftermath of slavery and
colonialism in the Caribbean, Xuela offers a singular account of power
and injury that is neither fully present nor fully past; it is partially shared
and partially hers alone. Evidence of historical injury is everywhere.
From kinship structures, governance, and formal education to architec-
ture and the economy, the legacies of colonialism are reproduced across
decolonization as corrupt local governments supplant colonial ones (a
topic about which Kincaid wrote memorably in *A Small Place*). Of the
affective remnants of colonialism, harm persists in the painful silence of
those whose lives are unmemorialized. Near the end of a life haunted by
her effort to speak out of this silence, Xuela says, "I can hear the sound of
much emptiness now. . . . I hear it, a soft rushing sound, waiting to grow
bigger, waiting to envelop me. . . . I only wish to know it so that I may one
day tell myself the story of my existence within it" (226). By articulating
how the silence is shaped, Kincaid contributes to the story of historical
trauma literary characters, like Xuela, who memorialize harm without
providing a ready language of response.

Kincaid's autobiographical fiction draws on history and the genealogy
of her family to offset the demand for sympathetic sufferers in humanitarian discourse. Its location at the limits of this discourse reveals compelling insights into the production of the human and thereby contributes
to the ongoing reclamation of lives from histories of violence. Benefits
arise from reading testimonial genres in relation to each other. Literary
witness broadens the testimonial archive beyond norms of storytelling
and the messages the genres carry about which lives and stories count. In
so doing, it holds open the possibility that we can become more engaged

readers not only of fiction but also, and indissolubly, of testimony. Xuela is guided in her project of witnessing by a grudging credo: "all that is impersonal I have made personal" (228). Her statement may be read as a definition of the work of testimony: to particularize violence, to give it not only a human face and form but also a voice, a record made for those who cannot offer an account. But, as Kincaid shows further, the testimonial contact zone (to use Mary Louise Pratt's helpful term), in which one struggles to inhabit a livable position, is always structured through the limitations imposed by violence. Given that the consequence of violence is to destroy the person who might otherwise render an account, we need an expanded sense of how history speaks that acknowledges and makes room for extrajudicial testimony. Certainly not all documents in a testimonial network have the same truth-value or facticity. They are not interchangeable across contexts. Nor can literary accounts supplant documentary records. But I would not want national and international courts, and the documents that circulate in them, to delimit the scope of what can be considered adequate speech about trauma when what is needed is a more acute sense of how trauma speaks.

Literary witness also offers readers an important role in elucidating how the testimonial imperative arises in many different kinds of texts. A wide variety of readers, including but not restricted to scholars of trauma and postcolonial studies, or the numerous and diverse efforts through which they address forms of power and politics, can and must offer not only specialized and specialists' analysis, but also a critical sense of genre's limitations, a sense that has actually been important in expanding the requirements for legal testimony. In the development of human rights discourse and over a range of juridical settings, testimony has played a crucial role in various efforts to redress crimes against humanity. Juridical settings accord a pivotal role to the testimony of those who have been wronged: they implicitly and explicitly conceive of the witness to and sufferer of injury as one who must speak, whose speaking is capable of shaping a just outcome, and on whose speech depends the project of asserting the category of the human in the face of its radical disavowal by genocide, apartheid, ethnic cleansing, and rape.

Traumatized persons called on to provide testimony endure the hardship of facing their abusers in court; they must repeat the tale of what happened to them. The protocols of some national and international courts permit witnesses to be vigorously questioned and to have their testimony subjected to unsympathetic scrutiny, even as they offer the possibility of redress. Legal testimony's aspirational horizon for those who have experienced injury is that this exposure repeats the founding injury (by retelling it) with a crucial transformation: in the telling, the injury will conclude differently and historical violence will be countered (through either trial or reparation or something that can be claimed as a just response). Legal testimony in this sense seeks to elaborate the notion of the human in locations of harm. In my literary example, Kincaid's *Autobiography of My Mother* details the intimate impact of colonial economy and kinship structures, but by choosing fiction and a close (even claustrophobic) focus on a particular character, as she did in her critique of tourism, *A Small Place*, Kincaid crafts a postcolonial particularity, suffused in melancholy and piteous and unpitiable in its wounding. She does not seek redress from any court. Instead, she probes the wound of historical trauma, represents the temporalities of this violence, and crafts a testimonial account unbounded by the strictures of testimonial protocols. Her literary texts alongside literal texts of testimony promise a fuller archive from which to draw understandings of the human, even when that account means refusing the category itself, as Xuela ultimately does.

When we yoke the legal and extralegal in a testimonial archive broadened beyond a single genre to an interdisciplinary critique, the category of legitimate testimony includes subjects rendered "inhuman." To probe the intimate wounds that have been transmitted over generations of kinship bonds violated by slavery and colonialism, Xuela must become human in order to be able to answer her question "What was I?" Her sense of futility, her belief that her life was cut off at its beginning when her mother died giving birth to her, prompts a series of agentic negotiations around her sexuality and includes her decision not to have children, a decision that has troubled many reviewers. It is seen as a hopeless capitulation, a refusal of the future. Xuela fails to overcome her suffering.

The expectation that she overcome her suffering or, in failing to, elude compassion obscures the context of her choice.

During the slave trade in the Caribbean, many women who were enslaved refused, as far as they were able, to bear children. Unable to resist rape and impregnation, they relied on knowledge passed among women to induce miscarriage. They refused to bear children for a slave economy that depended for its reproduction on their extreme coercion—that is, they refused, as Xuela does, to reproduce the category of the human without any hope of access to it. This knowledge, transmitted generationally and used by Xuela, carries the burden of history and is not simply the personal choice that reviewers and readers found difficult to open their hearts to. When Xuela uses the trope of reproduction to represent the labor of bringing forth the human in herself, the accounting is not for one person only: "In me is the voice I never heard, the face I never saw, the being I came from. In me are the voices that should have come from out of me, the faces I never allowed to form, the eyes I never allowed to see me. This account is an account of the person who was never allowed to be and an account of the person I did not allow myself to become" (227–28).

Xuela describes the conquerors, colonizers, and (mostly male) beneficiaries of colonialism as not quite human. Yet in the summarizing of her life, in which she poses and answers her own questions in a quasi-legal confession, she concludes that the category of the human has been so thoroughly violated by slavery and its aftermath that she cannot redeem it. All she can do is refuse its reproduction. In her representation of the persistence of colonialism, Kincaid articulates what colonialism consigns to silence: the effects of being rendered inhuman, of being stripped of the right of self-possession in its basic forms. She chooses to stage her argument with history in the form of autobiographical fiction and to attribute to the fictional character of Xuela the project of testimony. In her mobilization of autobiography in the service of a literary representation of the psychic and material contents of colonial history, Kincaid brings to the arena of human rights a thickened discursive context. She draws on the practices and philosophical underpinnings of autobiography, fiction, and history in order to explore the limits of articulating the human that arise from empire. She also insists on exploring the psychic effects and legacies of this history and in so doing illuminates the generational transmission of trauma. Thus a benefit—in addition to the expanded archive—is an understanding of the historical circumscription of the human. These benefits, taken together, mean that stories of hardship and overcoming sought and promoted in worthy campaigns will not mark the limits of the stories that can be told.

Through her use of autobiographical material, Kincaid amplifies the testimonial abilities of life narrative to bear witness. Notably, she does so in extrajudicial ways: in autobiographical novels, memoirs, and essays. Literary witness belongs to the complicated terrain of truth telling, justice, injury, and resistant agency. It can escape the narrower protocols of testimony yet, like the practice of *testimonio*, still assert its authority in the messy world where truth is often violently contested. Some might say that if testimony is Kincaid's end, autobiographical fiction is a less than adequate means. But if one adopts the view that autobiographical and literary texts can and do constitute public mourning, expand the limits of what it means to acknowledge and grieve the losses of history, and offer a traumatic witness capable not only of injury but also of speech, then it is possible to see in them the articulation of what is always on the verge of disappearing: the human subject of historical and intimate trauma. The key is to track the itinerary of the ethical across genres to bring out those selves and stories that might otherwise seem impossible to hear because they remain difficult, insufficiently transparent, and untranslated.

In moving beyond a single literary figure as witness, Kincaid offers the entire book as an example of literary witness. *Autobiography of My Mother* becomes a meditation on the shape of life that follows for women who have lost their mothers, for Xuela's mother died in childbirth and there is neither story nor body from which to weave a sense of life-in-time-and-space. The ethics of engaging with witnesses bereft of an uplifting story does not mean that others should supply them with one, but, instead, consists in the formation of publics that do not require it. Kincaid's work shows the undercurrents of empathy that structure testimony through characters who invite disidentification, and Kincaid tasks readers with bearing witness to narrated lives they cannot fully understand and about which they can do nothing. The figure of the literary witness, in this critical practice, denotes more than a character, a writer, or a reader. Instead it names a dynamic that conjoins the one whose experience propels the telling and the one who brings the story out by receiving it, within the mode of carrying the narrative to other witnesses.

Testimony seeks a witness. Testimony moves as multiple life narratives produced for different audiences circulate outside the locales in which they were elicited and absent the rules that shaped them. These narratives have a life of their own, an agentic force we associate with the power of discourse to mediate the translation of lived events into witness accounts. This chapter focuses on the transits of testimony as they engage with rape discourse; carry literary, legal, humanitarian, and neoliberal life narratives to diverse audiences; and influence and limit ethical witnessing. *Diallo v. Strauss-Kahn* provides a case study of how her testimony traveled, how it was heard and not heard in different legal, public, and popular contexts, and how it achieved its surprising conclusion after its currency as scandal had expired. The entire transit—often through contexts that place heavy demands of sympathy and purity on women who testify and those who bear witness—constitutes Diallo's testimony, which otherwise fragments into the judgment of others.

CONCLUSION

Testimonial Publics—#BlackLivesMatter and Claudia Rankine's *Citizen*

Occasionally it is interesting to think about the outburst if you
   would just cry out—
To know what you'll sound like is worth noting—

—CLAUDIA RANKINE, *CITIZEN: AN AMERICAN LYRIC*

Testimony is an increasingly central feature of contemporary life, as is the judgment that accompanies it and attaches, in specific ways, to the life stories of women. Anita Hill's testimony at Clarence Thomas's confirmation hearing, Rigoberta Menchú's *testimonio* about genocide in Guatemala, and Nafissatou Diallo's claim that she was raped by Dominique Strauss-Kahn demonstrate the vulnerabilities of women witnesses in the courts and in the public square but also the importance of these same witnesses to expose the contexts and histories that construct and perpetuate vulnerability. Similarly, dissonant autobiographical literary accounts that are not confessional and do not seek sympathy, such as Kathryn Harrison's memoir and Jamaica Kincaid's autobiographical fiction, provide an important counterweight to the preponderance of neoliberal life narratives that promote norms of gendered authority, affect, and agency. They also indicate how life story is mutating in the long memoir boom to include new forms and figures, as well as the political and market forces that shape permissible identities and voice, and render some lives "grievable"[1] and others as "salvage."[2] In addition to the verbal record of testimonial discourse, women's bodies are scrutinized as evidence of lying as much as truth. While either can be read in order to invoke doubt, both can and have also introduced new witnesses into testimonial networks where they force repressed histories and contexts into view.

New witnesses to the intersectional realities and poetics of race and gender in testimonial networks, specifically, highlight how witness accounts matter, how they unearth and make vivid the histories that animate contemporary life, how antiracist and feminist political and ethical commitments enter into scenes of judgment and shape them. Racism is inevitably incubated within concepts of personhood and agency from the very formation of law in the United States. The testimonial limitations imposed on people of color are traceable in the violence that greets their embodied presence prior to any opportunity to present a verbal account that would be heard. What does it mean to add #BlackLivesMatter to the testimonial network? How can it connect with the poetic discourse of Claudia Rankine's *Citizen* in order to place the black body's exposure to harm and its bearing of historical injury in the context of vivid protest? How do both also materialize the histories of testimony borne in human lives, in patterns of settlement and displacement, in the distribution of wealth away from the labor of those who were enslaved, and in the generational legacies that record this history? Can they reawaken the powerful feminist voices displaced within the memoir boom by neoliberal life narrative?

The journey from owned possession under chattel slavery to full citizenship describes the symbolic transition for African Americans in the United States from material possession to life. Designated as property that could be bought and sold, excluded from membership within the universalism of human life on which the nation was founded, and prevented by law from crossing a "perpetual and impassable barrier" between "the dominant race" and the "subordinate race of beings," African American lives not only did not matter, they represented mere matter.[3]

This rupture is part of a now discredited legacy of legalized racism, but the afterlife of slavery lingers in an ongoing struggle about whose lives matter and how. In her autobiographical account of searching for genealogical traces of her family along the Atlantic slave route, Saidiya Hartman writes of the persistence of this legacy: "I, too, live in the time of slavery, by which I mean I am living in the future created by it. It is the ongoing crisis of citizenship."[4] In the testimonial ecology of lives and matter, black witness has recently gained a vibrant political voice in the public square through the #BlackLivesMatter movement and its political and poetic kin. Their acts include protest, mourning, political organizing, and ethical action.

#BLACKLIVESMATTER: PUTTING ONE'S BODY ON THE LINE AND ONLINE

Words work as release—well-oiled doors opening and closing between intention, gesture. A pulse in a neck, the shiftiness of the hands, an unconscious blink, the conversations you have with your eyes translate everything and nothing. What will be needed, what goes unfelt, unsaid—what has been duplicated, redacted here, redacted there, altered to hide or disguise—words encoding the bodies they cover. And despite everything the body remains.

—CLAUDIA RANKINE, *CITIZEN: AN AMERICAN LYRIC*

From Tahrir Square to the Occupy movement and the digital images and videos documenting the flow of migrants across Europe, social media has become important to the evolving work of grassroots political movements. Social media as a testimonial space is developing so rapidly that it can be easy to forget how recently it and the technologies that make it possible appeared: Facebook in 2004, Twitter in 2006, the iPhone in 2007, and the launch by Apple of its app store in 2008. Yet even given the compressed time frame of news cycles and the brevity of public attention, #BlackLivesMatter's use of social media may offer a density of testimonial reference and supply historical context missing from the headlines and, through links and hashtags, propel these references forward.

#BlackLivesMatter emerged in the aftermath of Trayvon Martin's killing on February 26, 2012. Trayvon Martin, a seventeen-year-old African American high school student, was fatally shot by George Zimmerman, a neighborhood watch volunteer/vigilante, who stalked Martin as he walked to a convenience store in Sanford, Florida, to buy candy and a soda. When Zimmerman was not charged in the killing, a wave of protest was ignited nationwide, in part, through social activism online. An online petition calling for a full investigation and the criminal prosecution of Zimmerman garnered 2.2 million signatures in March 2012, and the name "Trayvon" was tweeted more than two million times in the thirty days following the shooting.[5] Debates about racial profiling and local "stand your ground laws" moved online, too, and sparked a national debate. When Zimmerman, who was subsequently charged and tried for Martin's killing, was acquitted of second-degree murder and manslaughter in July 2013, expressions of outrage circulated through #BlackLivesMatter and traditional news outlets.

An immediate observable difference between the two emerged. Media in the United States have a well-established propensity to report on "looting" and "rioting" when people of color are at the center of a news story.[6] For example, during the crisis that followed in the wake of Hurricane Katrina, residents of New Orleans were without electricity and drinking water. When residents who were people of color took bottled water from convenience stores, some mainstream news outlets covered this life-saving activity as looting. Where news outlets associate broken store fronts and people of color with looting no matter the scale of this activity in recent protests in Ferguson and Baltimore, #BlackLivesMatter augments images of protest, including property damage, with images of police brutality to provide context and humanize communities of color. #BlackLivesMatter establishes both a documentary and a commemorative politics around bearing witness and grieving in public through their integration into the everyday practices of social networks: they offset mug shots with childhood photos and selfies of victims of police abuse, they challenge the purposeful framing of events by photojournalists with an abundance of so-called amateur digital photographs of the same events but from different perspectives, and in the Trayvon Martin case, they posted video of his mother (Sybrina Fulton) who called for justice and calm. Through the feminist intersectional framing of #BlackLivesMatter's online witness, Trayvon Martin's mother was enabled to bear witness not only to her own loss but also to the legacy of African American children's vulnerability and the inability of mothers to protect them during slavery.

The Trayvon Martin case exposed the legacies of racial violence in the United States, including the lingering potency of Jim Crow laws, which instituted racial segregation in all aspects of life, and was reconfigured anew in the aftermath of civil rights legislation through the practice of unequal policing and the disproportionate incarceration of people of color. #BlackLivesMatter frames the killing of African American men through this historical context of racial violence. And it brings this framing online to a mass audience, confirming Laurie McNeill's observation that the Internet makes possible a collective scale of circulation that is simply "unimaginable" offline.[7] In other words, this use of social media by grassroots political groups connects what it means to put one's body on the line and online politically and ethically.

INTERSECTIONAL FEMINIST WITNESS

The founders of #BlackLivesMatter are feminist activists and community organizers of color. Cofounder Opal Tometi explains the movement's beginnings:

> #BlackLivesMatter, a project started by three black women, two of whom are queer women and one who is a Nigerian-American, has opened up the political space for that new leadership, and as a result, a new movement to emerge. Black trans people, Black queer people,

Black immigrants, Black incarcerated people and formerly incarcerated people, Black millennials, Black women, low income Black people, and Black people with disabilities are at the front, exercising a new leadership that is bold, innovative, and radical.[8]

In "A Herstory of the #BlackLivesMatter Movement," published online in the *Feminist Wire*, another cofounder, Alicia Garza, traces the movement's eventful life from founding to online dissemination: "I created #BlackLivesMatter with Patrisse Cullors and Opal Tometi, two of my sisters, as a call to action for Black people after 17-year-old Trayvon Martin was post-humously placed on trial for his own murder and the killer, George Zimmerman, was not held accountable for the crime he committed. It was a response to the anti-Black racism that permeates our society and also, unfortunately, our movements."[9] The #BlackLives-Matter origin story cites the failure of the law to hold George Zimmerman accountable for killing Trayvon Martin, rather than the killing itself, as catalyst, emphasizing the significance of political interpretation and critique in its founding. Garza continues: "BlackLivesMatter is an ideological and political intervention in a world where Black lives are systematically and intentionally targeted for demise. It is an affirmation of Black folks' contributions to this society, our humanity, and our resilience in the face of deadly oppression." The movement developed as "cultural workers, artists, designers and techies offered their labor and love to expand #BlackLivesMatter beyond a social media hashtag. Opal, Patrisse, and I created the infrastructure for this movement project— moving the hashtag from social media to the streets."[10] Tometi, Garza, and Cullors, writing in the Huffington Post, explain: "When we founded #BlackLivesMatter in 2013, we wanted to create a political space within and amongst our communities for activism that could stand firmly on the shoulders of movements that have come before us, such as the civil rights movement, while innovating on its strategies, practices and approaches to finally centralize the leadership of those existing at the margins of our economy and our society."[11]

Tying the evolution of #BlackLivesMatter primarily to its responses to a series of killings of African American men and boys by police officers, as some articles have, obscures the feminist focus on black lives broadly.[12] By refusing a presentist framing of the event, #BlackLivesMatter is not, as its founders make clear, only about what happened but about how to frame it, how to bear witness to histories of the present, and how to look at images of death, grief, and protest as a form of ethical engagement. Alicia Garza clarifies that such an ethics requires going beyond contemporary models of politics and includes world making premised in the altered framing that comes from broad participation and shared leadership:

> Black Lives Matter is a unique contribution that goes beyond extrajudicial killings of Black people by police and vigilantes. It goes beyond the narrow nationalism that can be prevalent within some Black communities, which merely call on Black people to love Black, live Black and buy Black, keeping straight cis Black men in the front of the movement while our sisters, queer and trans and disabled folk take up roles in the background or not at all. Black Lives Matter affirms the lives of Black queer and trans folks, disabled folks, Black-undocumented folks, folks with records, women and all Black lives along the gender spectrum. It centers those that have been marginalized within Black liberation movements. It is a tactic to (re)build the Black liberation movement."[13]

As Daunesia Yancey, a #BlackLivesMatter organizer in Boston, underlines in response to the criticism that decentralized leadership represents a lack of leadership and political naiveté: "It's absolutely wrong because we do know what we're doing, and we're very clear."[14]

I dwell on the feminist historicization of #BlackLivesMatter activists to counter the notion that social media cannot adequately bear witness to the specters of historical violence that haunt the infliction of violence on black bodies. Because, in its feminist focus on the body, #BlackLivesMatter does precisely that: makes legible and shareable a past as well as a present. That is, all those videos made by people getting their phones out of their pockets in exceedingly stressful situations, taking up the position of witness as they record violent acts in which they otherwise cannot intervene, and then tapping their screens to send evidence online are testifying to the iconic power of the mourned black body. When what is shared online carries the hashtag #BlackLivesMatter, those digital images and videos help to embed feminist witness within testimonial networks.

#BlackLivesMatter was up and running when Michael Brown, an eighteen-year-old recent high school graduate, was shot and killed by white police officer Darren Wilson on August 9, 2014, in Ferguson, Missouri, after Wilson confronted Brown and a friend for jaywalking. #BlackLivesMatter was positioned not only to document and share unfolding events but to frame them and to organize protests. In contrast to the recycling of caricatures of young African American men as thugs, #BlackLivesMatter intervened in the national narrative as it was being created. As with its centering of Trayvon Martin's mother's commitment to seek justice for her son, #BlackLivesMatter countered the stereotypes of men of color, especially young men, as criminally dangerous and, instead, in the lightning fast online environment, slowed the rush to judgment about Michael Brown. Through a feminist intersectional framing, men, like Michael Brown, are portrayed as members of families, and the histories and contexts of their personal lives and their communities are combined with analyses of systemic racism.

#BlackLivesMatter's model of civic dissent, public protest, and ethical witnessing also shaped the dissemination of information about the killing of Tamir Rice, an African American twelve-year-old boy, on November 22, 2014, in Cleveland, Ohio, by two white officers; the fatal choking of Eric Garner, forty-three years old, on July 17, 2014, by white police officers in Staten Island, New York; and the killing of Freddie Gray, twenty-six years old, on April 12, 2015 in Baltimore, Maryland, who was dragged by police officers to a police van, handcuffed, and driven around so violently that he died. All these incidents began with the initiation of contact by police with people of color as part of a permissible pattern of harassment and escalated to fatal ends. The very ordinariness of this activity, the ways in which it is undertaken with impunity, in public and often in full view, also provides the opportunity to record and share it.

In the rapidly evolving online environment, #BlackLivesMatter fended off some potential cooptation represented by the shift to "All Lives Matter," and added #SayHerName to address violence against cisgender and trans women of color. #BlackLivesMatter and #SayHerName project outward into the public square knowledge of the routine harassment and fear people of color experience daily. And they build feminist activism into the testimonial network. Here the black body resonates within a history of racial violence; its circulation becomes potent through repetition as the online testimonial network hosts a citational economy that creates value through repetition. This repetition registers the presence of women of color and consistently carries forward their intersectional politics as hashtags and links, which also make available pedagogical materials, guides to organizing, and other informational sites.

The example of #BlackLivesMatter helps us to see how social media can carry political and historical context about current events online and how it functions within a broader testimonial network of extrajudicial and judicial spaces of judgment, how it travels with a range of media to diverse audiences. Through practices of sharing and repetition, a feminist form of witness joins the testimonial network.

Judith Butler has argued that protest requires a sense of the public square. Drawn from Roman history, the public square represents the space of politics and "for politics to take place, the body must appear."[15] In #BlackLivesMatter, bodies appear online in part because the public square has historically been off limits to black bodies and policed by violence. In the videos that recorded Michael Brown's body as it lay face down in the street for four hours in the heat of an August day, the body was present and the public square took shape through the presence of technology. While we readily think of the power of bodies in protest as the massing of people in the ongoing, nightly protests in Ferguson and Baltimore, the significance of the dead body—witnessed and mourned, for whom justice is demanded—evokes histories of witnessing that stretch into the past and haunt the present. Here we confront the specters of African Americans lynched and whipped, raped and sold that form both the historical context of current violence and also the testimonial context of previous instances of bearing witness to the mutilated body. Here we think of Emmett Till, who in 1955 was tortured and killed at the age of fourteen in Mississippi for reportedly flirting with/talking with a white woman. At his mother's insistence, the violated body of her young son was returned to Chicago and placed in an open casket. The public funeral was attended by tens of thousands, and images of his body were published in newspapers and magazines circulated to black audiences. The images raised a public outcry, rallied cross-racial support, and brought critical attention to civil rights in Mississippi. Thus the material witness evoked by Emmett Till's mother's decision about her son's body precedes and resonates with the online witnessing #BlackLivesMatter practices. We also note the potent voice of female dissent to intervene on behalf of the dead body of one's kin.

BEARING WITNESS: SANDRA BLAND AND BREE NEWSOME

What does a victorious or defeated black woman's body
in historically white space look like?

—CLAUDIA RANKINE, *CITIZEN: AN AMERICAN LYRIC*

On July 10, 2015, Sandra Bland, a twenty-eight-year-old African American woman, was on her way to take a new job at her alma mater in Texas. The selfie she took at the outset of her trip shows her smiling face in close up. The next images of Sandra Bland come from the dashboard camera on the police car that pulled her over. Review of the evidence suggests that the officer was approaching Bland's car very rapidly and she pulled over to get out of his way. The ostensible reason for the traffic stop was her failure to use her turn signal when she changed lanes. From there, the white officer, Brian Encinia, aggressively questions her about her attitude, tells her to put out her cigarette, threatens to "light her up" as he aims a Taser at her face, hauls her from the car, throws her to the ground, knees in her back, and handcuffs her. The dashboard camera bears witness to Sandra Bland's continuous verbal challenge to the legality of the officer's actions as he assaults her.

Sandra Bland is taken to a jail and booked for resisting arrest. She is held in jail, and at the end of three days it is announced that she has hanged herself in her cell. None of this makes any sense to her friends or family. We know she protested her illegal and violent treatment and turned up dead in her cell. Her articulate witness and the live recording of a brutal encounter either renders her offstage suicide illegible as agentic act, as protest, or enables a framing of it as such. Her family has insisted on an investigation to determine what happened.

In the second case, following the mass killing on June 17, 2015, in the Emanuel African Methodist Episcopal Church in Charleston, South Carolina, of nine people by a young white racist man who posted photos of himself online with the Confederate flag and markers of apartheid South Africa, the old controversy about the Confederate flag flying over the South Carolina state house was reopened. Coalescing swiftly in the wake of the extraordinary testimony of forgiveness offered by members of the dead in a hearing to charge the killer, a new move to take down the flag quickly came together. But not quickly enough for Bree Newsome, an African American woman, who climbed to the top of the flagpole, removed the flag, climbed down, and presented herself for arrest. Her aim was perfectly clear: she announced it, she linked her civil disobedience to the murders in the church by reciting the twenty-seventh psalm: "The Lord is my light and my salvation. Whom shall I fear?" She took action and she bore witness.

Both women awaken specters of witnesses past who insist that the dead body deserves to be mourned and to have mourning and lamentation turn into just action. The black body as capable of voice, dissent, and agency and the vulnerable black body circulate online in digital images of Michael Brown's body, in video from dashboard and police body cameras, surveillance footage in jails, and the videos taken by citizens of violence. These citizen videos are often the only indicting evidence, as the strong presumption is the word of the police officer as law and law enforcement consolidate into an obdurate force. #BlackLivesMatter has not only seeded the testimonial network with a feminist intersectional analysis but has also renewed attention to figures like Emmett Till's mother who already circulate there and become potent in new configurations of event and interpretation. As a testimonial form, #BlackLivesMatter represents a new witness as it foregrounds its feminist origins and investments, references the history of slavery, conjures ghosts, and evokes buried histories of dissent.

CITIZEN

In 2015 Ta-Nehisi Coates published *Between the World and Me*,[16] an autobiographical essay written in the form of a letter to his son about the grinding violence directed at the vulnerable black body. As the site of injury and oppression, Coates places the black body in both human and historic scale: infinitely precious and impossible to protect, the black body represents a history of violence evident in all aspects of life for people of color in the United States. The previous year, Claudia Rankine published *Citizen: An American Lyric*, which shares with *Between the World and Me* a focus on narratives of the insecurity of human connection and the meaning of the body: how it can be read and misread in social spaces, the generalizations and anonymity imposed by racism, and the lasting harm of incidents of racism.[17] Rankine and Coates offer their autobiographical histories as illustrations at a cellular level of the whole ecology of racism. In this way, each person's history bears witness to the weight of history, to its capacity to order daily life, and in defiance of the commonsensical assertion that the past is past. Both employ a lyric "I," personal and hieratic, aggrieved and inconsolable, patient and terse, in narratives of contact that always carry the threat of undoing.

In *Citizen*, Rankine employs a lyric voice in brief narratives of intimacy denied by racism. Each vignette focuses on a microaggression, those incidents that interrupt daily life and reproduce the trauma of racial histories of violence in everyday occurrences. Like Saidiya Hartman, who argues that "slavery persists as an issue in the political life of black America, . . . because black lives are still imperiled and devalued by a racial calculus and a political arithmetic that were entrenched centuries ago,"[18] Rankine bears witness to an individual and a common life that is the "afterlife of slavery."[19] A literary witness, like Jamaica Kincaid, with the poetic and testimonial voice that distinguished Rigoberta Menchú, Rankine etches shard-like scenes of hurt in a racialized domestic vernacular. The "I" of *Citizen* rides in cars with colleagues, listens to lectures, teaches and gives readings, hangs out with friends, and stands in line at Starbucks. In any and all of these places she is at home in the world . . . until cast into the role of the stranger by the dislocating sense of being thrown into racist relief. A white friend calls her by the name of the woman who cleans the friend's house: is it because those are the only two women of color she knows? A colleague rants about being pressured to hire "a minority" when there are so many "qualified" applicants. Am I here? Rankine wonders. Who am I to you? The question haunts as intensely personal—she has access to these encounters through her work and social world—but it is the question of national belonging: is the stranger truly a citizen? The fragility of connection places the haunting presence of the past at the center of questions of citizenship.

AUTOBIOGRAPHICAL WITNESS: SELF-REPRESENTATION AND A FEMINIST "I"

Previous generations of women writers have evolved a feminist "I" as a voice of feminist theorizing, autobiographical narrative, and literary innovation: from Harriet Jacobs in the nineteenth century to Virginia Woolf's "I" in *A Room of One's Own*—"Call me Mary Beaton, Mary Seaton, or Mary Carmichael, it makes no difference"—in the early twentieth century to the generation of women writers whose autobiographical work placed a revelatory and intimate "I" as both participant in and witness to history. As inheritors and adapters alike of Walt Whitman's democratic and visionary "I," called both to aesthetic expression and political critique, the writers I have argued initiated a long memoir boom that continues to host earlier forms and incubate new ones persist within a feminist literary tradition as historical witnesses to the evolving limits on testimony. Often, they lead the way in evading the mechanisms whereby women are discredited as witnesses—often by writing in literary forms that do not require legal standards of evidence.[20]

Yet when women wish to bear witness in public, the protective devices of literature are not at hand, and the full risks of being deemed crazy or criminal exist. Whether we can add feminist dissidence to testimonial networks depends in no small part on insisting on the inclusion of histories of harm—slavery, colonialism, and the current crisis in the mass incarceration of people of color—as the context for understanding contemporary testimonial acts as they arise in protest and in poetry, online and in the streets, and within the proliferating jurisdictions and platforms that constitute the public square. Feminist dissidence is always potentially present as a witness to contemporary history: it is embedded in the words, bodies, and acts of those who have gone before, in the imagined witness of literary characters, and in the postmemory that present generations embody. These histories, immaterial as they may have been rendered through active practices of forgetting and erasure, matter.

NOTES

INTRODUCTION: TAINTED WITNESS
IN TESTIMONIAL NETWORKS

1. Feminist scholarship on testimony and witness is disciplinarily, geographically, and politically diverse and it is beyond the scope of this project to catalog it; however, some key texts that inform the theorization of race, gender, doubt, and ethics in this study include Kathryn Abrams and Irene Kacandes, eds., *WSQ: Women's Studies Quarterly, Special Issue on "Witness"* 36, no. 1–2 (2008); Wendy Kozol, *Distant Wars Visible: The Ambivalence of Witnessing* (Minneapolis: University of Minnesota Press, 2014); Wendy Hesford, *Spectacular Rhetorics: Human Rights Visions, Recognitions, Feminisms* (Durham, N.C.: Duke University Press, 2011); and Sidonie Smith and Kay Shaeffer, *Human Rights and Narrative Lives: The Ethics of Recognition* (New York: Palgrave Macmillan, 2004). Work that focuses on trauma and testimony associated with the subaltern, the geographical and historical contexts of the global South, and the politics of decolonialization includes Gayatri Spivak, "Can the Subaltern Speak?," in *Marxism and the Interpretation of Culture*, ed. Cary Nelson and Lawrence Grossberg, 271–313 (Urbana: University of Illinois Press, 1988). Interdisciplinary studies of race that consider the historical impact of slavery on American institutions and everyday life supply the analytical grounding for reading literary testimony as a cultural process connected to how publics engage with race, gender, truth-telling, doubt, and justice and include Michelle Alexander, *The New Jim Crow: Mass Incarceration in the Age of Colorblindness* (New York: New Press, 2010); Brittney Cooper, "Intersectionality," in *The Oxford Handbook of Feminist Theory*, ed. Lisa Disch and Mary Hawkesworth (Oxford: Oxford University Press, 2016); Kimberlé Crenshaw, "Mapping the Margins: Intersectionality, Identity Politics, and Violence Against Women of Color," *Stanford Law Review* 43 (July 1991): 1242–99; Angela Davis, *Are Prisons Obsolete?* (New York: Seven Stories Press, 2003); Ruth

Wilson Gilmore, *Golden Gulag: Prisons, Surplus, Crisis, and Opposition in Globalizing California* (Berkeley: University of California Press, 2007); and Saidiya Hartman, *Lose Your Mother: A Journey Along the Atlantic Slave Route* (New York: Farrar, Straus and Giroux, 2007).

2.   See, too, how Gillian Whitlock's notion of "testimonial transactions" (*Postcolonial Life Narrative: Testimonial Transactions* [New York: Oxford University Press, 2015]) and Rosanne Kennedy's "moving testimony" ("Moving Testimony: Human Rights, Palestinian Memory, and the Transnational Public Sphere," in *Transnational Memory Circulation, Articulation, Scales*, ed. Chiara De Cesari and Ann Rigney, 51–78 [Berlin: Walter de Gruyter, 2014]) seek to characterize and trace the movement of testimony across contexts and audiences.

3.   Note here how the Fifth Amendment acknowledges the need to balance the right against self-incrimination against the need to hear testimony from those who would incriminate themselves in the process of testifying. Granting immunity in exchange for self-incriminating testimony represents a form of testimonial transaction. Testimony has its own agency under these conditions because immunity protects testimony from its association with a compromised witness and enables testimony to possess a credibility in court that the witness who offers it does not have.

4.   This is very much in line with Lauren Berlant's theorization of impersonality developed in *Cruel Optimism* (Durham, N.C.: Duke University Press, 2011) and addressed again in an interview with Dana Luciano in *Social Text* (2013), http://socialtextjournal.org /periscope_article/conversation-lauren-berlant-with-dana-luciano/. Berlant captures how events that one cannot help but experience as personal arise from the impersonal forces of accidents, other people's motives, institutional norms, and so on. Berlant offers a new way to think about the critical error through which blameworthiness, including self-blame, takes hold.

5.   I am thinking of stickiness in a different, but allied, way as Sara Ahmed uses the term with reference to how racism attaches to black bodies (*The Cultural Politics of Emotion* [New York: Routledge, 2005]). Another allied way of thinking about bodies as bearing evidence they cannot fully control is offered by Gayle Salamon (*Assuming a Body: Transgender and Rhetorics of Materiality* [New York: Columbia University Press, 2010]) who analyzes how the felt sense of gendered embodiment travels in relation to various forms of cultural judgment about it.

6.   D. W. Winnicott, *Playing and Reality* (London: Tavistock/Routledge, 1971), 109.

7.   Ahmed, *The Cultural Politics of Emotion*, 44.

8.   Chandan Reddy, *Freedom with Violence: Race, Sexuality, and the U.S. State* (Durham, N.C.: Duke University Press, 2011), 16.

9.   See ibid. Reddy analyzes the legal and cultural accumulation of racism and sexism as "amending" citizenship.

10.   The phrase is Lauren Berlant's from *The Female Complaint: The Unfinished Business of Sentimentality in American Culture* (Durham, N.C.: Duke University Press, 2008), 5. For critical narratives of how racism and sexism shape intimate publics, see also

Ann Cvetkovich, "Public Feelings," *South Atlantic Quarterly* 106, no. 3 (2007): 459–68; Ahmed, *The Cultural Politics of Emotion*; and Paula Ioanide, *The Emotional Politics of Racism: How Feelings Trump Facts in an Era of Colorblindness* (Stanford, Calif.: Stanford University Press, 2015).

11. See the "human rights and narrated lives" paradigm developed by Smith and Schaeffer, *Human Rights and Narrative Lives*, that accounts for the significance and circulation of life stories in relation to human rights.

12. Lisa Lowe, *The Intimacies of Four Continents* (Durham, N.C.: Duke University Press, 2015), 8.

13. For an analysis of victim blaming as a large-scale cultural politics, see Susan Faludi's *Backlash: The Undeclared War on Women* (New York: Crown, 1991), written during the period I study here, which argues that women's outrage at Anita Hill's treatment helped to spur the massive prochoice demonstration in 1992, but that women's "political awakening provoked instant political reprisal" (xi). For analysis of victim blaming, see Michelle L. Meloy and Susan L. Miller, *The Victimization of Women: Law, Policies, and Politics* (Oxford: Oxford University Press, 2011), 3–5, which traces how women victims are associated with responsibility for the crimes men commit against them.

14. Lauren Berlant, *The Queen of America Goes to Washington City: Essays on Sex and Citizenship* (Durham, N.C.: Duke University Press, 1997); Berlant, *The Female Complaint*; Berlant, *Cruel Optimism*.

15. Lauren Berlant and Lisa Duggan, eds., *Our Monica, Ourselves: The Clinton Affair and the National Interest* (New York: New York University Press, 2001).

16. See Berlant's notion of "juxtapolitical" reading in *The Female Complaint*, 155.

17. See Crenshaw, "Mapping the Margins"; and Brittney Cooper, "Intersectionality."

18. See Raymond Williams's discussion in *Marxism and Literature* (Oxford: Oxford University Press, 1977), chap. 9, 128ff., in which he connects an affective history to the structures of lived experience.

19. See Sidonie Smith and Julia Watson's critical field guide to life writing, *Reading Autobiography: A Guide for Interpreting Life Narratives*, 2nd ed. (Minneapolis: University of Minnesota Press, 2010), and related work on human rights narratives by Schaeffer and Smith (*Human Rights and Narrative Lives*); Gillian Whitlock, *Postcolonial Life Narratives* (New York: Oxford University Press, 2015); and Joseph Slaughter, *Human Rights, Inc.: The World Novel, Narrative Form, and International Law* (New York: Fordham University Press, 2007).

20. Leigh Gilmore, *Autobiographics: A Feminist Theory of Women's Self-Representation* (Ithaca, N.Y.: Cornell University Press, 1994).

21. Jacques Derrida, *Demeure: Fiction and Testimony*, trans. Elizabeth Rottenberg (Stanford, Calif.: Stanford University Press, 2000); Mark Sanders, *Ambiguities of Witnessing: Law and Literature in the Time of a Truth Commission* (Stanford, Calif.: Stanford University Press, 2007).

22. See Donna Haraway, "Situated Knowledges: The Science Question in Feminism and the Privilege of Partial Perspective," *Feminist Studies* 14, no. 3 (1988): 575–99.

23. See Leigh Gilmore, "Learning from Fakes: Memoir, Confessional Ethics, and the Limits of Genre," in *Contemporary Trauma Narratives: Liminality and the Ethics of Form*, ed. Jean-Michel Ganteau and Susana Onega, 21–35 (New York: Routledge, 2014); Leigh Gilmore, "Boom/lash: Fact-Checking, Suicide, and the Lifespan of a Genre," *a/b: Auto/ Biography Studies* 29, no. 2 (2014): 211–24.

24. Avery Gordon's notion of haunting is apposite here; see her *Ghostly Matters: Haunting and the Sociological Imaginary* (Minneapolis: University of Minnesota Press, 1997). See Reddy, *Freedom with Violence*, for a critical narrative of how racist histories of law and violence persist in contemporary notions and enactments of freedom.

25. Hartman, *Lose Your Mother*, 133.

26. *Time* magazine, October 21, 1991.

27. I echo here Simone de Beauvoir's "One is not born woman, but rather becomes a woman."

28. Anita Miller, ed. *The Complete Transcripts of the Clarence Thomas–Anita Hill Hearings: October 11, 12, 13, 1991* (Chicago: Academy Chicago Publishers, 1994), 89.

29. See Jon Krakauer's account of rape culture in Missoula, Montana: *Missoula: Rape and the Justice System in a College Town* (New York: Doubleday, 2015). Krakauer's account focuses on white male criminals, but the association of black masculinity, sexuality, and criminality is well studied in criminology and media studies. The racial logics of "boys will be boys" asserts that white male aggression is natural and permissible while black male violence, actual and falsely conjured, is animalistic and criminal.

30. Jon Krakauer (*Missoula*) makes a key point about rape and doubt. Women lie about rape in the same percentage that all people lie about all crimes (2–10%). But police and others presume *all* women to be lying about *all* rape. Commenting specifically on the retracted *Rolling Stone* article about a gang rape in a fraternity, Krakauer said: "The overwhelming majority, you know, of victims do not lie about rape. I mean, there's this mythology out there that women lie about being raped. In fact, some women *do* lie about being raped—between 2 and 10 percent is the best research. Many studies show this. So it's really a small amount. It's not too different from other crimes. The difference is in other crimes the victim isn't assumed to be lying . . . the way rape victims are treated is different than any other crime" (NPR Staff, "Jon Krakauer Tells a 'Depressingly Typical' Story of College Town Rapes," *NPR*, April 19, 2015, http://www.npr.org/2015/04/19/400185648/jon-krakauer-tells-a-depressingly-typical-story-of-college-town-rapes).

31. See Hortense J. Spillers, "Mama's Baby, Papa's Maybe: An American Grammar Book," *Diacritics* 17, no. 2 (Summer 1987): 64; and bell hooks, *Black Looks: Race and Representation* (Boston: South End Press, 1992, 120).

32. Peter Brook, *Law's Stories: Narrative and Rhetoric in the Law* (New Haven, Conn: Yale University Press, 1998).

33. See Danielle S. Allen, *The World of Prometheus: The Politics of Punishing in Democratic Athens* (Princeton, N.J.: Princeton University Press, 2000), 260.

34. Greg Mortenson and David Oliver Relin, *Three Cups of Tea: One Man's Mission to Fight Terrorism and Build Nations . . . One School at a Time* (New York: Penguin, 2007);

Nicholas Kristof and Sheryl WuDunn, *Half the Sky: Turning Oppression into Opportunity for Women Worldwide* (New York: Knopf, 2009).

35.   Claudia Rankine, *Citizen: An American Lyric* (Minneapolis: Graywolf Press, 2014).

36.   Judith Butler, *Antigone's Claim: Kinship Between Life and Death* (New York: Columbia University Press, 2002); Butler, *Precarious Life: The Powers of Mourning and Violence* (New York: Verso, 2004); Butler, *Frames of War: When Is Life Grievable?* (New York: Verso, 2009).

1. ANITA HILL, CLARENCE THOMAS, AND THE SEARCH FOR AN ADEQUATE WITNESS

1.   Toni Morrison emphasizes the profusion of speech during the nomination process in "Friday on the Potomac," in *Race-ing Justice, Engendering Power: Essays on Anita Hill, Clarence Thomas, and the Construction of Social Reality*, ed. Toni Morrison (New York: Pantheon, 1993), viii–ix.

2.   Anita Miller, ed., *The Complete Transcripts of the Clarence Thomas–Anita Hill Hearings: October 11, 12, 13, 1991* (Chicago: Academy Chicago Publishers, 1994), 118.

3.   On the elements of haunting especially relevant to the presence of histories of racial violence, slavery, gender, and law in the United States, see Avery Gordon, *Ghostly Matters: Haunting and the Sociological Imaginary* (Minneapolis: University of Minnesota Press, 1997), 63–65.

4.   Anita Hill, *Speaking Truth to Power* (New York: Doubleday, 1997), 139.

5.   Miller, *Complete Transcripts*, 71.

6.   Gordon, *Ghostly Matters*, 63.

7.   Jim Crow laws enforced segregation by legally excluding African Americans from nearly all the privileges of citizenship achieved after the Civil War. Jim Crow effectively restricted voting rights through poll taxes, literacy tests, and white primaries and civic amenities like libraries, parks, swimming pools, and public beaches, and enforced second-class citizenship by requiring black citizens to enter through separate doors, use separate washrooms and drinking fountains, and be sworn in using separate Bibles in court. Schools and health care were segregated. Jim Crow legalized and regulated Chief Justice Roger Taney's ruling in *Dred Scott* (1857): a Negro "had no rights which the white man was bound to respect."

8.   In his self-described hatchet job, *The Real Anita Hill: The Untold Story* (New York: Free Press, 1993), David Brock misrepresented every gap in the testimony against Thomas into an intentional lie and hurled at Hill every possible accusation he was fed by the Thomas team as if it were research. He later recanted, and has described the combination of feckless zeal on his part and over-the-top political character assassination, on the part of Thomas supporters that encouraged him to concoct utter falsehoods about Hill's testimony and also Thomas's character and actions. It should be noted that Brock lied plenty about Thomas, too, as the fabrication of a nefarious Hill was tied to the fabrication of an idealized Thomas. Brock details how he was fed false information

during and after the hearings (though he claims not to have known it at the time and even doubts it would have dissuaded him) and, as a result of undertaking a similar smear of Hillary Clinton, has recanted his previous publications (Brock, *Blinded by the Right: The Conscience of an Ex-Conservative* [New York: Three Rivers Press 2003], 107–9). He identifies himself as the coiner of "a little bit nutty and a little bit slutty" (*Blinded*, 109).

9. See Jane Mayer and Jill Abramson, *Strange Justice: The Selling of Clarence Thomas* (Boston: Houghton Mifflin, 1994); Jeffrey Toobin, "Unforgiven," *New Yorker*, November 12, 2007, http://www.newyorker.com/magazine/2007/11/12/unforgiven; Hendrik Hertzberg, "Leaks, Lies and the Law," *Washington Post*, December 1, 1991, https://www .washingtonpost.com/archive/opinions/1991/12/01/leaks-lies-and-the-law/871a0b36 -a52c-46c5-8632-9fca4ac039eb; Hertzberg, "A Cold Case," *New Yorker*, August 12, 2008, http://www.newyorker.com/news/hendrik-hertzberg/a-cold-case; Morrison, "Friday on the Potomac"; Amy Richards and Cynthia Greenberg, *I Still Believe Anita Hill: Three Generations Discuss the Legacies of Speaking Truth to Power* (New York: Feminist Press, 2013); Jane Flax, *The American Dream in Black and White: The Clarence Thomas Hearings* (Ithaca, N.Y.: Cornell University Press, 1998).

10. See excellent compilations of feminist views in Morrison, "Friday on the Potomac," and Richards and Greenberg, *I Still Believe Anita Hill.*

11. At the time of the hearing, 41 percent of persons polled believed Thomas and 27 percent believed Hill. This was during a period of intensive campaigning against her in which falsehoods and innuendo were presented as fact. In 1993, after the publication of *The Selling of Clarence Thomas*, the percentage shifted.

12. Thomas confirms and elaborates this strategy in his memoir published fifteen years after his confirmation: *My Grandfather's Son: A Memoir* (New York: HarperCollins, 2007).

13. As Nina Totenberg explains, following Bork's failed confirmation in which he detailed his conservative views at length, Thomas denied any such views whatsoever. On such landmark cases as *Roe v. Wade*, the court's 1973 abortion ruling, that occurred while Thomas was in law school and which could reasonably be expected to draw his interest, Thomas denied ever discussing it and asserted he had no view whatsoever. Vermont Democrat Patrick Leahy was incredulous: "You're not suggesting that there wasn't any discussion at any time of *Roe v. Wade*?" Thomas demurred: "I cannot remember personally engaging in those discussions." According to Harvard Law professor Noah Feldman: "Most people had trouble believing that someone who had been to Yale Law School [and] had spent a public career in jobs connected to law, could possibly have no opinion on the most controversial legal topics of his generation." The twist was that Thomas's outright refusal to engage was read as strategy rather than lying. Feldman observes: "And yet somehow those answers not only did not stand in the way of Justice Thomas' confirmation, but were seen in some way as good politics." Nina Totenberg, "Thomas Confirmation Hearings Had Ripple Effect," *NPR*, October 11, 2011, http://www.npr.org/2011/10/11/141213260/ thomas-confirmation-hearings-had-ripple-effect.

14. Robert Bork's nomination hearings were so politically divided that the strategy of sinking a candidate on his or her actual jurisprudence and ideology came to be known as "borking."

15. According to Mayer and Abramson, "Thomas's grandfather was an active member of the NAACP; at one point he was dubbed a 'sharpshooter' for the effectiveness of the boycotts he lead against white businesses that wouldn't hire blacks" (*Strange Justice*, 43).

16. Ibid., 41–42.

17. Lani Guinier, "But Some of Us Are Brave," in *I Still Believe Anita Hill: Three Generations Discuss the Legacies of Speaking Truth to Power*, ed. Amy Richards and Cynthia Greenberg (New York: Feminist Press, 2013).

18. Ibid., 55.

19. Ibid., 83.

20. Quoted in Hill, *Speaking Truth to Power*, 131.

21. Miller, *Complete Transcripts*.

22. See Hendrik Hertzberg's writing on the conspiracy claim. Hertzberg wrote in the *Washington Post*'s Sunday Outlook section ("Leaks, Lies and the Law") and again in the *New Yorker* ("A Cold Case") that "if Thomas and his supporters were speaking the truth, then not only he but also the entire nation were being victimized by a monstrous plot to use perjured testimony in order to undermine a solemn process mandated by the Constitution itself—and, thereby, to alter the course of American government for decades to come. A considerable number of people would necessarily have committed serious crimes in furtherance of this plot, beginning, of course, with Anita Hill herself. . . . It would have been a simple matter to collect the evidence from e-mail and telephone records and from the testimony, immunized and compelled if necessary, of her co-conspirators and other witnesses. Nothing of the kind happened, of course. . . . From Thomas's supporters, there were no calls for a special prosecutor, no demands to bring in the F.B.I., no expressions of outrage that Hill and the other plotters were being permitted to get away scot-free, no attempts to uphold the rule of law and the Constitutional order by ensuring that the guilty were indicted, tried, and imprisoned for their crimes" (Hertzberg, "A Cold Case").

23. See Hertzberg, "A Cold Case."

24. Kate Phillips, "Biden and Anita Hill, Revisited," *New York Times* blog, August 23, 2008, http://thecaucus.blogs.nytimes.com/2008/08/23/biden-and-anita-hill-revisited.

25. Angela Wright was prepared to testify that she dated Thomas at his importuning when she worked for him. Thomas's team worked to minimize the damage she could do, including providing her a letter of recommendation that presented her firing by Thomas as her decision to move on and seek other professional opportunities. Lest this be interpreted as something other than an implied quid pro quo for her continued silence, Thomas's aide was explicit about the link. As to Biden's claims that Wright was not prepared to testify, court records indicate otherwise: she waited without being called.

26. Phillips, "Biden and Anita Hill."

27. At one point during the questioning, Senator Alan Simpson brandished a stack a papers while referencing "the faxes" he had received about Hill. Mayer and Abramson describe this as purposeful deception with Simpson using a prop, basically, to conjure the image of concerned citizens informing on Hill (*Strange Justice*, 314).

28. Brock, *Blinded by the Right*, 107.

29. Mayer and Abramson, *Strange Justice*, 314–16.

30. Ibid., 315.

31. Ibid., 314.

32. The office of the public prosecutor in the United States emerged with the founding of the nation and is engrained in legal training and practice. See Danielle S. Allen, *The World of Prometheus: The Politics of Punishing in Democratic Athens* (Princeton, N.J.: Princeton University Press, 2000), 3–5.

33. As I write this chapter, the United States is gripped by a series of murders of unarmed African Americans pursued by white racist actions. A number of these killings have occurred as police officers seek and escalate conflict into one-sided violence: from Michael Brown in Ferguson to Eric Garner in the Bronx to Freddie Gray in Baltimore to Sandra Bland in Texas. The legal protections offered to police (access to weapons, forms of impunity for their actions, protection of police by police) were exploited during Jim Crow in the South. This history is not past, but is part of a continuation, as Michelle Alexander, Ruth Wilson Gilmore, Angela Davis, and others argue, of racial violence in the post–civil rights era.

34. Morrison, "Friday on the Potomac," xvi.

35. See Kendall Thomas, "Strange Fruit" in Morrison, *Race-ing Justice*, 364–89.

36. Scholars testify to the power of watching the hearings. See, for example, Flax, *The American Dream in Black and White*, 3.

37. "Kendall Thomas by Lynn Tillman," an interview in *BOMB: Artists in Conversation* 59 (Spring 1997), http://bombmagazine.org/article/2059/kendall-thomas.

38. Joseph Biden ruled two areas of questioning off limits: Thomas's qualifications for the court and corroboration of Hill's report on his pornography use. When the American Bar Association rated Thomas "qualified," Biden was concerned that further questioning would appear as ganging up on a black man, so no line of questioning regarding his qualifications was permitted. Nor would Biden question Thomas on pornography and its centrality to Hill's testimony, for similar reasons. Thus the confirmation hearings were permitted under Biden to proceed exactly as orchestrated for years: a fait accompli to place a young conservative vote on the court. See Mayer and Abramson, *Strange Justice*, on how Biden has defended his role in the hearings. He suppressed evidence about sexual harassment through a claim to uphold decency standards and failed to press Thomas on his legal thinking and conservative politics out of racial deference. Biden told Mayer and Abramson he felt this deference was "misplaced."

39. Anita Faye Hill and Emma Coleman Jordan, *Race, Gender, and Power in America: The Legacy of the Hill–Thomas Hearings* (New York: Oxford University Press, 1995), 273.

40. Feminists have fully critiqued the existence of a private sphere outside law and contract as a false notion (Carole Pateman, *The Sexual Contract* [Cambridge: Polity, 1988]). The private/public spheres suggest a false balance, as does the he said/she said pairing. The notion that there is a separate private sphere obscures the legal extension of male rule and privilege beyond the public sphere of citizenship in Athens and into the household. Thus the public/private split is not a split at all but an extension of the rights of the father to exercise law over the inhabitants of the household who lack any footing in the polis (women, slaves, children, nonhuman animals). Hence the notion that men's territorial, aggressive, and proprietary sexual conduct is "private," and that criticism of it is a violation of privacy.

41. Allen, *World of Prometheus*, 51.

42. Mayer and Abramson, *Strange Justice*, 7.

43. Ibid., 8.

44. Thomas, *My Grandfather's Son*, 280.

45. Toobin, "Unforgiven."

46. See Hill, *Speaking Truth to Power*; Hill and Jordan, *Race, Gender, and Power in America*; Thomas, *My Grandfather's Son*; and *Anita: Speaking Truth to Power*, directed by Freida Mock (First Run Features, 2013).

47. Thomas, *My Grandfather's Son*, 244.

48. Ibid., 171.

49. Ibid., 170.

50. Ibid., 156.

51. Ibid., 171, 179.

52. Ibid., 16, 17.

53. Mayer and Abramson, *Strange Justice*, 60.

54. Hill, *Speaking Truth to Power*, 187.

55. "The Thomas Hearings: Excerpts from Senate's Hearings on the Thomas Nomination," *New York Times*, September 13, 1991, http://www.nytimes.com/1991/09/13/us/the-thomas-hearings-excerpts-from-senate-s-hearing-on-the-thomas-nomination.html.

56. Linda Greenhouse, "Clarence Thomas, Silent but Sure," Opinionator, *New York Times*, March 11, 2010, http://opinionator.blogs.nytimes.com/2010/03/11/.

57. Totenberg, "Thomas Confirmation Hearings Had Ripple Effect."

58. Ibid.

59. Ibid.

60. Michelle Alexander, *The New Jim Crow: Mass Incarceration in the Age of Colorblindness* (New York: New Press, 2010), 180.

61. Morrison, "Friday on the Potomac," x.

2. JURISDICTIONS AND TESTIMONIAL NETWORKS: RIGOBERTA MENCHÚ

1. Rigoberta Menchú, *I, Rigoberta Menchú: An Indian Woman in Guatemala*, trans. Ann Wright, ed. Elisabeth Burgos-Debray (New York: Verso, 1984).

2. John Beverly's definition of *testimonio* informs the debate about genre and truth telling. See his *Against Literature* (Minneapolis: University of Minnesota Press, 1993).

3. See Greg Grandin, "It Was Heaven That They Burned: Who Is Rigoberta Menchú?" *Nation*, September 8, 2010, http://www.thenation.com/article/it-was-heaven-they -burned.

4. Ibid. The controversy was covered comprehensively in essays collected by Arturo Arias in *The Rigoberta Menchú Controversy* (Minneapolis: University of Minnesota Press, 2001). See also Greg Grandin, Open School of Ethnography and Anthropology/ Community Institute for Transcultural Exchange, "Rigoberta Menchu Debates, Redux," *Osea-cite.org*, n.d., http://www.osea-cite.org/history/redux_rigoberta-menchu-debate .php; James Dawes, *Evil Men* (Cambridge, Mass.: Harvard University Press, 2013), 156–59.

5. Dinesh D'Souza, "Liar, Rigoberta Menchú," *Boundless*, 1999, http://www.boundless. org/2005/articles/a0000074.cfm.

6. Grandin, "It Was Heaven That They Burned."

7. In 1999 Juan Jesús Aznárez, in an interview with Menchú, offered these numbers: "100,000 people dead, 40,000 disappeared, 200,000 orphans, and a wandering legion of 100,000 widows" (Rigoberta Menchú, "Those Who Attack Me Humiliate the Victims," an interview with Juan Jesús Aznárez, January 24, 1999, in Arias, *The Rigoberta Menchú Controversy*, 109). Most current sources place the number at over 200,000 killed (http://www.pbs.org/newshour/updates/latin_america-jan-june11-timeline_03–07/).

8. Ibid.

9. David Stoll, *Rigoberta Menchú and the Story of All Poor Guatemalans* (Boulder, Colo.: Westview Press, 1999). Challenges emerge from political scientists, historians, and anthropologists, in addition to political activists. See, for example, Victoria Sanford, *Buried Secrets: Truth and Human Rights in Guatemala* (New York: Palgrave Macmillan, 2004); Julieta Rostica, "The Naturalization of Peace and War: The Hegemonic Discourses on the Political Violence in Guatemala," in *The Struggle for Memory in Latin America: Recent History and Political Violence*, 183–201, ed. Eugenia Allier-Montaño and Emilio Crenzel (New York: Palgrave Macmillan, 2015); and Grandin, "It Was Heaven That They Burned."

10. See Menchú, "Those Who Attack Me Humiliate the Victims," 109–20, for Menchú's immediate disputation of Stoll's assertions and the *New York Times* story. The *Times* did not report her response.

11. Dante Liano, "The Anthropologist with the Old Hat," in Arias, *The Rigoberta Menchú Controversy*, 123.

12. Larry Rohter, "Tarnished Laureate: A Special Report: Nobel Winner Finds Her Story Challenged," *New York Times*, December 15, 1998, http://www.nytimes.com/1998/12/15 /world/tarnished-laureate-a-special-report-nobel-winner-finds-her-story-challenged. html.

13. Liano, "The Anthropologist with the Old Hat," 123, 124.

14. Ibid., 124. Stoll's methodology has been assessed by anthropologists, though it was not reported on as his claims against Menchú circulated in global media. Stoll interviewed 120 people, many of whom gave hearsay accounts of Menchú, and created a story

from the interviewees who supported his views. See also Kay B. Warren's comment in "Telling Truths: Taking David Stoll and the Rigoberto Menchú Exposé Seriously," in Arias, *The Rigoberta Menchú Controversy*, 208: "Stoll's dominant focus is on *the facts* so as to question the veracity of the testimonial account. What more could there be? Not much if one accepts this framing. But this is where Stoll chooses a distinctive path from ethnographers who are interested in the *cultural and social contexts* of their informants' lives and portrayals as in the particular facts they provide" (emphasis in original).

15. Menchú, "Those Who Attack Me Humiliate the Victims," 111.

16. "Efrain Rios Montt and Mauricio Rodriguez Sanchez: Background," *International Justice Monitor*, n.d., http://www.ijmonitor.org/efrain-rios-montt-and-mauricio-rodriguez-sanchez-background.

17. According to Arturo Taracena in an interview with Luis Aceituno for *El periódico de Guatemala*, Guatemala City, on January 3, 1999, Burgos-Debray was interested in publishing a testimony by a Guatemalan Mayan woman after the idea was suggested to her by a Canadian friend. The status of Burgos-Debray's "ownership" of the interview continues to be controversial. See dialogue between Greg Grandin and David Stoll following Grandin's article in the *Nation* (2010). Grandin describes how the publisher, Verso Books, rejected his preface to a new edition of *I, Rigoberta Menchú* when rights-holder Burgos-Debray objected. Grandin comments: "Subsequently, I have learned that Burgos has kept all of the money/royalties from all editions since the early 1990s—a fact rarely mentioned in all the commentary on Menchú. This was confirmed by both Gallimard publishers (which acknowledges that Burgos is the legal 'author' of the book) and Burgos herself—in an email she admitted that she kept all the money since the 1990s, saying that 'si vous souhaitez faire votre promotion de faiseur de vendettas personnelles, je serais heureuse d'expliquer à l'occasion pourquoi j'ai cessé l'envoie des droits d'auteur. . . . ' It no doubt takes a life steeped in the excitements of the international left to summon such drama to a simple query, but there it is. Considering the early 90s forward was the period when the book really took off in sales, this must be a considerable amount of money. *I'm not especially politically correct, and have always thought that defenses of Menchú's memoir based on her position—that is, as an indigenous woman with claims to ways of knowing or speaking distinct from colonial knowledge—came up short. Yet this particular perverse arrangement does say something about the international division of labor.* Menchú, having barely escaped unimaginable terror to live with unbearable sorrow, got the opprobrium, while someone else, living far away, got the cash." Grandin, "Rigoberta Menchu Debates, Redux" (emphasis and formatting in original).

18. For an account of this process, see Arturo Taracena's interview: Luis Aceituno, "Arturo Taracena Breaks His Silence," in Arias, *The Rigoberta Menchú Controversy*, 82–94.

19. Quoted in Grandin, "It Was Heaven That They Burned."

20. Aceituno, "Arturo Taracena Breaks His Silence," 84.

21. Ibid., 85.

22. Grandin, "It Was Heaven That They Burned."

23. Ibid.

24. Beverly, *Against Literature*; John Beverly, *Testimonio: On the Politics of Truth* (Minneapolis: University of Minnesota Press, 2004); Doris Sommer, "Las Casas's Lies and Other Language Games," in Arias, *The Rigoberta Menchú Controversy*, 237–50.

25. Pamela Yates, "Trial on Guatemala's Spanish Embassy Resumes Today: The Rest of History," *NACLA.org*, January 19, 2015, https://nacla.org/news/2015/01/19/trial-guatemala% E2%80%99s-spanish-embassy-fire-resumes-today-rest-history-video.

26. Pamela Yates, *Granito: How To Nail a Dictator*, *Skylight.is*, n.d., http://skylight.is/films /granito.

27. Pamela Yates, *Dictator in the Dock*, *Skylight.is*, n.d., http://skylight.is/films/dictator -in-the-dock.

28. Skylight filmed the entire genocide trial of Ríos Montt from the day it started on March 19, 2013, to its conclusion on May 10, 2013, when Riós Montt was found guilty. Although the verdict was overturned and the key judge and prosecutor (both women) were dismissed on technicalities, the fact of the trial and the verdict were unprecedented and profoundly meaningful.

29. Yates, *Dictator in the Dock*.

30. Ibid. Another spin-off project, *Granito: Every Memory Matters*, is the companion project to *How to Nail a Dictator*. It is a multimedia, multiplatform project meant to make young people in Guatemala who did not live through the genocide and do not remember it aware, and to awaken memory in the elders (https://vimeo.com/28082375). The documentary archive that developed around Menchú was instrumental in court, and also an example of restorative justice via the means Nicholas Mirzoeff calls "visual activism," in which "artists, academics, community groups and many others . . . are linking visible online presence to real-world interventions to create social change." Nicholas Mirzoeff, "Nicholas Mirzoeff on the Real Impact of Sharing 700 Million Snapchats Every Day," *It's Nice That*, June 4, 2015, http://www.itsnicethat.com/articles /nicholas-mirzoeff.

31. See Sidonie Smith and Kay Schaeffer's framework of human rights and narrated lives (*Human Rights and Narrative Lives* [New York: Palgrave Macmillan, 2004]), and Gillian Whitlock's testimonial transactions (*Postcolonial Life Narrative: Testimonial Transactions* [New York: Oxford University Press, 2015]).

32. Arjun Appaduri, "Introduction: Commodities and the Politics of Value," in *The Social Life of Things: Commodities in Cultural Perspective*, ed. Arjun Appaduri (Cambridge: Cambridge University Press, 1986), 5.

33. I have written on this previously: Leigh Gilmore, *The Limits of Autobiography: Trauma and Testimony* (Ithaca, N.Y.: Cornell University Press, 2001).

34. I take "forum of judgment" as my definition of jurisdiction from Peter Goodrich, *Law in the Courts of Love: Literature and Other Minor Jurisprudences* (New York: Routledge, 1996), 1. I use *memoir* to refer to autobiographical texts that make a claim to historical accuracy and constrain their focus to a particular set of events, duration of time, relationship of interest, or some other specifiable focus within the broader purview of the genre of autobiography. Memoir's typical evidence is memory, though it may incorporate more documentary materials. I use *testimonio* to refer to testimonial literature

that offers first-person accounts of historical and political struggle in which it is not the sovereign subject of universalism but the resistant subject who speaks. For this usage, I draw on Beverley, *Against Literature*, and Caren Kaplan, "Resisting Autobiography: Out-Law Genres and Transnational Feminist Subjects," in *De/Colonizing the Subject: The Politics of Gender in Women's Autobiography*, ed. Sidonie Smith and Julia Watson, 115–38 (Minneapolis: University of Minnesota Press, 1992). I concur with Julie Rak that these terms do double and triple duty in the field and the histories of these terms do not fully register in the current omnibus usage *life narrative* (Rak, *Boom! Manufacturing Memoir for the Popular Market* [Waterloo: Wilfrid Laurier University Press, 2013]).

35. Lauren Berlant, *The Female Complaint: The Unfinished Business of Sentimentality in American Culture* (Durham, N.C.: Duke University Press, 2008), 5.

36. Bruno Latour, *Reassembling the Social: An Introduction to Actor-Network-Theory* (Oxford: Oxford University Press, 2005).

37. Jürgen Habermas describes the public sphere as "a domain of our social life in which such a thing as public opinion can be formed. Access to the public sphere is open in principle to all citizens. A portion of the public sphere is constituted in every conversation in which private persons come together to form a public" (Habermas, *The Structural Transformation of the Public Sphere: An Inquiry into a Category of Bourgeois Society*, trans. Thomas Burger and Frederick Lawrence [Cambridge, Mass.: MIT Press, 1989], 231). Critiques of Habermas's definition of the public sphere that examine the ambiguities of intimacy and privacy, often under the rubric of "publics," "intimate publics," or "counterpublics," have deepened and historicized more fully the complexities that attend any use or enactment of "public" and "private." See, e.g., Berlant, *The Female Complaint*, and Noëlle McAfee, *Habermas, Kristeva, and Citizenship* (Ithaca, N.Y.: Cornell University Press, 2000).

38. Michel Foucault, *Power: The Essential Works of Foucault, 1954–1984*, vol. 3, trans. James Hurley, ed. James Faubion (New York: New Press, 2000).

39. Richard Ford, "Law's Territory (A History of Jurisdiction)," *Michigan Law Review* 97, no. 4 (1999): 843.

40. Ibid., 898.

41. Holloway Sparks offers a crisp definition of dissent as "the public contestation of prevailing arrangements of power by marginalized citizens through oppositional, democratic, noninstitutionalized practices that augment or replace institutionalized channels of democratic opposition when those channels are inadequate or unavailable" (Sparks, "Dissident Citizenship: Democratic Theory, Political Courage, and Activist Women," *Hypatia* 12, no. 4 [1997]: 83–84).

42. Nancy K. Miller, *Bequest and Betrayal: Memoirs of a Parent's Death* (New York: Oxford University Press, 1996), 2.

43. See David Horowitz, "I, Rigoberta Menchú, Liar," *FrontPageMagazine.com*, February 26, 1999, http://archive.frontpagemag.com/readArticle.aspx?ARTID=24278; D'Souza, "Liar."

44. David Stoll, *Rigoberta Menchú and the Story of All Poor Guatemalans* (Boulder, Colo.: Westview Press, 1998), 70. In some interviews Stoll withholds this epithet, although other critics of Menchú do not.

45. As Arturo Arias argues, "David Stoll finds her, on the one hand, not Western enough when it comes to the rigor of her logic and her use of facts. He thus accuses her of invention, of fibbing. On the other hand, he finds her too Western in her politics, and he therefore claims that her ideas are not representative of what he judges to be authentic 'native' Mayan thought" (Arturo Arias, "Authorizing Ethnicized Subjects: Rigoberta Menchú and the Performative Production of the Subaltern Self," *PMLA* 116, no. 1 [2001], 75).

46. Arias, *The Rigoberta Menchú Controversy*, 79.

47. Wendy Brown, *States of Injury: Power and Freedom in Late Modernity* (Princeton, N.J.: Princeton University Press, 1995).

3. NEOLIBERAL LIFE NARRATIVE: FROM TESTIMONY TO SELF-HELP

1. See Leigh Gilmore, *The Limits of Autobiography: Trauma and Testimony* (Ithaca, N.Y.: Cornell University Press, 2001); Julie Rak, *Boom! Manufacturing Memoir for the Popular Market* (Warterloo: Wilfrid Laurier University Press, 2013).

2. Berlant's work across several major books has transformed the understanding of what Habermas theorizes as the public sphere and Benedict Anderson analyzes as imagined communities by theorizing how the gender-sexuality-citizenship-affect nexus works in popular culture and intimate life and is rooted in the form of the nation.

3. See my description of the emergence of a "boom/lash" in Leigh Gilmore, "Boom/lash: Fact-Checking, Suicide, and the Lifespan of a Genre," *a/b: Auto/Biography Studies* 29, no. 2 (2014): 211–24.

4. See Julie Rak's parsing of scholarly accounts of the popularity of memoir (including Gilmore, Miller, and Couser). See, too, Rak's account of the rise in a popular readership for nonfiction as cause (*Boom!*, 6–12).

5. Susanna Kaysen, *Girl, Interrupted* (New York: Vintage, 1993); Mary Karr, *The Liar's Club: A Memoir* (New York: Penguin, 1995); Frank McCourt, *Angela's Ashes* (New York: Scribner, 1996).

6. For documentation of the memoir boom, see Leigh Gilmore, "Limit-Cases: Trauma, Self-Representation, and the Jurisdictions of Identity," *Biography* 24, no. 1 (2001): 128–39. See Rak, *Boom!*, for a case study of bookstore practices in Canada during the memoir boom.

7. For discussion of how the meaning of the term "memoir" migrated during these years, see Sidonie Smith and Julia Watson, *Reading Autobiography: A Guide for Interpreting Life Narratives*, 2nd ed. (Minneapolis: University of Minnesota Press, 2010), 2–6; and Rak, *Boom!*.

8. Gilmore, *Limits of Autobiography*.

9. See Hillary L. Chute, *Graphic Women: Life Narrative and Contemporary Comics* (New York: Columbia University Press, 2010), for an account of innovative women's comics as life narrative; and Gillian Whitlock, *Soft Weapons: Autobiography in*

Transit (Chicago: University of Chicago Press, 2006) for a reading of blogs, journalism, book design, and marketing as significant elements in life narrative.

10.   Paul Eakin, for example, organizes a reading of what I call nonnormative life writing around rule breaking (Eakin, *Making Selves: How Our Lives Become Stories* [Ithaca: Cornell University Press, 1999]). For a study of censorious responses to Kaysen and Harrison, see Elizabeth Marshall, "The Daughter's Disenchantment: Incest as Pedagogy in Fairy Tales and Kathryn Harrison's *The Kiss*," *College English* 66, no. 4 (March 2004): 395–418.

11.   See Wendy Brown, *Undoing the Demos: Neoliberalism's Stealth Revolution* (Cambridge, Mass.: MIT Press, 2015), for the soul-crushing consequences of the demand within neoliberalism to transform human experience into capital.

12.   I follow Lauren Berlant, whose analysis of sentimentality and intimate publics describes the consumption of what I call neoliberal life narrative and the identification of a gendered audience for these narratives. Elizabeth Gilbert, whose *Eat, Pray, Love* marks an important moment in the formation of neoliberal life narrative, genders the target audience as female.

13.   Jeanette Walls, *The Glass Castle: A Memoir* (New York: Scribner, 2005).

14.   For the publishing and marketing history of *The Glass Castle*, see Leigh Gilmore and Elizabeth Marshall, "Trauma and Young Adult Literature: Representing Adolescence and Knowledge in David Smalls's *Stitches: A Memoir*," *Prose Studies: History, Theory, Criticism* 35, no. 1 (2013): 16–38.

15.   "Jeannette Walls," *Kepplerspeakers.com*, n.d., http://www.kepplerspeakers.com/speakers /?speaker=Jeannette%20Walls.

16.   Maya Angelou, *I Know Why the Caged Bird Sings* (New York: Random House, 1969); Maxine Hong Kingston, *The Woman Warrior: Memoirs of a Girlhood Among Ghosts* (New York: Vintage, 1976); Audre Lorde, *Zami: A New Spelling of My Name: A Biomythography* (New York: Crossing Press, 1982); Cherríe Moraga, *Loving in the War Years: Lo Que Nunca Pasó por Sus Labios* (Brooklyn: Sound End Press, 1983); Sandra Cisneros, *The House on Mango Street* (Houston: Arte Público Press, 1984); Cherríe Moraga and Gloria Anzaldúa, eds., *This Bridge Called My Back: Writings By Radical Women of Color* (London: Persephone Press, 1981); Gloria Anzaldúa, *Borderlands/La Frontera: The New Mestiza* (San Francisco: Spinsters/Aunt Lute, 1987).

17.   Carolyn Steedman, *Landscape for a Good Woman: A Story of Two Lives* (London: Virago, 1986); Monique Wittig, *The Lesbian Body*, trans. Peter Owen (New York: Avon, 1975). See Hillary Chute's related and relevant historicization of women's life narrative in comics at the beginning of the twenty-first century, *Graphic Women: Life Narrative and Contemporary Comics* (New York: Columbia University Press, 2010). Lynda Barry's "autobiofictionalography" *One!Hundred!Demons* (Seattle: Sasquatch Press 2002), Phoebe Gloeckner's *A Child's Life and Other Stories* (Berkeley, Calif.: Frog, 1998) and *Diary of a Teenage Girl: An Account in Words and Pictures* (Berkeley, Calif.: North Atlantic Books, 2002), and Alison Bechdel's *Dykes to Watch Out For* (1983–2008) and graphic memoir *Fun Home: A Family Tragicomic* (New York: Houghton Mifflin, 2006) testify to the dynamism of feminism, comics, and life narrative in the period I study

and are part of the alternative history of memoir I offer here. See also Kate Douglas's historicization of published childhood trauma narratives within the 1990s and 2000s in *Contesting Childhood: Autobiography, Trauma, and Memory* (New Brunswick, N.J.: Rutgers University Press, 2010).

18. Sara Ahmed identifies the predicament of the feminist killjoy as the one at risk of losing her place at the family table At risk of losing her place, at risk if she stays, the feminist killjoy is blamed for the dissonance she unmasks, the dissonance she is. See Ahmed, "Feminist Killjoys (and Other Willful Subjects)," *The Scholar and Feminist Online* 8, no. 3 (2010), http://sfonline.barnard.edu/polyphonic/ahmed_01.htm.

19. See Lauren Berlant on the "false distinction between the merely personal and the profoundly structural" in *The Queen of America Goes to Washington City: Essays on Sex and Citizenship* (Durham, N.C.: Duke University Press, 1997), 9.

20. See Elizabeth Gilbert, Eckhart Tolle, Byron Katie, and the sorrowing pretexts of their transformation.

21. In contrast, and to tie these examples to my earlier discussion, consider Menchú's experience of civil war and Anita Hill's entrapment within Washington politics.

22. Queer studies scholars have shown how neoliberalism absorbs radical formations of gender, sexuality, and race into its own programs, thereby neutralizing their capacity to transform social reality. My analysis is indebted to these insights. Scholars have described how the child, for example, a figure allied with the self-made man I described in chapter 1, is used to compel national morality to uphold and confirm the centrality of guilt and innocence. See Berlant, *Queen of America*; Lee Edelman, *No Future: Queer Theory and the Death Drive* (Durham, N.C.: Duke University Press, 2004); Jamaica Kincaid, *Autobiography of My Mother* (New York: Penguin, 1996); Kathryn Bond Stockton, *The Queer Child, or Growing Sideways in the Twentieth Century* (Durham, N.C.: Duke University Press, 2009). Queer formations around kinship have been absorbed: Lisa Duggan, *The Twilight of Equality? Neoliberalism, Cultural Politics, and the Attack on Democracy* (New York: Beacon, 2003); Roderick Ferguson, *Aberrations in Black: Toward a Queer of Color Critique* (Minneapolis: University of Minnesota Press, 2004); Chandan Reddy, *Freedom with Violence: Race, Sexuality, and the U.S. State* (Durham, N.C.: Duke University Press, 2011).

23. See, for example, Judith Herman's *Trauma and Recovery: The Aftermath of Violence—from Domestic Abuse to Political Terror* (New York: Basic Books, 1992); and Jennifer J. Freyd, *Betrayal Trauma: The Logic of Forgetting Childhood Abuse* (Cambridge, Mass.: Harvard University Press, 1998).

24. Dorothy Allison, *Bastard Out of Carolina* (New York: Penguin, 1992); David Wojnarowicz, *Close to the Knives: A Memoir of Disintegration* (New York: Vintage, 1991).

25. See Gilmore, *Limits of Autobiography*.

26. See Gillian Harkins, "Aye, and Neoliberalism," *Journal of Homosexuality* 59, no. 7 (2012): 1073–80; Jane Elliott and Gillian Harkins, "Genres of Neoliberalism," *Social Text* 31, no. 2 (2013): 1–17.

27. A reporter did track down Harrison's father, who, when questioned, sidestepped a flat-out denial. Warren St. John, "Kathryn Harrison's Dad Responds to Her Memoir," *New York Observer*, April 21, 1997.

28. See Wendy Brown, *States of Injury: Power and Freedom in Late Modernity* (Princeton, N.J.: Princeton University Press, 1995), for a feminist analysis of the complexity of claiming injury as a basis of feminist identity or of addressing a plea to the state to provide relief.

29. Kathryn Harrison, *The Kiss* (New York: Harper Perennial, 1998), 61, 65, 68–70.

30. Colin Harrison, "Sins of the Father," *Vogue*, April 1, 1997.

31. Robert Coles, *The Moral Lives of Children* (New York: Grover, 1986).

32. Christopher Lehmann-Haupt, "Life with Father: Incestuous and Soul-Deadening," *New York Times*, February 27, 1997, C18.

33. Cynthia Crossen, "Know Thy Father," *Wall Street Journal*, March 4, 1997, A16.

34. Robin Pogrebin quoting Paul Bogaards, director of promotion at Knopf, "The Naked Literary Come-On," *New York Times*, August 17, 1997, http://www.nytimes.com/1997/08/17/weekinreview/the-naked-literary-come-on.html.

35. Nathan Schneider, "Religious Liberty, Minorities, and Islam: An Interview with Saba Mahmood," *Immanent Frame*, August 7, 2011, http://blogs.ssrc.org/tif/2011/08/17/religious-liberty-minorities-and-islam/

36. Gillian Harkins, *Everybody's Family Romance: Reading Incest in Neoliberal America* (Minneapolis: University of Minnesota Press, 2009), 215.

37. James Frey, *A Million Little Pieces* (New York: Random House, 2003); Elizabeth Gilbert, *Eat, Pray, Love: One Woman's Search for Everything Across Italy, India and Indonesia* (New York: Penguin, 2006); Eckhart Tolle, *The Power of Now: A Guide to Spiritual Enlightenment* (Novato, Calif.: New World Publishing, 1999); Cheryl Strayed, *Wild: From Lost to Found on the Pacific Crest Trail* (New York: Vintage, 2012).

38. Eva Illouz, *Oprah Winfrey and the Glamour of Misery: An Essay on Popular Culture* (New York: Columbia University Press, 2003), 5.

39. Patricia J. Williams, *The Alchemy of Race and Rights: Diary of a Law Professor* (Cambridge, Mass.: Harvard University Press 1991), 48.

40. Michel Foucault, *History of Sexuality*, vol. 1: *An Introduction*, trans. Robert Hurley (New York: Vintage, 1978), 28.

41. Several insightful scholars have considered this democratization in analyses of Oprah Winfrey's impact on popular culture, including Cecilia Konchar Farr, *Reading Oprah: How Oprah's Book Club Changed the Way America Reads* (Albany: State University of New York Press, 2005); Kathleen Rooney, *Reading with Oprah: The Book Club That Changed America* (Fayetteville: University of Arkansas Press, 2005); and Trysh Travis, *The Language of the Heart: A Cultural History of the Recovery Movement from Alcoholics Anonymous to Oprah Winfrey* (Chapel Hill: University of North Carolina Press, 2009).

42. A foundational text in autobiography studies, Philippe Lejeune's *Le Pacte Autobiographique* (Paris: Seuil, 1975) argues that the writer and reader are bound through the guarantee of the autobiographer's production of historically verifiable truth. Lejeune acknowledges normal stumbling blocks to rendering this truth, including memory and subjectivity,

but these essential characteristics of self-consciousness and narrative are subordinate to the contractual definition of genre. In contrast to this view, Judith Butler argues that the limitations on self-knowing, including not simply lapses in memory but the opacities of self-awareness that constitute the psyche and that place violence in relation to the moral self, make such transparency impossible, and further, that it is unethical to construe such an impossibility as the criterion of ethicity. This powerful counterweight to Lejeune's valuable effort to distinguish autobiography's specificity would push autobiography studies to contend more seriously with morality, ethics, and violence.

43.   I follow many scholars in referring to Oprah Winfrey by her first name, not to indicate an overly familiar or nonscholarly relation to her but to acknowledge that she is best known as "Oprah," a potent name of her own forging.

44.   For an analysis of how Oprah resists and is constrained by racialization, see Patricia Hill Collins, *Black Sexual Politics: African Americans, Gender, and the New Racism* (New York: Routledge, 2005). For differing analyses of her place in self-help culture, see Illouz, *Oprah Winfrey and the Glamour of Misery*, and Janice Peck, *The Age of Oprah: Cultural Icon for the Neoliberal Era* (Boulder, Colo.: Paradigm, 2008).

45.   Such negotiations around sexism and racism are mediated by stereotype, as described in Collins, *Black Sexual Politics*, and in Jennifer Harris and Ellwood Watson, eds., *The Oprah Phenomenon* (Lexington: University of Kentucky Press, 2007).

46.   Eckhart Tolle, *A New Earth: Awakening to Your Life's Purpose* (New York: Penguin, 2005).

47.   Peck, *The Age of Oprah*, 15.

48.   Ibid., 7.

49.   Illouz, *Oprah Winfrey and the Glamour of Misery*, 98–99.

50.   Lauren Berlant, *The Female Complaint: The Unfinished Business of Sentimentality in American Culture* (Durham, N.C.: Duke University Press, 2008), 3.

51.   Ibid., 6.

52.   Tolle, *Power of Now*, 3–4.

53.   Ibid., 5.

54.   Cheryl Strayed, *Tiny Beautiful Things: Advice on Love and Life from Dear Sugar* (New York: Vintage, 2012).

55.   "*Brave Enough*: Cheryl Strayed," Amazon.com, n.d., http://www.amazon.com/Brave-Enough-Cheryl-Strayed/dp/1101946903.

56.   Elizabeth Gilbert, *The Signature of All Things* (New York: Penguin, 2013); Elizabeth Gilbert, *Big Magic: Creative Living Beyond Fear* (New York: Penguin, 2015).

57.   See Rak's description of the ends of Frey, who exits the fray calling memoir "bullshit" (*Boom!*, 14).

4. WITNESS BY PROXY: GIRLS IN HUMANITARIAN STORYTELLING

1.   Leigh Gilmore and Elizabeth Marshall, "Girls in Crisis: Rescue and Transnational Feminist Autobiographical Resistance," *Feminist Studies* 36, no. 3 (2010): 680.

2. Marjane Satrapi's *Persepolis: The Story of a Childhood*, trans. L'Association (New York: Pantheon, 2003), appealed to this new literary market. For an analysis of life writing in the post-9/11 global context, see Gillian Whitlock, *Soft Weapons: Autobiography in Transit* (Chicago: University of Chicago Press, 2006).

3. Around 2004 the U.S. military began training social scientists to be placed in the field to gain local knowledge. A series of programs, including Human Terrain, involved mixing academically trained civilians into military operations in the global war on terror. See the film and website for *Human Terrain*, the movie, for a timeline and critical analysis (http://humanterrainmovie.com). Greg Mortenson and David Oliver Relin receive shared authorship for *Three Cups of Tea*. Relin is described as a "globe-trotting journalist" in the book's credits.

4. Jon Krakauer, "Is It Time to Forgive Greg Mortenson?" *Daily Beast*, April 8, 2013, http://www.thedailybeast.com/articles/2013/04/08/is-it-time-to-forgive-greg-mortenson.html.

5. Mortenson followed up *Three Cups* with another "saving girls through education" effort, *Stones into Schools: Promoting Peace with Education in Afghanistan and Pakistan* (New York: Viking, 2009), on which he is sole author but credits two writers for assistance with structure, and Pennies for Peace, a service-learning fundraising project and nonprofit he launched in U.S. schools. Mortenson credits Mike Bryan and Kevin Fedarko with help in research and structure, respectively.

6. Nicholas Kristof, "Dr. Greg and Afghanistan," *New York Times*, October 20, 2010, http://www.nytimes.com/2010/10/21/opinion/21kristof.html. Thomas Friedman also wrote positive stories in the op-ed pages of the *New York Times* praising Mortenson's school-building strategy ("Teacher, Can We Leave Now? No.," *New York Times*, July 18, 2009, http://www.nytimes.com/2009/07/19/opinion/19friedman.html).

7. Jon Krakauer, *Into Thin Air: A Personal Account of the Mt. Everest Disaster* (New York: Anchor, 1997), and *Into the Wild* (New York: Anchor, 1996). He has shifted to explorations of toxic masculinity in *Under the Banner of Heaven: A Story of Violent Faith* (New York: Anchor, 2003) and *Missoula: Rape and the Justice System in a College Town* (New York: Doubleday, 2015).

8. Jon Krakauer's exposé of Mortenson, *Three Cups of Deceit: How Greg Mortenson, Humanitarian Hero, Lost His Way*, was initially offered free online for seventy-two hours on *byliner.com* in April 2011, and a print edition was published by Random House in July 2011. A *60 Minutes* story aired April 12, 2011.

9. Associated Press, " 'I Feel Like a Criminal Coming Back': 'Three Cups of Tea' Author Who Lied About Being Kidnapped by the Taliban Returns as Figurehead for Mismanaged Charity," *Daily Mail*, September 19, 2014, http://www.dailymail.co.uk/news/article-2760931/Three-Cups-Tea-author-plans-reluctant-return.html.

10. Eun Kyung Kim, " 'Three Cups' Author Greg Mortenson: 'I Let a Lot of People Down,' " *Today.com*, January 21, 2014, reporting on an interview with Tom Brokaw, http://www.today.com/popculture/three-cups-author-greg-mortenson-i-let-lot-people-down-2D11961320.

11. Sidonie Smith and Julia Watson elaborate how "metrics of authenticity" arise to help readers navigate the hoaxy terrain where testimony, humanitarian narratives, and

frauds coexist. See their "Witness or False Witness: Metrics of Authenticity, Collective I-Formations, and the Ethic of Verification in First-Person Testimony," *Biography* 35, no. 4 (2012): 590–626.

12.   David Oliver Relin, "Introduction: In Mr. Mortenson's Orbit," in Mortenson and Relin, *Three Cups of Tea*, 5.

13.   After the book came under scrutiny, Relin was caught up in the controversy and named in a lawsuit alleging that readers had been duped (a similar lawsuit was filed against James Frey, the publisher offered to refund the cost of the book, and subsequent editions of *A Million Little Pieces* carry a disclaimer). David Oliver Relin took his life by kneeling on the tracks in front of an oncoming train on November 14, 2012. Within the testimonial network, it is important to remember that some witnesses, like Relin, do not survive long enough for their side of the story to receive an adequate hearing. As controversies erupt, the zeal with which cases are enjoined is hardly consequence free.

14.   See Whitlock, *Soft Weapons*, on how life narratives function as "soft weapons" in the war on terror. Her analysis suggests that the humanitarian hero and proxy witnesses are new devices in the context she analyzes.

15.   Joseph Slaughter, *Human Rights, Inc.: The World Novel, Narrative Form, and International Law* (New York: Fordham University Press, 2007), 2.

16.   See Clare Hemmings, *Why Stories Matter: The Political Grammar of Feminist Theory* (Durham, N.C.: Duke University Press, 2011), 197, on the work certain stories perform within feminism, especially regarding empathy. See also Leela Fernandes, *Transnational Feminism in the United States: Knowledge, Ethics, Power* (New York: New York University Press, 2013), on how transnational feminism travels alongside humanitarianism in global markets.

17.   Whitlock, *Soft Weapons*, 122.

18.   See Gilmore and Marshall, "Girls in Crisis," on the tendency of "girls in crisis" narratives to avoid focus on women as political agents.

19.   Whitlock, *Soft Weapons*, 130.

20.   Ibid., 48.

21.   Hillary Chute, *Graphic Women: Life Narrative and Contemporary Comics* (New York: Columbia University Press, 2010), 138; Azar Nafisi, *Reading Lolita in Tehran: A Memoir in Books* (New York: Random House, 2003); Satrapi, *Persepolis*.

22.   Özlem Sensoy and Elizabeth Marshall, "Missionary Girl Power: Saving the 'Third World,' One Girl at a Time," *Gender and Education* 22, no. 3 (2010): 295–311.

23.   The durability of this formation into the second decade of the twenty-first century suggests the resilience of the long boom in life narratives, including its capacity to generate ongoing forms of entertainment/education across multiple texts, images, and platforms, as I will show in my discussion of the journalist/activist/adventurer Nicholas Kristof.

24.   Hamid Dabashi, "Native Informers and the Making of the American Empire," *Al-Ahram*, June 1, 2006.

25.   Images of women bearing witness often become a visual signature and exemplify the body's openness to interpretation. A photograph of Anita Hill, one hand on the Bible

and the other raised as she is sworn in, is iconic, as is the image of a smiling Rigoberta Menchú facing the gaze of the camera, wearing traditional Mayan dress.

26. Wendy Kozol, *Distant Wars Visible: The Ambivalence of Witnessing* (Minneapolis: University of Minnesota Press, 2014); Nicholas Mirzoeff, "Nicholas Mirzoeff on the Real Impact of Sharing 700 Million Snapchats Every Day," *It's Nice That*, June 4, 2015, http://www.itsnicethat.com/articles/nicholas-mirzoeff.

27. Kozol, *Distant Wars Visible*, 57.

28. Slaughter, *Human Rights, Inc.*; Kay Schaffer and Sidonie Smith, *Human Rights and Narrative Lives: The Ethics of Recognition* (New York: Palgrave Macmillan, 2004).

29. Whitlock, *Soft Weapons*, 77.

30. Schaeffer and Smith, *Human Rights*, 31.

31. Sanders, *Ambiguities of Witnessing*.

32. Ibid.

33. Kennedy, "Moving Testimony."

34. Whitlock, *Soft Weapons*, 78.

35. I have elsewhere argued that neoliberal storytelling is evolving into its own genre. See Leigh Gilmore, "'What Was I?' Literary Witness and the Testimonial Archive," *Profession* (2011): 77–84.

36. Feminist scholarship addressing the unintended negative consequences of neoliberal humanitarianism includes, among others, Wendy Hesford, *Spectacular Rhetorics: Human Rights Visions, Recognitions, Feminisms* (Durham, N.C.: Duke University Press, 2011); Gilmore and Marshall, "Girls in Crisis"; and Caren Kaplan and Inderpal Grewal, "Transnational Practices and Interdisciplinary Feminist Scholarship: Refiguring Women's and Gender Studies," in *Women's Studies On Its Own: A Next Wave Reader in Institutional Change*, ed. Robyn Wiegman, 66–81 (Durham, N.C.: Duke University Press, 2002).

37. See Sensoy and Marshall, "Missionary Girl Power," for how this phenomenon is remediated in young adult fiction that focuses on humanitarianism, saving the Muslim girl, and girl power.

38. Nicholas Kristof and Sheryl WuDunn, *Half the Sky: Turning Oppression into Opportunity for Women Worldwide* (New York: Knopf, 2009), xxi.

39. In some circumstances, local groups are able to make use of humanitarian work and the resources provided by nongovernmental organizations to further work that they define and to challenge the notion that they need saving. See Lila Abu-Lughod, *Do Muslim Women Need Saving?* (Cambridge, Mass.: Harvard University Press, 2013). See, too, for example, the Afghan Women's Writing Project (AWWP, http://awwproject .org) and Revolutionary Association of the Women of Afghanistan (RAWA, http:// rawa.org).

40. This is in contrast to truth and reconciliation commissions that address apartheid in South Africa, stolen generations in Australia, and First Nations rights in Canada. All of these aim for national conversations and entail legal outcomes of differing sorts.

41. When Spivak raised the gambit of strategic essentialism in the 1980s, it represented a fraught and canny maneuver. Spivak considered a strategic use of essentialism, not an

embrace or even reconsideration of essentialism, as she clarified in an interview with Sara Danius and Stefan Jonsson in *Boundary 2* 20, no. 2 (1993): 24–50.

42.   Carol S. Vance, "Innocence and Experience: Melodramatic Narratives of Sex Trafficking for Law and Policy," *History of the Present: A Journal of Critical History* 2, no. 2 (2012): 208.

43.   I rely here on Gayatri Spivak's formulation, "white men are saving brown women from brown men," in "Can the Subaltern Speak?" in *Marxism and the Interpretation of Culture*, ed. Cary Nelson and Lawrence Grossberg (Urbana: University of Illinois Press, 1988), 297, and the generation of postcolonial feminist criticism it has informed. See also Gilmore and Marshall, "Girls in Crisis," 685–87, for analysis of this point in Spivak.

5. TAINTED WITNESS IN LAW AND LITERATURE: NAFISSATOU DIALLO AND JAMAICA KINCAID

1.   See Susan Brownmiller, *Against Our Will: Men, Women, and Rape* (New York: Ballantine, 1975) and the documentary film *Rape Culture* (Cambridge Documentary Films, prod. Margaret Lazarus and Renner Wunderlich, 1975). When it emerged, the notion of rape culture exposed marital rape and rape by acquaintances, as well as the broader forms of violence to which women are routinely exposed. In its more recent revival, the term signifies the view that access to women's sexuality is a male right and privilege and traces the production of that view across multiple sites.

2.   In October 2010 members of the Delta Kappa Epsilon fraternity at Yale University marched through an area of campus where first-year women students live and chanted, "No means yes, yes means anal." See the recent documentary film *The Hunting Ground* (dir. Kirby Dick, Weinstein Company, 2015) on sexual assault on campus and a report released in September 2015 on sexual assault on campus that estimates that one in four college women have experienced forced sexual contact.

3.   See Estelle B. Friedman, *Redefining Rape: Sexual Violence in the Era of Suffrage and Segregation* (Cambridge, Mass.: Harvard University Press, 2013).

4.   I follow the convention of referring to an unproven accusation as an *alleged* incident. Although the case against Dominique Strauss-Kahn was dropped by the Attorney General's Office in Manhattan Criminal Court, he was found guilty by a preponderance of the evidence in civil court in the Bronx, as this essay details; thus the harm is no longer alleged but proven.

5.   For this reason, rape discourse represents a far more serious and pervasive threat to the testimonial dimension of life narrative than hoaxes or fake memoirs do.

6.   See Rachel Hall, "'It Can Happen to You': Rape Prevention in the Age of Risk Prevention," *Hypatia* 19, no. 3 (Summer 2004): 1–19.

7.   See Kay Schaffer and Sidonie Smith, *Human Rights and Narrative Lives: The Ethics of Recognition* (New York: Palgrave Macmillan, 2004); Wendy Hesford, *Spectacular Rhetorics: Human Rights Visions, Recognitions, Feminisms* (Durham, N.C.: Duke University Press, 2011); Wendy Kozol, *Distant Wars Visible: The Ambivalence of Witnessing* (Minneapolis: University of Minnesota Press, 2014).

8. Rob Nixon, "The Great Acceleration and the Great Divergence: Vulnerability in the Anthropocene," Presidential Forum, *Profession*, March 19, 2014, http:/profession.commons .mla.org/2014/03/19/the-great-acceleration-and-the-great-divergence-vulnerability -in-the-anthropocene/

9. Rosanne Kennedy uses the notion of "moving testimony" to describe transnational memory practices. See her case study of Palestinian testimony in the Goldstone Report: Kennedy, "Moving Testimony: Human Rights, Palestinian Memory, and the Transnational Public Sphere," in *Transnational Memory Circulation, Articulation, Scales*, ed. Chiara De Cesari and Ann Rigney (Berlin: Walter de Gruyter, 2014), 51–78.

10. In addition to very good work done on the complexity of affect, see also the skepticism engendered by the notion that personal stories prompt justice in recent Tanner Lectures given by Rowan Williams, "The Paradoxes of Empathy," Tanner Lectures on Human Values, April 8–10, 2014, Harvard University, Cambridge, Mass.

11. I will move between sympathy and empathy in this chapter. Sympathy, or feeling with, often describes the capacity to imagine oneself in the place of another. Empathy, or feeling one's way into, often arises from shared experience. Both sympathy and empathy prove difficult to sustain in the encounter with testimony about women's injuries. It is not because audiences cannot feel sympathy for women who have been harmed or themselves are immune to injury but because the experience many audiences also share and which is persistently reinforced as a response to women's testimony is doubt. Neither sympathy nor empathy offers secure grounds from which ethical witness will emerge when women testify.

12. I draw here on Erwin Schrödinger's well-known example of how two contradictory claims are true at the same time. In his example, because it is not possible to know whether a cat in a closed box is alive or dead in the presence of a reactive element, the cat is both dead and alive (potentially) before one opens the box.

13. Patricia J. Williams, "Sex Lies, and the DSK Case," *Nation*, August 31, 2011, http://www. thenation.com/article/sex-lies-and-dsk-case.

14. See Strauss-Kahn's trial on charges of "aggravated pimping": Angelique Chrisafis, "Dominique Strauss-Kahn's 'Swinging Lifestyle' Shocks France," *Guardian*, February 13, 2015, http://www.theguardian.com/world/2015/feb/13/france-dominic-strauss-kahn -prostitutes-pimping-trial-lille.

15. Wai Chee Dimock, "Literature for the Planet," *PMLA* 116, no. 1 (January 2001): 174.

16. Patricia J. Williams, *The Alchemy of Race and Rights: Diary of a Law Professor* (Cambridge, Mass.: Harvard University Press 1991), 169.

17. Nicholas Kristof and Sheryl WuDunn, "The Women's Crusade," *New York Times*, August 17, 2009, http://www.nytimes.com/2009/08/23/magazine/23Women-t.html.

18. http://www.halftheskymovement.org.

19. Moira Ferguson and Jamaica Kincaid, "A Lot of Memory: An Interview with Jamaica Kincaid," *Kenyon Review* 16, no. 1 (1994): 175.

20. For example, Cathleen Schine's review, "A World as Cruel as Job's," *New York Times*, February 4, 1996, led with this synopsis: "This is a shocking book. Elegantly and delicately composed, it is also inhuman, and unapologetically so. Jamaica Kincaid has

written a truly ugly meditation on life in some of the most beautiful prose we are likely to find in contemporary fiction."

21. Jamaica Kincaid, *Autobiography of My Mother* (New York: Penguin, 1996), 3.

22. Jamaica Kincaid, *Lucy: A Novel* (New York: Farrar, Straus and Giroux, 1990), 150.

CONCLUSION: TESTIMONIAL POLITICS—#BLACKLIVESMATTER AND CLAUDIA RANKINE'S *CITIZEN*

1. Judith Butler, *Frames of War: When is Life Grievable?* (New York: Verso, 2009).

2. Gillian Whitlock, *Postcolonial Life Narrative: Testimonial Transactions* (New York: Oxford University Press, 2015).

3. I draw this language from *Dred Scott v. Sanford*, 60 U.S. 393 (1857), which encoded the legal distinction between "races."

4. Saidiya Hartman, *Lose Your Mother: A Journey Along the Atlantic Slave Route* (New York: Farrar, Straus and Giroux, 2007), 133.

5. Frances S. Robles, "What Is Known, What Isn't About Trayvon Martin's Death," *Miami Herald*, March 31, 2012, archived from the original on September 27, 2013, https://web.archive.org/web/20130927021942/http://www.miamiherald.com/2012/03/31/2725442/what-is-known-what-isnt-about.html.

6. That the destruction of property, congregation of bodies in public space, and the presence of police to control crowds is called "rioting" when people of color are involved, with an especial fascination with "looting," and something else when crowds of white people are involved has been highlighted in the reporting on post–football game violence and the Pumpkin Festival in Keene, New Hampshire (2014). In a story covering the postgame mass violence in Columbus, Ohio, that involved police in riot gear and their use of pepper spray and other crowd controlling tactics, the people being controlled (who were lighting cars and other property on fire, and who pulled down the goalposts) were referred to as "revelers." Andrew Welsh-Huggins, "Ohio State Fans Set Fires, Tear Down Goal Post After Football Win," *Huffington Post*, January 13, 2015, http://www.huffingtonpost.com/2015/01/13/ohio-state-football-riot_n_6463620.html.

7. Laurie McNeill, "Life Bytes: Six-Word Memoir and the Exigencies of Auto/tweetographies," in *Identity Technologies: Constructing the Self Online*, ed. Anna Poletti and Julie Rak, 144–66 (Madison: University of Wisconsin Press, 2014).

8. Opal Tometi, Alicia Garza, and Patrisse Cullors-Brignac, "Celebrating MLK Day: Reclaiming Our Movement Legacy," *Huffington Post*, January 18, 2015, http://www.huffingtonpost.com/opal-tometi/reclaiming-our-movement-l_b_6498400.html.

9. Alicia Garza, "A Herstory of the #BlackLivesMatter Movement," *Feminist Wire*, October 7, 2014, http://www.thefeministwire.com/2014/10/blacklivesmatter-2.

10. Ibid.

11. Tometi, Garza, and Cullors-Brignac, "Celebrating MLK Day."

12. Khury Petersen-Smith, "Black Lives Matter: A New Movement Takes Shape," *International Socialist Review* 96 (2015), http://isreview.org/issue/96/black-lives-matter.

13. Garza, "A Herstory of the #BlackLivesMatter Movement."

14. "Black Lives Matter Activist: Hillary Clinton's Racial Justice Record is 'Abysmal,'" *NPR*, August 20, 2015, http://www.npr.org/2015/08/20/433257673/black-lives-matter -activist-hillary-clintons-racial-justice-record-is-abysmal.

15. Judith Butler, "Bodies in Alliance and the Politics of the Street," State of Things Lecture Series, Office for Contemporary Art, Norway, Venice, September 7, 2011, http://www .eipcp.net/transversal/1011/butler/en.

16. Ta-Nehisi Coates, *Between the World and Me* (New York: Spiegel & Grau, 2015).

17. Claudia Rankine, *Citizen: An American Lyric* (Minneapolis: Graywolf Press, 2014).

18. Hartman, *Lose Your Mother*, 6.

19. Ibid.

20. Leigh Gilmore, *The Limits of Autobiography: Trauma and Testimony* (Ithaca, N.Y.: Cornell University Press, 2001).

BIBLIOGRAPHY

Abrams, Kathryn, and Irene Kacandes, eds., *WSQ: Women's Studies Quarterly, Special Issue on "Witness"* 36, no. 1–2 (2008).

Abu-Lughod, Lila. *Do Muslim Women Need Saving?* Cambridge, Mass.: Harvard University Press, 2013.

Aceituno, Luis. "Arturo Taracena Breaks His Silence." In *The Rigoberta Menchú Controversy*. Edited by Arturo Arias, 82–94. Minneapolis: University of Minnesota Press, 2001.

Ahmed, Sara. *The Cultural Politics of Emotion*. New York: Routledge, 2005.

——. "Feminist Killjoys (and Other Willful Subjects)." *The Scholar and Feminist Online* 8, no. 3 (2010). http://sfonline.barnard.edu/polyphonic/ahmed_01.htm.

Alexander, Michelle. *The New Jim Crow: Mass Incarceration in the Age of Colorblindness*. New York: New Press, 2010.

Allen, Danielle S. *The World of Prometheus: The Politics of Punishing in Democratic Athens*. Princeton, N.J.: Princeton University Press, 2000.

Allison, Dorothy. *Bastard Out of Carolina*. New York: Penguin, 1992.

Angelou, Maya. *I Know Why the Caged Bird Sings*. New York: Random House, 1969.

Anita: Speaking Truth to Power. Directed by Freida Mock. First Run Features, 2013.

Anzaldúa, Gloria. *Borderlands/La Frontera: The New Mestiza*. San Francisco: Spinsters/Aunt Lute, 1987.

Appadurai, Arjun. "Introduction: Commodities and the Politics of Value." In *The Social Life of Things: Commodities in Cultural Perspective*. Edited by Arjun Appadurai, 3–63. Cambridge: Cambridge University Press, 1986.

Arias, Arturo. "Authorizing Ethnicized Subjects: Rigoberta Menchú and the Performative Production of the Subaltern Self." *PMLA* 116, no. 1 (2001): 75–88.

Arias, Arturo, ed. *The Rigoberta Menchú Controversy*. Minneapolis: University of Minnesota Press, 2001.

Associated Press. "'I Feel Like a Criminal Coming Back': 'Three Cups of Tea' Author Who Lied About Being Kidnapped by the Taliban Returns as Figurehead for Mismanaged Charity." *Daily Mail*, September 19, 2014. http://www.dailymail.co.uk/news/article-2760931/Three -Cups-Tea-author-plans-reluctant-return.html.

Barry, Lynda. *One!Hundred!Demons*. Seattle: Sasquatch Press, 2002.

Bechdel, Alison. *Dykes to Watch Out For*. 1983–2008.

——. *Fun Home: A Family Tragicomic*. New York: Houghton Mifflin, 2006.

Berlant, Lauren. *Cruel Optimism*. Durham, N.C.: Duke University Press, 2011.

——. *The Female Complaint: The Unfinished Business of Sentimentality in American Culture*. Durham, N.C.: Duke University Press, 2008.

——. *The Queen of America Goes to Washington City: Essays on Sex and Citizenship*. Durham, N.C.: Duke University Press, 1997.

Berlant, Lauren, and Lisa Duggan, eds. *Our Monica, Ourselves: The Clinton Affair and the National Interest*. New York: New York University Press, 2001.

Beverly, John. *Against Literature*. Minneapolis: University of Minnesota Press, 1993.

——. *Testimonio: On the Politics of Truth*. Minneapolis: University of Minnesota Press, 2004.

"Black Lives Matter Activist: Hillary Clinton's Racial Justice Record is 'Abysmal.'" *NPR*, August 20, 2015. http://www.npr.org/2015/08/20/433257673/black-lives-matter-activist-hillary -clintons-racial-justice-record-is-abysmal.

"Brave Enough: Cheryl Strayed." Amazon.com, n.d. Accessed October 22, 2015. http://www .amazon.com/Brave-Enough-Cheryl-Strayed/dp/1101946903.

Brock, David. *Blinded by the Right: The Conscience of an Ex-Conservative*. New York: Three Rivers Press, 2003.

——. *The Real Anita Hill: The Untold Story*. New York: Free Press, 1993.

Brook, Peter. *Law's Stories: Narrative and Rhetoric in the Law*. New Haven, Conn.: Yale University Press, 1998.

Brown v. Board of Education, 347 U.S. 483 (1954).

Brown, Wendy. *States of Injury: Power and Freedom in Late Modernity*. Princeton, N.J.: Princeton University Press, 1995.

——. *Undoing the Demos: Neoliberalism's Stealth Revolution*. Cambridge, Mass.: MIT Press, 2015.

Brownmiller, Susan. *Against Our Will: Men, Women, and Rape*. New York: Ballantine, 1975.

Butler, Judith. *Antigone's Claim: Kinship Between Life and Death*. New York: Columbia University Press, 2002.

——. "Bodies in Alliance and the Politics of the Street." State of Things Lecture Series. Office for Contemporary Art, Norway, Venice. September 7, 2011. http://www.eipcp.net /transversal/1011/butler/en.

——. *Frames of War: When is Life Grievable?* New York: Verso, 2009.

——. *Precarious Life: The Powers of Mourning and Violence*. New York: Verso, 2004.

Chrisafis, Angelique. "Dominique Strauss-Kahn's 'Swinging Lifestyle' Shocks France." *Guardian*, February 13, 2015. http://www.theguardian.com/world/2015/feb/13/france -dominic-strauss-kahn-prostitutes-pimping-trial-lille.

Chute, Hillary L. *Graphic Women: Life Narrative and Contemporary Comics*. New York: Columbia University Press, 2010.

Cisneros, Sandra. *The House on Mango Street*. Houston: Arte Público Press, 1984.

Coates, Ta-Nehisi. *Between the World and Me*. New York: Spiegel & Grau, 2015.

Coles, Robert. *The Moral Lives of Children*. New York: Grover, 1986.

Collins, Patricia Hill. *Black Sexual Politics: African Americans, Gender, and the New Racism*. New York: Routledge, 2005.

Cooper, Brittney. "Intersectionality." *The Oxford Handbook of Feminist Theory*. Edited by Lisa Disch and Mary Hawkesworth. Oxford and New York: Oxford University Press, 2016.

Crenshaw, Kimberlé. "Mapping the Margins: Intersectionality, Identity Politics, and Violence Against Women of Color." *Stanford Law Review* 43 (July 1991): 1242–1299.

Crossen, Cynthia. "Know Thy Father." *Wall Street Journal*, March 4, 1997, A16.

Cvetkovich, Ann. "Public Feelings." *South Atlantic Quarterly* 106, no. 3 (2007): 459–68.

Dabashi, Hamid. "Native Informers and the Making of the American Empire." *Al-Ahram*, June 1, 2006.

Daily Show with Jon Stewart. Interview with Anita Hill. Comedy Central, June 13, 2014. http://www.cc.com/video-clips/7xxm6h/the-daily-show-with-jon-stewart-anita-hill.

Davis, Angela. *Are Prisons Obsolete?* New York: Seven Stories Press, 2003.

Dawes, James. *Evil Men*. Cambridge, Mass.: Harvard University Press, 2013.

Derrida, Jacques. *Demeure: Fiction and Testimony*. Translated by Elizabeth Rottenberg. Stanford, Calif.: Stanford University Press, 2000.

Dimock, Wai Chee. "Literature for the Planet." *PMLA* 116, no. 1 (January 2001): 174.

Donoghue, Emma. *Kissing the Witch: Old Tales in New Skins*. New York: HarperCollins, 1997.

Douglas, Kate. *Contesting Childhood: Autobiography, Trauma, and Memory*. New Brunswick, N.J.: Rutgers University Press, 2010.

Dred Scott v. Sanford, 60 U.S. 393 (1857).

D'Souza, Dinesh. "Liar, Rigoberta Menchú." *Boundless*, 1999. http://www.boundless.org/2005 /articles/a0000074.cfm.

Duggan, Lisa. *The Twilight of Equality? Neoliberalism, Cultural Politics, and the Attack on Democracy*. New York: Beacon, 2003.

Eakin, Paul John. *Making Selves: How Our Lives Become Stories*. Ithaca, N.Y.: Cornell University Press, 1999.

Edelman, Lee. *No Future: Queer Theory and the Death Drive*. Durham, N.C.: Duke University Press, 2004.

"Efrain Rios Mott and Mauricio Rodriguez Sanchez: Background." *International Justice Monitor*, n.d. Accessed October 21, 2015. http://www.ijmonitor.org/efrain-rios-montt-and -mauricio-rodriguez-sanchez-background.

Elliott, Jane, and Gillian Harkins. "Genres of Neoliberalism." *Social Text* 31, no. 2 (2013): 1–17.

Faludi, Susan. *Backlash: The Undeclared War on Women*. New York: Crown, 1991.

Farr, Cecilia Konchar. *Reading Oprah: How Oprah's Book Club Changed the Way America Reads*. Albany: State University of New York Press, 2005.

Ferguson, Moira, and Jamaica Kincaid. "A Lot of Memory: An Interview with Jamaica Kincaid." *Kenyon Review* 16, no. 1 (1994): 163–88.

Ferguson, Roderick. *Aberrations in Black: Toward a Queer of Color Critique*. Minneapolis: University of Minnesota Press, 2004.

Fernandes, Leela. *Transnational Feminism in the United States: Knowledge, Ethics, Power*. New York: New York University Press, 2013.

Flax, Jane. *The American Dream in Black and White: The Clarence Thomas Hearings*. Ithaca, N.Y.: Cornell University Press, 1998.

Ford, Richard. "Law's Territory (A History of Jurisdiction)." *Michigan Law Review* 97, no. 4 (1999): 843–930.

Foucault, Michel. *History of Sexuality*. Vol. 1: *An Introduction*. Translated by Robert Hurley. New York: Vintage, 1978.

——. *Power: The Essential Works of Foucault, 1954–1984*. Vol. 3. Translated by James Hurley. Edited by James Faubion. New York: New Press, 2000.

Frey, James. *A Million Little Pieces*. New York: Random House, 2003.

Freyd, Jennifer J. *Betrayal Trauma: The Logic of Forgetting Childhood Abuse*. Cambridge, Mass.: Harvard University Press, 1998.

Friedman, Estelle B. *Redefining Rape: Sexual Violence in the Era of Suffrage and Segregation*. Cambridge, Mass.: Harvard University Press, 2013.

Friedman, Thomas. "Teacher, Can We Leave Now? No." *New York Times*, July 18, 2009. http://www.nytimes.com/2009/07/19/opinion/19friedman.html.

Garza, Alicia. "A Herstory of the #BlackLivesMatter Movement." *Feminist Wire*, October 7, 2014. http://www.thefeministwire.com/2014/10/blacklivesmatter-2.

Gilbert, Elizabeth. *Big Magic: Creative Living Beyond Fear*. New York: Penguin, 2015.

——. *Eat, Pray, Love: One Woman's Search for Everything Across Italy, India and Indonesia*. New York: Penguin, 2006.

——. *The Signature of All Things*. New York: Penguin, 2013.

Gilmore, Leigh. "American Neoconfessional: Memoirs, Self-Help, and Redemption on Oprah's Couch." *Biography* 33, no. 4 (2010): 657–79.

——. *Autobiographics: A Feminist Theory of Women's Self-Representation*. Ithaca, NY: Cornell University Press, 1994.

——. "Boom/lash: Fact-Checking, Suicide, and the Lifespan of a Genre." *a/b: Auto/Biography Studies* 29, no. 2 (2014): 211–24.

——. "Jurisdictions: *I, Rigoberta Menchú, The Kiss*, and Scandalous Self-Representation in the Age of Memoir and Trauma." *Signs* 28, no. 2 (2003): 695–719.

——. "Learning from Fakes: Memoir, Confessional Ethics, and the Limits of Genre." In *Contemporary Trauma Narratives: Liminality and the Ethics of Form*. Edited by Jean-Michel Ganteau and Susana Onega, 21–35. New York: Routledge, 2014.

——. "Limit-Cases: Trauma, Self-Representation, and the Jurisdictions of Identity." *Biography* 24, no. 1 (2001): 128–39.

——. *The Limits of Autobiography: Trauma and Testimony*. Ithaca, N.Y.: Cornell University Press, 2001.

——. "'What Was I?' Literary Witness and the Testimonial Archive." *Profession* (2011): 77–84.

Gilmore, Leigh, and Elizabeth Marshall. "Girls in Crisis: Rescue and Transnational Feminist Autobiographical Resistance." *Feminist Studies* 36, no. 3 (2010): 667–90.

——. "Trauma and Young Adult Literature: Representing Adolescence and Knowledge in David Smalls's *Stitches: A Memoir*." *Prose Studies: History, Theory, Criticism* 35, no. 1 (2013): 16–38.

Gilmore, Ruth Wilson. *Golden Gulag: Prisons, Surplus, Crisis, and Opposition in Globalizing California*. Berkeley: University of California Press, 2007.

Gloeckner, Phoebe. *A Child's Life and Other Stories*. Berkeley, Calif.: Frog, 1998.

——. *Diary of a Teenage Girl: An Account in Words and Pictures*. Berkeley, Calif.: North Atlantic Books, 2002.

Goodrich, Peter. *Law in the Courts of Love: Literature and Other Minor Jurisprudences*. New York: Routledge, 1996.

Gordon, Avery. *Ghostly Matters: Haunting and the Sociological Imaginary*. Minneapolis: University of Minnesota Press, 1997.

——. "Some Thoughts on Haunting and Futurity." *borderlands* 10, no. 2 (2011). http://www .borderlands.net.au/vol10no2_2011/gordon_thoughts.pdf.

Grandin, Greg. *The Blood of Guatemala: A History of Race and Nation*. Raleigh, NC: Duke University Press, 2000.

——. "It Was Heaven That They Burned: Who is Rigoberta Menchú?" *The Nation*, September 8, 2010. http://www.thenation.com/article/it-was-heaven-they-burned.

——. Open School of Ethnography and Anthropology/Community Institute for Transcultural Exchange, "Rigoberta Menchu Debates, Redux," *Osea-cite.org*, n.d. Accessed October 4, 2010. http://www.osea-cite.org/history/redux_rigoberta-menchu-debate.php.

Guinier, Lani. "But Some of Us Are Brave." In *I Still Believe Anita Hill: Three Generations Discuss the Legacies of Speaking Truth to Power*. Edited by Amy Richards and Cynthia Greenberg. New York: Feminist Press, 2013.

Habermas, Jürgen. *The Structural Transformation of the Public Sphere: An Inquiry into a Category of Bourgeois Society*. Translated by Thomas Burger and Frederick Lawrence. Cambridge, Mass.: MIT Press, 1989.

Hall, Rachel. "'It Can Happen to You': Rape Prevention in the Age of Risk Management." *Hypatia* 19, no. 3 (Summer 2004): 1–19.

Haraway, Donna. "Situated Knowledges: The Science Question in Feminism and the Privilege of Partial Perspective." *Feminist Studies* 14, no. 3 (1988): 575–99

Harkins, Gillian. "Aye, and Neoliberalism." *Journal of Homosexuality* 59, no. 7 (2012): 1073–80.

——. *Everybody's Family Romance: Reading Incest in Neoliberal America*. Minneapolis: University of Minnesota Press, 2009.

Harris, Jennifer, and Ellwood Watson, eds. *The Oprah Phenomenon*. Lexington: University of Kentucky Press, 2007.

Harrison, Colin. "Sins of the Father." *Vogue*, April 1, 1997.

Harrison, Kathryn. *The Kiss*. New York: Harper Perennial, 1998.

Hartman, Saidiya. *Lose Your Mother: A Journey Along the Atlantic Slave Route*. New York: Farrar, Straus and Giroux, 2007.

Hemmings, Clare. *Why Stories Matter: The Political Grammar of Feminist Theory*. Durham, N.C.: Duke University Press, 2011.

Herman, Judith. *Trauma and Recovery: The Aftermath of Violence—From Domestic Abuse to Political Terror*. New York: Basic Books, 1992.

Hertzberg, Hendrik. "A Cold Case." *New Yorker*, August 12, 2008. http://www.newyorker.com /news/hendrik-hertzberg/a-cold-case.

——. "Leaks, Lies and the Law." *Washington Post*, December 1, 1991. https://www.washingtonpost .com/archive/opinions/1991/12/01/leaks-lies-and-the-law/871a0b36-a52c-46c5-8632– 9fca4aco39eb.

Hesford, Wendy. *Spectacular Rhetorics: Human Rights Visions, Recognitions, Feminisms*. Durham, N.C.: Duke University Press, 2011.

Hill, Anita. *Speaking Truth to Power*. New York: Doubleday, 1997.

Hill, Anita Faye, and Emma Coleman Jordan. *Race, Gender, and Power in America: The Legacy of the Hill-Thomas Hearings*. New York: Oxford University Press, 1995.

Horowitz, David. "I, Rigoberta Menchú, Liar." *FrontPageMagazine.com*, February 26, 1999. http://archive.frontpagemag.com/readArticle.aspx?ARTID=24278.

The Hunting Ground. Directed by Kirby Dick. Weinstein Company, 2015.

Illouz, Eva. *Oprah Winfrey and the Glamour of Misery: An Essay on Popular Culture*. New York: Columbia University Press, 2003.

Ioanide, Paula. *The Emotional Politics of Racism: How Feelings Trump Facts in an Era of Color-blindness*. Stanford, Calif.: Stanford University Press, 2015.

"Jeannette Walls." *Kepplerspeakers.com*, n.d. Accessed October 29, 2015. http://www.keppler speakers.com/speakers/?speaker=Jeannette%20Walls.

Kaplan, Caren. "Resisting Autobiography: Out-Law Genres and Transnational Feminist Subjects." In *De/Colonizing the Subject: The Politics of Gender in Women's Autobiography*. Edited by Sidonie Smith and Julia Watson, 115–38. Minneapolis: University of Minnesota Press, 1992.

Kaplan, Caren, and Inderpal Grewal. "Transnational Practices and Interdisciplinary Feminist Scholarship: Refiguring Women's and Gender Studies." In *Women's Studies on Its Own: A Next Wave Reader in Institutional Change*. Edited by Robyn Wiegman, 66–81. Durham, NC: Duke University Press, 2002.

Karr, Mary. *The Liar's Club: A Memoir*. New York: Penguin, 1995.

Kaysen, Susanna. *Girl, Interrupted*. New York: Vintage, 1993.

Kennedy, Rosanne. "Moving Testimony: Human Rights, Palestinian Memory, and the Transnational Public Sphere." In *Transnational Memory Circulation, Articulation, Scales*. Edited by Chiara De Cesari and Ann Rigney, 51–78. Berlin: Walter de Gruyter, 2014.

Kim, Eun Kyung. "'Three Cups' Author Greg Mortenson: 'I Let a Lot of People Down.'" Interview with Tom Brokaw. *Today.com*, January 21, 2014. http://www.today.com/popculture /three-cups-author-greg-mortenson-i-let-lot-people-down-2D11961320.

Kincaid, Jamaica. *Autobiography of My Mother*. New York: Penguin, 1996.

Kingston, Maxine Hong. *The Woman Warrior: Memoirs of a Girlhood Among Ghosts*. New York: Vintage, 1976.

Kozol, Wendy. *Distant Wars Visible: The Ambivalence of Witnessing*. Minneapolis: University of Minnesota Press, 2014.

Krakauer, Jon. *Into the Wild*. New York: Anchor, 1996.

——. *Into Thin Air: A Personal Account of the Mt. Everest Disaster*. New York: Anchor, 1997.

——. "Is It Time to Forgive Greg Mortenson?" *Daily Beast*, April 8, 2013. http://www.thedaily beast.com/articles/2013/04/08/is-it-time-to-forgive-greg-mortenson.html.

——. *Missoula: Rape and the Justice System in a College Town*. New York: Doubleday, 2015.

——. *Three Cups of Deceit: How Greg Mortenson, Humanitarian Hero, Lost His Way*. New York: Anchor, 2011.

——. *Under the Banner of Heaven: A Story of Violent Faith*. New York: Anchor, 2003.

Kristof, Nicholas. "Dr. Greg and Afghanistan." *New York Times*, October 20, 2010. http://www .nytimes.com/2010/10/21/opinion/21kristof.html.

Kristof, Nicholas, and Sheryl WuDunn. *Half the Sky: Turning Oppression into Opportunity for Women Worldwide*. New York: Knopf, 2009.

——. "The Women's Crusade." *New York Times*, August 17, 2009. http://www.nytimes.com /2009/08/23/magazine/23Women-t.html.

Larry King Live. Interview with James Frey. *CNN.com*, January 11, 2006. http://edition.cnn .com/TRANSCRIPTS/0601/11/lkl.01.html.

Latour, Bruno. *Reassembling the Social: An Introduction to Actor-Network-Theory*. Oxford: Oxford University Press, 2005.

Lehmann-Haupt, Christopher. "Life with Father: Incestuous and Soul-Deadening." *New York Times*, February 27, 1997, C18.

Lejeune, Philippe. *Le Pacte Autobiographique*. Paris: Seuil, 1975.

Lorde, Audre. *Zami: A New Spelling of My Name: A Biomythography*. New York: Crossing Press, 1982.

Marshall, Elizabeth. "The Daughter's Disenchantment: Incest as Pedagogy in Fairy Tales and Kathryn Harrison's *The Kiss*." *College English* 66, no. 4 (March 2004): 395–418.

Mayer, Jane, and Jill Abramson. *Strange Justice: The Selling of Clarence Thomas*. Boston: Houghton Mifflin, 1994.

McAfee, Noëlle. *Habermas, Kristeva, and Citizenship*. Ithaca, N.Y.: Cornell University Press, 2000.

McCourt, Frank. *Angela's Ashes*. New York: Scribner, 1996.

McNeill, Laurie. "Life Bytes: Six-Word Memoir and the Exigencies of Auto/tweetographies." In *Identity Technologies: Constructing the Self Online*. Edited by Anna Poletti and Julie Rak, 144–66. Madison: University of Wisconsin Press, 2014.

Meloy, Michelle L., and Susan L. Miller. *The Victimization of Women: Law, Policies, and Politics*. Oxford: Oxford University Press, 2011.

Menchú, Rigoberta. *I, Rigoberta Menchú: An Indian Woman in Guatemala*. Translated by Ann Wright. Edited by Elisabeth Burgos-Debray. New York: Verso, 1984.

Miller, Anita, ed. *The Complete Transcripts of the Clarence Thomas–Anita Hill Hearings: October 11, 12, 13, 1991*. Chicago: Academy Chicago Publishers, 1994.

Miller, Nancy K. *Bequest and Betrayal: Memoirs of a Parent's Death*. New York: Oxford University Press, 1996.

Mirzoeff, Nicholas. "Nicholas Mirzoeff on the Real Impact of Sharing 700 Million Snapchats Every Day." *It's Nice That*, June 4, 2015. http://www.itsnicethat.com/articles/nicholas -mirzoeff.

Moraga, Cherríe. *Loving in the War Years: Lo Que Nunca Pasó por Sus Labios*. Brooklyn: Sound End Press, 1983.

Moraga, Cherríe, and Gloria Anzaldúa, eds. *This Bridge Called My Back: Writings By Radical Women of Color*. London: Persephone Press, 1981.

Morrison, Toni. "Introduction: Friday on the Potomac." In *Race-ing Justice, En-gendering Power: Essays on Anita Hill, Clarence Thomas, and the Construction of Social Reality*. Edited by Toni Morrison, vii–xxx. New York: Pantheon, 1992.

Mortenson, Greg. *Stones into Schools: Promoting Peace with Education in Afghanistan and Pakistan*. New York: Viking, 2009.

Mortenson, Greg, and David Oliver Relin. *Three Cups of Tea: One Man's Mission to Fight Terrorism and Build Nations . . . One School at a Time*. New York: Penguin, 2006.

Nafisi, Azar. *Reading Lolita in Tehran: A Memoir in Books*. New York: Random House, 2003.

Nixon, Rob. "The Great Acceleration and the Great Divergence: Vulnerability in the Anthropocene." *MLA Profession* (2014).

NPR Staff. "Jon Krakauer Tells a 'Depressingly Typical' Story of College Town Rapes." *NPR*, April 19, 2015. http://www.npr.org/2015/04/19/400185648/jon-krakauer-tells-a-depressingly-typical-story-of-college-town-rapes.

Open School of Ethnography and Anthropology/Community Institute for Transcultural Exchange. "Rigoberta Menchu Debates, Redux." *Osea-cite.org*. n.d. Accessed October 29, 2015. http://www.osea-cite.org/history/redux_rigoberta-menchu-debate.php.

Pateman, Carol. *The Sexual Contract*. Cambridge: Polity, 1988.

Peck, Janice. *The Age of Oprah: Cultural Icon for the Neoliberal Era*. Boulder, Colo.: Paradigm, 2008.

Petersen-Smith, Khury. "Black Lives Matter: A New Movement Takes Shape." *International Socialist Review* 96 (2015). http://isreview.org/issue/96/black-lives-matter.

Phillips, Kate. "Biden and Anita Hill, Revisited." *New York Times* blog, August 23, 2008. http://thecaucus.blogs.nytimes.com/2008/08/23/biden-and-anita-hill-revisited.

Pogrebin, Robin. "The Naked Literary Come-On." *New York Times*, August 17, 1997. http://www.nytimes.com/1997/08/17/weekinreview/the-naked-literary-come-on.html.

Rak, Julie. *Boom! Manufacturing Memoir for the Popular Market*. Warterloo: Wilifrid Laurier University Press, 2013.

Rankine, Claudia. *Citizen: An American Lyric*. Minneapolis: Graywolf Press, 2014.

Rape Culture. Produced by Margaret Lazarus and Renner Wunderlich. Cambridge Documentary Films, 1975.

Reddy, Chandan. *Freedom with Violence: Race, Sexuality, and the U.S. State*. Durham, NC: Duke University Press, 2011.

Richards, Amy, and Cynthia Greenberg, eds. *I Still Believe Anita Hill: Three Generations Discuss the Legacies of Speaking Truth to Power*. New York: Feminist Press, 2013.

Robles, Frances S. "What Is Known, What Isn't About Trayvon Martin's Death." *Miami Herald*, March 31, 2012. Archived from the original on September 27, 2013. https://web.archive.org/web/20130927021942/http://www.miamiherald.com/2012/03/31/2725442/what-is-known-what-isnt-about.html.

Rohter, Larry. "Tarnished Laureate: A Special Report: Nobel Winner Finds Her Story Challenged." *New York Times*, December 15, 1998. http://www.nytimes.com/1998/12/15

/world/tarnished-laureate-a-special-report-nobel-winner-finds-her-story-challenged
.html.

Rooney, Kathleen. *Reading with Oprah: The Book Club That Changed America*. Fayetteville: University of Arkansas Press, 2005.

Rostica, Julieta. "The Naturalization of Peace and War: The Hegemonic Discourses on the Political Violence in Guatemala." In *The Struggle for Memory in Latin America: Recent History and Political Violence*. Edited by Eugenia Allier-Montaño and Emilio Crenzel, 183–201. New York: Palgrave Macmillan, 2015.

St. John, Warren. "Kathryn Harrison's Dad Responds to Her Memoir." *New York Observer*, April 21, 1997.

Salamon, Gayle. *Assuming a Body: Transgender and Rhetorics of Materiality*. New York: Columbia University Press, 2010.

Sanders, Mark. *Ambiguities of Witnessing: Law and Literature in the Time of a Truth Commission*. Stanford, Calif.: Stanford University Press, 2007.

Sanford, Victoria. *Buried Secrets: Truth and Human Rights in Guatemala*. New York: Palgrave Macmillan, 2004.

Satrapi, Marjane. *Persepolis: The Story of a Childhood*. Translated by L'Association. New York: Pantheon, 2003.

Schaffer, Kay, and Sidonie Smith. *Human Rights and Narrative Lives: The Ethics of Recognition*. New York: Palgrave Macmillan, 2004.

Sensoy, Özlem, and Elizabeth Marshall. "Missionary Girl Power: Saving the 'Third World,' One Girl at a Time." *Gender and Education* 22, no. 3 (2010): 295–311.

Slaughter, Joseph. *Human Rights, Inc.: The World Novel, Narrative Form, and International Law*. New York: Fordham University Press, 2007.

Smith, Sidonie. "Narrating the Right to Sexual Well-being and the Global Management of Misery: Maria Rosa Henson's *Comfort Woman* and Charlene Smith's *Proud of Me*." *Literature and Medicine* 24, no. 2 (2005): 153–80.

Smith, Sidonie, and Kay Shaeffer. *Human Rights and Narrative Lives: The Ethics of Recognition*. New York: Palgrave Macmillan, 2004.

Smith, Sidonie, and Julia Watson. *Reading Autobiography: A Guide for Interpreting Life Narratives*. 2nd edition. Minneapolis: University of Minnesota Press, 2010.

——. "Witness or False Witness: Metrics of Authenticity, Collective I-Formations, and the Ethic of Verification in First-Person Testimony." *Biography* 35, no. 4 (2012): 590–626.

Sommer, Dorris. "Las Casas's Lies and Other Language Games." In *The Rigoberta Menchú Controversy*. Edited by Arturo Arias, 237–50. Minneapolis: University of Minnesota Press, 2001.

Sparks, Holloway. "Dissident Citizenship: Democratic Theory, Political Courage, and Activist Women." *Hypatia* 12, no. 4 (1997): 74–110.

Spillers, Hortense J. "Mama's Baby, Papa's Maybe: An American Grammar Book." *Diacritics* 17, no. 2 (Summer 1987): 64–81.

Spivak, Gayatri Chakravorty. "Can the Subaltern Speak?" In *Marxism and the Interpretation of Culture*. Edited by Cary Nelson and Lawrence Grossberg, 271–313. Urbana: University of Illinois Press, 1988.

——. *Outside in the Teaching Machine*. New York: Routledge, 1993.

Steedman, Carolyn. *Landscape for a Good Woman: A Story of Two Lives*. London: Virago, 1986.

Stockton, Kathryn Bond. *The Queer Child, or Growing Sideways in the Twentieth Century.* Durham, N.C.: Duke University Press, 2009.

Stoll, David. *Rigoberta Menchú and the Story of All Poor Guatemalans.* Boulder, Colo.: Westview Press, 1999.

Strayed, Cheryl. *Tiny Beautiful Things: Advice on Love and Life from Dear Sugar.* New York: Vintage, 2012.

——. *Wild: From Lost to Found on the Pacific Crest Trail.* New York: Vintage, 2012.

Thomas, Clarence. *My Grandfather's Son: A Memoir.* New York: HarperCollins, 2007.

"The Thomas Hearings: Excerpts from Senate's Hearings on the Thomas Nomination," *New York Times,* September 13, 1991. http://www.nytimes.com/1991/09/13/us/the-thomas -hearings-excerpts-from-senate-s-hearing-on-the-thomas-nomination.html.

Tolle, Eckhart. *A New Earth: Awakening to Your Life's Purpose.* New York: Penguin, 2005.

——. *The Power of Now: A Guide to Spiritual Enlightenment.* Novato, Calif.: New World Publishing, 1999.

Tometi, Opal, Alicia Garza, and Patrisse Cullors-Brignac. "Celebrating MLK Day: Reclaiming Our Movement Legacy." *Huffington Post,* January 18, 2015. http://www.huffingtonpost.com /opal-tometi/reclaiming-our-movement-l_b_6498400.html.

Toobin, Jeffrey. "Unforgiven," *New Yorker,* November 12, 2007. http://www.newyorker.com/ magazine/2007/11/12/unforgiven.

Totenberg, Nina. "Thomas Confirmation Hearings Had Ripple Effect." *NPR,* October 11, 2011. http://www.npr.org/2011/10/11/141213260/thomas-confirmation-hearings-had-ripple-effect.

Travis, Trysh. *The Language of the Heart: A Cultural History of the Recovery Movement from Alcoholics Anonymous to Oprah Winfrey.* Chapel Hill: University of North Carolina Press, 2009.

Vance, Carole S. "Innocence and Experience: Melodramatic Narratives of Sex Trafficking for Law and Policy." *History of the Present: A Journal of Critical History* 2, no. 2 (2012): 200–218.

Walls, Jeanette. *The Glass Castle: A Memoir.* New York: Scribner, 2005.

Welsh-Huggins, Andrew. "Ohio State Fans Set Fires, Tear Down Goal Post After Football Win." *Huffington Post,* January 13, 2015. http://www.huffingtonpost.com/2015/01/13/ohio-state -football-riot_n_6463620.html.

Whitlock, Gillian. *Postcolonial Life Narrative: Testimonial Transactions.* New York: Oxford University Press, 2015.

——. *Soft Weapons: Autobiography in Transit.* Chicago: University of Chicago Press, 2006.

Williams, Patricia J. *The Alchemy of Race and Rights: Diary of a Law Professor.* Cambridge, Mass.: Harvard University Press 1991.

——. "Sex, Lies and the DSK Case." *Nation,* August 31, 2011. htttp://www.thenation.com /articles/sex-lies-and-dsk-case.

——. "Slouching Toward Faux. *The Nation,* July 13, 2011. http://www.thenation.com/article /slouching-towards-faux.

Williams, Raymond. *Marxism and Literature.* Oxford: Oxford University Press, 1977.

Williams, Rowan. "The Paradoxes of Empathy." Tanner Lectures on Human Values. April 8–10, 2014. Harvard University. Cambridge, Mass.

Wittig, Monique. *The Lesbian Body.* Translated by Peter Owen. New York: Avon, 1975.

Wojnarowicz, David. *Close to the Knives: A Memoir of Disintegration.* New York: Vintage, 1991.

Yates, Pamela. *Dictator in the Dock*. *Skylight.is*, n.d. Accessed October 21, 2015. http://skylight
.is/films/dictator-in-the-dock.

——. *Granito: How To Nail a Dictator*. *Skylight.is*, n.d. Accessed October 21, 2015. http://
skylight.is/films/granito.

——. "Trial on Guatemala's Spanish Embassy Resumes Today: The Rest of History."
NACLA.org, January 19, 2015. https://nacla.org/news/2015/01/19/trial-guatemala%E2%80
%99s-spanish-embassy-fire-resumes-today-rest-history-video.

INDEX

GENDER AND CULTURE READERS